THE HARD SELL

Colin Clark is Research Fellow in Negotiation at Surrey European Management School, Surrey University. He is also a visiting professor of marketing at the Ecole Supérieure de Commerce de Rennes.

Trevor Pinch is Professor of Sociology at the Department of Science and Technology Studies, Cornell University.

THE HARD SELL

The Language and Lessons of
Street-wise Marketing

Colin Clark
and Trevor Pinch

HarperCollinsPublishers

HarperCollins*Publishers*
77–85 Fulham Palace Road,
Hammersmith, London W6 8JB

A Paperback Original 1995
1 3 5 7 9 8 6 4 2

A catalogue record for this book
is available from the British Library

ISBN 0 00 638465 X

Set in Linotron Galliard
at The Spartan Press Ltd,
Lymington, Hants

Printed in Great Britain by
HarperCollinsManufacturing Glasgow

CONTENTS

ACKNOWLEDGEMENTS

The research project which led to this book was funded by two small grants from the Nuffield Research Foundation. Additional financial support was also provided by the Institute for Research in the Social Sciences, University of York, the Department of Sociology, University of York, and the Ecole Supérieure de Commerce de Rennes, France. The extracts from the sales interactions from retail settings (which feature in Chapter 4) were collected for a research project funded by the Economic and Social Research Council grant number: F00232393.

We would like to thank the following people:
Richard Wrightson, David Holmes and members of the Audio-Visual Centre, University of York, for technical advice and assistance; Vince Cooper for helping us record one of the 'Market Pitcher of the Year' competitions; Neil Brisley, for reading through a draft of this book; Annelies Kosijungan and Ellen Van Oost for collecting and translating videos of a Dutch market; and Corinne Fourny and Virginie Villepontoux for translating our videos of, respectively, a Parisian fire-eating escapologist and French market and *braderie* pitchers. We would also like to thank Suzanne Moon and Todd La Porte.

This book would, of course, never have been started, let alone completed, without the help of the market pitchers themselves . . .

Colin Clark and Trevor Pinch
'La Berline' bistro,
Rennes, France and Ithaca, New York

INTRODUCTION

Our study began by accident.

It was that dingy, wet autumn of 1985, and the rain had spoiled yet another Saturday afternoon's shopping. We were taking a short-cut through our local market in a small town in the north of England, trying to find somewhere – anywhere – that was dry, when we heard a commotion about fifty yards in front of us. It sounded as if someone was getting on the wrong side of a hell of a one-sided argument. As sociologists, it didn't take us long to convince ourselves that we had a professional duty to investigate. After all, we were already as wet as we'd ever get. Threading our way through the rows of stalls, we eventually came upon the source. A market trader was ridiculing one of his sales assistants. We were not alone in our curiosity: a crowd had gathered to listen shamelessly to the incident, which sounded as if it was already well under way.

'*Go on*, look at the bloody plight of her,' the trader barked, pointing an accusing finger at the hapless teenager standing beside him with her head hanging low. 'She's just out of Holloway and she can go straight back there as far as I'm concerned.' He was seriously upset about some aspect of her behaviour. The veins were standing right out on his neck, and his face was so flushed that it threatened to overwhelm his tan.

He shook his head slowly while he tried to get his breath back. 'I'll tell you something, ladies and gentlemen,' he confided to us all in a world-weary, resigned tone, 'you can't get decent staff these days. What's the problem? I'll tell you what the bloody problem is – *she's serving her friends!* I've got no alternative but to sack her after today.'

THE HARD SELL

(full text)

He wasn't interested in hearing any pleas of clemency from the crowd. 'It's no use you saying "Poor lass",' he shouted, 'I can't allow *anyone* to get any preferential treatment at my stall. As far as I'm concerned it's *first come, first served.*'

The girl had turned beetroot red with embarrassment. She was as wet as the rest of us and looked absolutely pitiful. Spinning back round towards her, the trader continued with his tirade.

'The customer *always* comes *first*, right? *Right?*'

The girl nodded sheepishly.

'Remember that, you lot,' he advised us all, 'and you won't go far wrong in life. Always, *always* remember that the customer comes *first.*'

He let this pearl of wisdom hang out to dry for a moment. But then, almost as an afterthought, and through a hint of a mischievous grin, he added: 'Yeah. *A prostitute told me that!*'

When the joke hit home a wave of laughter swept through the crowd. Even his assistant broke into a small smile. Intrigued, we decided to listen a little longer. We even tried to edge our way nearer to the front of his stall to get a better view, but we were hemmed in on every side by all the other 'incident watchers'.

Quick as a flash he conjured up a child's toy from one of the many cardboard boxes that littered his stall. It was a plastic tandem tricycle. Sitting astride the miniature saddles were two small dolls, a boy and a girl – just like Ken and Barbie. Poking out of the saddle-bag at the back was the head of a plastic baby. *'FAMILY RIDERS! FAMILY RIDERS!'* he yelled. He wound the toy up, placed it on the long trestle table in front of him, and let the dolls' little legs peddle away along the counter.

'Here. *Look at this one go!* And that includes you, Doris.'

An elderly woman near the front of the crowd smiled back, obviously pleased about being made the centre of attention.

'This toy is specially for the kids,' he added, 'but I know all you adults will absolutely love it too. In fact, I like to call it my summer line. You know, summer paid for, and summer not.'

The sniggers from the crowd just shaded the groans on that one.

He continued, unperturbed. 'You get the "Sindy" boy, the "Sindy" girl, and the baby in the back there. And the only reason the baby's there is that when we got here this morning and unloaded the van we found little Sindy *in the same bloody box as Action Man!*'

The crowd exploded with laughter. Holding the tricycle aloft, he then assured us that it 'wasn't made in Hong Kong, ding-dong they go wrong. It's a *British-made product!*'

We were spellbound.

He wasn't finished. '*Look,*' he continued, 'I know you can go and buy the same thing round the corner at "Shivery Dick's" for a tenner and, yes, love, I'll admit it, they *are* cheap there. But I'll tell you what, *his* price is not *nearly* cheap enough for you lot here. I *know* you're after a bargain, and that's *exactly* what I'm gonna give you. Just leave it *all* to me. I will do you *RIGHT*. I will *NOT* do you *WRONG*.'

He started caressing the plastic dolls, as if he were comforting his own children. His face began to look pensive; upset even. Suddenly, and without a single word of explanation, he began packing the tricycle back into its box. There were murmurs of protest throughout the crowd.

'No, I'm sorry, I *can't* give them to you,' he replied sorrowfully, 'my kids'll never forgive me. This toy is part of our family now. It'd be like getting rid of one of my own babies. You wouldn't want me to do that, now, *would you?*'

Yet that is precisely what the crowd wanted him to do. One or two people even started to voice their objections more forcefully as he finished packing the toy away. Eventually, under the growing pressure, he relented.

'All right. *All right*, you can have them,' he conceded reluctantly. 'But I'm not at all happy about it.' Out they came again, their little legs still peddling away frantically.

'*Look,*' he shouted, holding the toy up again, 'if you went to a fancy store, you'd pay a fancy price for this, like *well over* thirty quid. And even if you bought something like this out of the catalogue it'd still cost you *at least* fifteen quid. But by the time you've finished paying it off at twenty pence a week for the next ten years, your kids'll have grown up and left you *and probably had kids of their own*. Listen to *me*, because *I'm* cheaper than credit. In fact, *I'm* the *cheapest* of them *all*! And if you don't believe me you can go and get that copper that's walking round the corner there, he'll be more than pleased to nick me, I can assure you.'

We quickly glanced to where he'd pointed but we obviously weren't quick enough; there was no 'copper' in sight.

He started to reel off a list of prices that the toy was worth but which he, in all his generosity, was not even thinking of going to sell it for.

'And you can *forget* fifteen quid too. And by the look of your bloody faces I think we'd *better* forget fifteen quid. It's not a tenner either. *They're nothing like that price*! In fact, *never* mind nine, or *even* eight . . .'

He stopped shouting, but only to wipe the sweat from his face. A man who was squashed up next to us in an anorak and a flat cap took advantage of this brief lull in the proceedings to inform his wife quietly that the toy would end up being sold for £7.

'And they're *not* seven pounds either, so you're wrong,' the trader replied, looking as if he'd just been stabbed in the heart by the man. 'I haven't even *started* with the price yet. But I'll tell you what. *Sir*, if I *gave them away to you* at *seven* quid you'd have got the *deal of the century* from me here today, *is that right*?'

The man acknowledged the point with a small, self-conscious nod.

We looked around us again. A few people had already made their decision, whatever the final price was going to be – they were waving ten-pound notes frantically in the air, trying to attract the stall-holder's attention. Most of the rest seemed to be jostling one another to get even closer to the stall.

'Put your money away,' the trader shouted, waving his hands disdainfully at everyone, '*I don't want your money*. I'll tell you *who* to pay, *when* to pay, and *what* to pay.'

Not one person with a hand in the air lowered even a finger.

'In fact, never mind six-fifty, or six-twenty.' He clapped his hands. 'And *today* they're *not even* six. I'm going to clear them all out of the way *right now*. *WATCH THIS*! I want *level* and *silly* money for an *even sillier* price . . .'

He grabbed hold of an auctioneer's mallet and waved it thoughtfully, high above his head.

There was a long, long silence.

Then . . . *wham*! He brought the mallet crashing down mercilessly onto the sales counter.

'GIMME *FIVE POUNDS* for the buggers to clear them out of the way before I change my mind!'

Mayhem broke out. Practically everyone lunged forward to snap up the bargain.

'*Get them gone*!' he shouted to his assistant, 'and *don't* be just serving your friends either and I *might* just let you stay.'

His assistant had found more tricycles. She started running around like a headless chicken, trying to quell the demand and grab the money that was being thrust into her face from every direction. 'Over there!' she pleaded to the trader. 'There's a lady – *there*! *That man wants serving too*!'

The rush of eager buyers to the front of the stall meant that we were soon left standing at the back along with one or two other ditherers. The man in the anorak was still standing next to us, and he started warning his wife to be careful about buying things from 'these kinds of people'. But the trader had already marked his card.

'HURRY UP,' he shouted, 'because you'll *never, EVER* get them at this price again. I've only got about ten of them left and after that they're gone. *There'll be no more*. I *can't* serve the eleventh person *even if he gives me a thousand pounds*! It'll be like backing the half past three race at quarter to four – you *won't* be in it.'

This was obviously the clincher. The man's wife broke free, and stormed forward with her purse already open – a triumph of the power of marketing over the ties of matrimony. Less than five minutes later every available tricycle was on its way to a new home. All twenty of them, at least.

That afternoon was *not* our first encounter with this form of street market selling. We'd seen these types of traders hundreds of times before, when we were children, on other street markets, at the old hiring fairs, and even at special indoor trade shows such as the 'Ideal Home' exhibition. As adults, we'd passed them by when walking through our local markets on our way to the more orthodox retail stores nearby. On each and every one of these occasions, though, we hadn't really given them anything more than a second glance. Today we had, and, as a consequence, we were both enthralled and perplexed.

As we sat in a nearby café waiting for our next bus to the university, we started to reflect on what we'd just witnessed. What was puzzling us more than anything else was that before the 'incident' between this trader and his assistant began there must have been nothing in front of his stall except a patch of bare waste ground and the occasional uninterested and wet passer-by. A few minutes later and a sea of eager purchasers had gathered, holding money aloft in their outstretched hands. We wanted to know what lay behind this trader's almost alchemical ability to transform all the hard-bitten and poker-faced weekend shoppers who had congregated into willing and eager buyers. How had he been able to persuade so many people to dip into their purses and pockets and then, in some cases, practically fight their way to the front of his stall for the privilege of being allowed to compete with one another for the opportunity to purchase his goods?

It didn't take us too long to develop a few ideas to account for this trader's sales success. Maybe the goods were stolen or were 'seconds'. How else could he have sold them so cheaply?

And where do the authorities always seem to go first in their search for the lead-filled and the lethal? Perhaps he'd also paid someone to stand surreptitiously in the crowd and initiate the frenzy of buying that took place. Why else would so many people suddenly develop an urgent need to own a toy tricycle with a plastic baby's head sticking out of the back pannier? Perhaps the people who'd bought the goods were just gullible suckers. After all, as the showman Barnum had once said, there's one born every minute. Was it just a fortuitous coincidence that over an hour's worth had been standing at the stall when we were there?

By the time we'd reached the university we'd decided that the only way to find out, once and for all, exactly what this trader had been up to was to return to the market, next weekend. But on this next occasion we would be more prepared. We would bring a video camera to capture everything on tape if – and we thought it was a big 'if' – the trader was still there.

We were already quite familiar with the benefits of using videotapes of real-life human behaviour for sociological research. We had used them in our studies of courtroom trials and scientists. We were also aware of a study of rhetoric conducted by the sociologist Max Atkinson. He had collected hundreds of video recordings of politicians speaking at party political conferences. His research had shown that the most successful political orators used a small number of rhetorical devices – 'clap-traps', as he called them – that elicited applause and other expressions of appreciation from an audience. In conjunction with a TV producer and a voice coach, he'd even trained a neophyte politician to use the same devices. Judging from the *World in Action* TV programme which reported his findings, and which included an excerpt from this woman's maiden speech at a party conference, these skills could be taught and employed with some success by practically anyone.

Maybe this stall-holder was using the same techniques? He certainly had something in common with the politicians that

Atkinson had studied. Both were using rhetoric to obtain a demonstrable result – one was seeking applause, the other was seeking sales.

Both were also using contrasts – a strategy that places two pieces of related information in opposition and contradiction to one another. When John F. Kennedy, in his inaugural speech as President of the United States, appealed for an era of service from the American public with the phrase 'Ask not what your country can do for you, ask what you can do for your country', he packaged this appeal in a contrast. When Churchill talked of the debt that the British owed to the pilots of the RAF during the Battle of Britain with 'Never in the field of human conflict has so much been owed by so many to so few', he was using a contrast device too. The trader we had seen was exploiting essentially the same rhetorical technique; for example, when he informed the crowd that the tricycle was not made in Hong Kong ('ding-dong they go wrong') but was a British-made product. The way he came to the selling price of the tricycle was via an elaborate series of higher and contrasting prices which he could but was not going to charge for his goods.

Video would allow us to view and review this trader's rhetoric and its effect on his audience at will, and in extremely fine detail. Atkinson had found, for example, that the politicians' clap-traps were being supplemented and reinforced with finely co-ordinated gestures and postural shifts that helped to hammer home their political messages and also to telegraph the place where the onset of applause was most appropriate. It was obvious to us that such subtle skills, if they were being used by this market trader, could not easily be studied by means of other data-collection methods employed by social scientists, such as experiments, surveys, or unaided observation.

But there was one big unanswered question – would this market trader give us permission to film him? One colleague we spoke to – whose father had been a market trader – insisted that we were wasting our time because 'the last thing these types of people would tolerate were namby-pamby academics like you two filming on the market and interfering with their livelihood'.

The already slim prospect of obtaining permission to film seemed to recede even further when, during the week following our initial encounter with this trader, we paid a visit to the university library to see what had been written on these types of salespeople. We searched through the textbooks on economics, marketing and consumer behaviour. There was practically nothing, except a few studies by anthropologists of markets in other societies, and one or two opening paragraphs in student-edition economic textbooks which, before going on to seemingly bigger and more important things, conceded that street markets are similar to other types of markets. Although selling on street markets is perhaps the oldest and most elementary form of economic exchange, it had seemingly been ignored and even dismissed by experts.

One week later we found ourselves sitting in the same café, with piles of video equipment stacked around us, trying to figure out how we could convince this stall-holder, if we could find him, to let us record his sales spiel. We'd turned up more out of hope than expectation. The obvious way in which we could attempt to record him — surreptitiously — was out of the question. Apart from ethical considerations, 1985 was not yet the era of the palm-sized camcorder. In fact, the tapes we'd brought along were bigger than today's camera and recorder put together. Lamenting the fact that we, like Captain Kirk of the Starship *Enterprise*, did not have the Klingon ability to invoke a 'cloak of invisibility', we resigned ourselves to the inevitable — we would just have to seek his permission to make a recording.

When we reached the market the Family Rider-seller was, somewhat surprisingly, still at the same spot, spieling his heart out. This time he was talking up a storm about some towels that he'd managed to acquire at a knock-down price from a liquidation sale. We edged our way up to the side of the stall, intending

THE HARD SELL

to wait for the most opportune moment to ask permission to record. We didn't have to wait long. The trader stopped, right in the middle of his routine, and came over to speak to *us*.

'Can I help you lads?'

'Um, yeah,' we replied. 'We're sociologists from the university. We're studying selling. Can— can we— um— film you, please?

'You're not the taxman are you?'

The crowd laughed.

We thought he was being serious so we flashed some ID – a library card – but he didn't even glance at it.

'No problem.' He smiled, shook our hands and told someone called Betty in the crowd to hurry up and tidy her hair because she was going to be famous. Then he nonchalantly went back to work.

While we waited for the shock of our good fortune to wear off, we watched him selling as the camera automatically recorded his sales patter. If this trader had planted any confederates in his crowd then they must have been masters of quick-change disguise, because different people were raising their hands and buying the goods in each sale. If the goods he was selling were seconds then the puzzle remained as to how the same towels, in the same cellophane wrapping, were on sale at a higher price in a department store (not named 'Shivery Dick's') round the corner. If his stock was stolen then how come he was still trading in such a highly public place? The market inspector and even some of the crowd knew him by his first name.

When he'd finished serving his last customer he strode over to talk to us again. He told us that he was a market 'pitcher' or 'grafter' – someone whose job involved attracting a crowd of people to his stall and then persuading them, with an elaborate sales spiel, that the goods on offer were bargains and worth buying. He assured us that he used nothing more than talk to sell ('Don't need to'), that the goods he was selling had been bought from a warehouse and, if we didn't believe him, we

xvi

could always come back home with him ('Anytime you like') to see the receipts for his stock. He told us that we'd find other pitchers at other markets nearby ('You'll find them all over the world if you're that interested') and suggested that we should go and study them too.

We followed his advice. By the end of that same weekend we had recorded five other pitchers at nearby markets selling things as diverse as sweets, towels, clothing, pens, pans, toys, meat, china and dinner services. One pitcher had even been selling boxes of Tampax. In fact, they'd been selling so well, apparently, that he'd had to warn everyone that they were only available at his stall 'for a limited period'.

Playing the tapes we had recorded back in our social psychology laboratory was an eye-opening experience. Because we were using the latest video technology, we could study the pitchers' sales spiels word for word and inspect the audience's reaction to them frame by frame. We quickly realized we had stumbled upon a bunch of spellbinding orators and patter merchants. What astounded us more than anything else was the sheer subtlety of the selling skills that these people were using. Sales were often obtained, *en masse*, not by shouting loudly, or by relying on some general, pre-scripted set of crude or illegal sales tactics, but by the employment, at an appropriate point in the sale, of a barely noticeable well-timed gesture, look or touch. Many of these skills could only be discerned after repeated inspection of the videotapes.

Since our first accidental encounter with this pitcher we have collected over seventy-five recordings of pitching routines from street markets all over Britain. We have recorded pitching routines in France and the Netherlands; pitchers selling the same goods at different times on the same as well as different markets; pitchers selling one item of stock (typically 'demonstrators') as well as a range of different products at any one time; and the same pitchers selling different goods on different markets and under different conditions (such as summer and winter, sunshine and rain, etc.). Only one pitcher ever refused to allow us to record him. Another pitcher, who had been working the same market on the same day, wasn't at all surprised at his refusal. When we asked him why, he informed us that he was 'a shit pitcher'.

To supplement these recordings we also interviewed many of the traders as well as some of the shoppers who bought (and did not buy) from them. To gain additional 'insider' knowledge, one of the authors learned to pitch and worked with a group of market pitchers for five months.

On a few occasions we also recorded pitchers surreptitiously, so as to check the extent to which our presence as researchers, with all our video equipment, disturbed and distorted the practices we observed. Apart from the occasional opportunistic references both to us (such as 'Watch your pockets, ladies and gentlemen, Dr Pinch is about') and to our equipment (such as 'Is that a microphone in your hand or are you pleased to see me?' and, once or twice, things like: 'All we're doing is making a commercial for the television'), we found no other obvious differences between this type of data and the recordings we had collected secretly.

In fact, wherever we went, whoever we studied, and however we obtained our recordings, we found more similarities than differences between these pitchers. Although each product offered for sale was being talked up with its own tailor-made patter and humour, these salesmen and women were all doing essentially the same thing. What we had stumbled upon was a kind of folk marketing activity based on a body of lay knowledge that was rarely found in academic texts. This was a skill disseminated, *in situ*, by word of mouth, and handed down from father and mother to son and daughter. None of the pitchers we studied had ever been to business school; not one of them had a business diploma, an MBA, or even a degree in sociology. Some were quite critical of what they could learn from these types of courses and the applicability of academic theories of selling, marketing and consumer behaviour in the real world. Indeed, for some pitchers the acronym 'MBA' stands for 'Master of Bugger All'.

One reason for this scepticism on the part of pitchers is that they deem marketing and selling to be, above all else, a social and communicative skill rather than a purely economic act. In their sales world, talk is by no means cheap and goods will never sell themselves without the assistance of this communicative skill. In this book it is these communicative skills which we will examine.

At first glance the sales and marketing techniques used by pitchers appear to have little relevance to other types of selling and marketing activity. Many people assume, as we had initially, that this form of exchange is archaic and simplistic – that pitcher's coax money out of the shoppers' pockets by a mixture of verbal conjuring, showmanship and chicanery. But pitching is a serious, sophisticated and, on many occasions, highly lucrative business. Moreover, as we shall see, there are skills at work which have a relevance far removed from the street market setting.

We will show that the various methods pitchers use to sell their goods display an intimate understanding of the informal 'rules' and shared economic reasoning that their audience of prospective purchasers hold about what it is that makes goods valuable bargains. This grass-roots knowledge goes beyond the standard models of economic and marketing behaviour whereby it is often assumed, for example, that consumers behave rationally and always search in advance for the lowest prices for goods they plan to purchase. Pitching, as we shall see, is certainly not simply a matter of these sellers equating their supply of goods with the demand (or even the demands) of prospective customers. Pitchers do not create or satisfy demand simply by offering goods at a 'low' price. Their task is far harder than this. It will become clear that persuading people to purchase goods is a complex affair, and rests upon pitchers attending to, appealing to and capitalizing upon a variety of taken-for-granted social conventions in order to persuade people to buy.

Pitchers deal directly, and on a very personal level, with their customers, and have direct access to their social worlds. Their sales patter forms a barometer for what their customers are thinking, what they are buying and, more to the point, what they can afford to buy and what motivates them to buy. Built into the pitchers' talk is an analysis of selling, shopping and consumer behaviour which is based upon their own direct experience of how people actually behave in real-life marketing situations. It is their gifts, their 'gab', their lay theories and their homespun 'psychology' which form the main focus of this book. It is the lessons that these marketeers have learned from doing their own 'market research' which our research has tried to capture, and which, in what follows, we attempt to describe, analyse and explain.

In Chapters 1 to 5 we examine the various stages of a typical market pitching routine – attracting and building an audience (Chapter 1); describing and demonstrating the goods (Chapter 2); building up the value of the goods on offer and announcing the selling price (Chapter 3); securing commitments and encouraging people to buy immediately (Chapter 4) – and the various ways in which pitchers attempt to deal with any problems, such as trouble-makers, that may arise during the course of a sale (Chapter 5). Chapter 6 reports what happened when one of the authors worked as a market pitcher.

However, this book is more than just an in-depth study of the rhetorical and interactional skills used by market pitchers. Even though many pitchers undoubtedly have a way with words, and their method of selling, although unorthodox, is, more often than not, both spellbinding and entertaining, they also have much more than this to tell us. The insights we have gained from studying this type of selling have, we believe, a much wider applicability and importance.

For instance, why is it that these so called street-wise 'barrow boys' seem to be equally at home (and equally successful and, by all accounts, equally indispensable) shouting about their wares on the street markets or yelling out a multi-million-pound 'position' across the pit of a financial futures market in the City? Is it also just a coincidence that some of the most successful companies in the UK, such as Marks and Spencer, Amstrad, Tesco (original motto: 'Pile 'em high and sell 'em cheap') originally started their business life by trading on street markets? Or are there some fundamental and forgotten lessons that can be learned by going back to this most 'elementary' form of selling and studying it seriously?

We must also ask ourselves the question: why is it that one of the most successful types of television advertising – 'home shopping' – is based directly on the techniques used by market pitchers? QVC – the home shopping channel (annual sales in 1992 $1.3 billion) has recently branched out from the USA and Canada into the UK. In the USA, home shopping is the fastest-growing retail sector and is a business with a turnover in excess of $2 billion annually. This figure is predicted to rise to $100 billion by the end of the decade. Some home shopping companies run twenty-to-thirty-minute 'infomercials' which are almost verbatim copies of market pitching routines, complete with stall and audience.

We believe that the techniques used by market pitchers to sell their goods on street markets are not novel. They are essentially the very same techniques that are used, and used successfully, by people in other situations as a means of persuading others to 'buy' things, whether it be goods or services in a high-street retail store or a point of view in a political or courtroom speech. Consequently, our study of market pitching has also been supplemented by examining videos of other people who 'sell' by oral means. For instance, we look at other types of street traders, such as the illegal street hawkers called 'fly pitchers' (Chapter 7), and 'con artists' such as mock auction fraudsters in the UK and USA (Chapter 8), as well as street entertainers and urban hustlers in the UK, USA, France and India (Chapter 9). Chapter 10 shows some of the similarities between pitching and TV 'home shopping' shows (in the USA, Canada and Europe).

Each of these chapters contains detailed verbatim passages, taken directly from our recordings, of the various techniques under discussion. An explanation of the transcription process we have employed follows. A glossary of unfamiliar words and phrases can be found at the end of the book. All the names of the pitchers and other salespeople we studied have been changed to preserve their anonymity. For the same reason we have altered, on one or two occasions, references to specific products and market venues in the transcripts.

KEY TO TRANSCRIPTIONS

SPEAKERS

A	Individual member of audience
AS	The audience as a group
CD	Card dealer
D	Demonstrator
EP	Edge Puller
FW	Floor worker
H	Host
L	Lurker
N	Nause/complainer
P	Pitcher
PC	Pitch Crew
R	Rick
S	Salesperson
SE	Street Entertainer
TM	Top Man
V	Volunteer

DIALOGUE

Talk	Dialogue in italics is spoken louder or emphasized
TALK	Dialogue in capitals is shouted or spoken even louder than that in italics
(Talk)	Brackets are used to represent dialogue that was difficult to hear and transcribe. An estimation of what may have been said is provided.

THE HARD SELL

CHAPTER 1

Building an Edge

According to Gary, a former bingo caller and disc jockey, now a market pitcher, the street market economy, like life itself, has its winners and its losers. He claims to be a winner, and after we had filmed him spieling one afternoon he told us why.

'You see all those silly idiots standing on the market with prices on their gear and their mouths shut? You know, those nutters who sit reading the newspaper waiting for everybody to come to *them*?'

We looked round, then nodded.

'Yes, love, can I help you?' he whimpered in a pathetic, high-pitched voice. 'That's what they say to people who stop at their stall.' He shook his head incredulously. '*That's* no good. *That don't sell gear.*' He thrust a pointed finger to his open mouth. '*That's what sells gear*! They just stand there all day wondering why they're skint. You've seen it yourselves, when we're having a break and not spieling, *nobody* buys *nothing*!'

'Yeah.' We'd noticed this, yet we still had our doubts. 'But it can't be as simple as that,' we ventured timidly. 'Surely the people who shop on markets aren't genetically programmed to stop, listen and buy from pitchers as soon as they've opened their mouths, are they?'

'*Of course they're not*,' Gary snapped, looking at us as if we were stupid or something. 'You've got to get an edge first.'

'An *edge*?'

'Rhyming slang. It's cockney.'

We obviously looked none the wiser.

3

'It's from "hedge and ditch" – it means pitch.'

'Um . . . pitch?' The penny still hadn't dropped.

'Y'know,' he broke in patiently, 'punters. *People-at-your-stall!*'

It turns out that the term 'edge' not only describes the crowd of shoppers who gather at a pitching stall, it also refers to the financial advantage that pitchers gain by seeking out the public's custom with an elaborate sales talk and deploying a sophisticated set of crowd-attracting and audience-management tactics. Whereas most market traders (or 'lurkers', as they are referred to by many spielers) usually remain content to let passers-by make their own decision as to whether they should stop and make a purchase, pitchers do not. Pitchers actively tout for the public's custom. 'We'd work our balls off for the next pound,' one (male) pitcher remarked. 'We're not called grafters for nothing, you know.'

Enterprising lurkers sometimes put prices on their stock to attract customers, but pitchers never do. This is because once the cost of the goods on offer is clearly marked, then there would be little point in going through the whole rigmarole of the selling spiel with its step-by-step build-up and slow but sure run-down to the final selling price. Some lurkers, though, do use speech to sell. Now and again they will attempt to draw attention to their goods by shouting out their prices and, for good measure, they will sometimes throw in a phrase or two about why their stock is worth buying. This shouting is, however, rather rudimentary. Even when it is successful in terms of generating sales, only individual buyers are attracted; rarely, if ever, will a crowd gather, let alone buy *en masse*. Their shouting is similar to the way in which street-corner newspaper vendors traditionally attempt to garner attention and, although lurkers appear to have the edge on their news-spieling counterparts in terms of clarity of pronunciation, the sales of both are usually sporadic and unpredictable. This is partly because lurkers simply use speech to announce, rather than to manage a sale. Often the name and price of a particular item is repeatedly (and somewhat monotonously) called out in a sing-song voice, as happens in the following example of a lurker struggling to sell her cauliflowers:

L   Come on, *clear 'em out*. Twenty-five pence your caulis.
     Come on, *clear 'em out*. Twenty-five pence your caulis.
     Come on! . . .

Sometimes, though only rarely, this shouting will be more elaborate, as in the following case where an Asian lurker is extolling the virtues of his stock of socks:

L   *Four for a pound*. Come on, ladies, the bargains are here.
     Now! Anything on here four for a pound. [To a passer-by]
     Not bad, is it? Get them before I go bankrupt. *Cheap?*
     Must be good, four for a pound. It's got to go, ladies. I
     have to do it because I got to do it. We are not foreigners
     any more, we are *British*. [To another passer-by] What are
     you looking at me like that for, brother? I am not a nig-
     nog any more. Here, I'm English. *British*. They call me
     George. By the way, I am sending all the foreigners back,
     one by one. [To somebody who is suspiciously fingering
     his stock] She [his assistant] has got you covered, *all right*?
     Black Power to the people. Let's have the bargains. Come
     on, ladies, give me the money. [To someone else who is
     touching the goods] No pinching, you American. Oh, I
     go to America. *Lovely country*. Come on, we're doing four
     for a pound. *Let's go!* We have got to do it, *got to do it*. We
     are going to make it here for you, how can you beat my
     prices?

For most lurkers, shouting seems to be used as a last resort – as a final, desperate act to get shot of goods at the end of the day, especially if they are perishable stock such as fruit and vegetables.

We asked Terry, a successful pitcher who started off as a quiet trader, whether he had ever employed any special shopper-attracting techniques when he was lurking.

'No.'

'*None?*' Now it was our turn to look incredulous.

'No. Not really. You see, you fall into the trap of having your bright little orange stars with "only five pounds" or whatever written on them – that's the biggest marketing ploy you've ever discovered. You think, "This is it! I've found the answer!" Instead of writing it out on bits of old cardboard you've cut out yourself you find that somebody actually prints them, so all of a sudden, you're like a "professional" trader.'

The reason why pitchers spend so much time and effort trying to attract a crowd is simple: the larger the number of people standing at the stall, the greater the likelihood of obtaining mass sales. But as we shall see later, pitching is not simply a 'numbers game'; members of the pitcher's edge are often employed unwittingly as 'free advertising' in order to sell to other people. Moreover, the various individuals who stop at a stall have to be turned into a homogeneous crowd – an 'audience' – and the first step in any pitching routine is, therefore, to attract a large number of tightly compacted shoppers ('as tightly packed as the leaves in a hedge') to listen to the sales patter.

The location of the stall and its visibility to the market public play a significant part in the quest for a crowd. Many pitchers will pay the market authorities extra to obtain an advantageous 'prime site' location in close proximity to a major pedestrian thoroughfare. A corner site at the intersection of two highly populated pedestrian walkways is ideal. Interestingly enough, some of the more astute lurkers favour a site situated next to a pitching stall for their own joints, because they find that with the larger numbers of people who gather for the pitcher, their own sales tend to go up too. ('Yeah, I can work individuals off the edge of his edge,' one lurker told us.)

Many pitchers work from an elevated stall position – usually from out of the side of a pantechnicon lorry – and use amplification systems to project their voices to the far corners of the market. Bright lights are also deployed to illuminate the stall. On the typically dull afternoons of a British market, a pitcher's lorry often stands out like a neon beacon crying out for people to participate. Close attention is always paid to the 'flash', or layout of the goods on offer, to make the stock look as attractive as possible. Pot-sellers, in particular, use a very elaborate flash with cut-glass chandeliers, giant Chinese vases and other ornaments bedecking every spare inch of their stalls. 'Flash', as practically every market trader we spoke to assured us, 'means cash.'

Although all these factors undoubtedly help to attract the odd individual passer-by, they do not guarantee that a large number of people will stop at the stall at any one point in time. Indeed, many of the pitchers we talked to claimed that they would have gone out of business long ago if they had had to live off the profits that accrued from their flash alone. To acquire a crowd, however, is a task worthy of Hercules. Gary put us in the picture once again.

'The easiest part of pitching is serving people at the end. The hardest part is at the beginning – getting people to stop and watch.'

In particular, pitchers always seem to experience a problem in attracting and keeping the very first individual.

GETTING THE FIRST PERSON TO STOP AT THE STALL

Mack the potato-peeler demonstrator, who continually faces the same problem as pitchers in getting that first person to stop, reckons that the cause of this difficulty is that individuals prefer to be part of crowds. People find shelter and safety in numbers, and because of this it is much easier to attract the *second* person to the stall than the first.

'Sometimes I'll have a walk round the market and I'll stand talking to another grafter who's also taking a break. So I stand right up in front of his joint and we'll be talking about having a drink or whatever. All of a sudden we'll have two people standing behind me.'

We'd experienced this type of situation for ourselves. To get permission to record the pitchers we would often hang around the fringe of an audience until the pitcher had finished spieling and was about to take a break. Once the shoppers had dispersed we would then go up to the front of the stall, announce who we were, and ask if we could record a couple of routines. Yet on many of these occasions, before we'd even plucked up the courage to ask to record a sale, there would be a couple of passers-by who had stopped at the stall behind us, thinking that we were the first customers for the next sale. More often than not the pitcher would then start his next sale using us, and the small crowd that had gathered, to attract an even larger crowd.

One obvious solution to the problem of attracting the first person to the stall is for the pitcher to provide his own member of staff solely for this purpose; that is, to use a plant or a 'rick'. By having a confederate who appears just to have stopped to listen planted at the front of the stall, other passers-by will be less reluctant to stop themselves.

The vast majority of the pitchers we studied, however, did not employ plants or ricks at the beginning of their sales, nor, indeed, at any other point in their routines. They didn't need to. They claimed that it was cheaper, and certainly more effective, to capitalize on their knowledge of how humans behave as individuals in crowd situations. What pitchers tended to do, instead, was to structure their patter in a way that made it more likely that people would already be standing at the stall at the beginning of a sale. Many spielers who sell a variety of goods can do this by conducting a 'running' or 'rolling' pitch. Before reaching the end of one sale – usually the point where they announce the selling price of the goods on offer – they will give the audience a brief taster of the line of goods that will be offered in the next sale. This induces some of the people already standing at the stall to stay for the next routine. In the following extract the pitcher has been attempting to sell sets of striped 'Habitat' bath and hand towels. He has elaborately described these goods and obtained displays of interest in them from members of the crowd, but he hasn't as yet announced their selling price. Now, instead of doing so, he proceeds to talk about some other items of stock he will sell in the next sale:

P   Very, *very* quickly, because you've stood here *long enough*. I appreciate that. *You see these here?* [P picks up a king-sized towel] *No stories*! I'll come straight to the price. Who bought those Habitat sets?

AS   [Hands raised]

P   Right. *No stories*! When I tell you what I want for these to match your Habitat. [P spreads the king-sized towel over the front of the stall] Look at the size of those. *FABU-LOUS*! If anyone wants a matching set I'll do those next. Or what about one of these? [P spreads another king-sized towel over the front of the stall] These are made in France. Anyone like a 'French bit'? Look at those. *Fabulous*! Anyway, *first of all* (. . .) *This is the price*. For your two bath, and your two hand . . .

This strategy works on the same principle as the cliff-hanging final scenes in the old Flash Gordon adventure series starring Buster Crabbe shown in Saturday-morning cinemas in the 1950s and 1960s. It is also a technique commonly used in many soap operas. In each case the audience is primed with information (usually in the form of an appetizing but un-finished plot line) designed to make them want to see more. Thus, when a grafter uses this type of running pitch spiel, by the time the next sale actually has started it is very likely that there will already be a small number of people standing at the stall eagerly waiting for the next sale. A running pitch, however, does not solve either the problem of getting started in the first place, or how to attract an edge if you are only pitching a single item of stock.

THE PULL UP

One technique that is used to attract a first edge is known as the 'pull-up'. Instead of passively waiting for someone to come to them, as many lurkers do, the pitcher may try to persuade an individual passer-by to stop. This individual, once at the stall, will then attract others. With this strategy, then, the pitcher is able to get people to 'rick for free'.

Attracting that first person is far easier said than done. Linda, an iron-pad demonstrator, who was adamant that 'Getting people to stop is definitely the most difficult thing to do', explained the method she uses:

'You start off by asking a passer-by a question. For instance, "What is this made of?" So you ask them something and put the product in front of them so they've got to answer you and stop. If you ask them a question, they don't know what it is to do with. And then . . .' She started laughing. '. . . they realize!'

Many of the demonstrators who ply their wares in large department stores use this procedure. The 'pull-up' relies on catching people off guard, and getting them to react positively before they fully appreciate what they have done and what they have thus let themselves in for. (Try waving at strangers in passing cars for a similar type of automatic and unthinking response.)

But the 'pull-up' has two fundamental flaws, both of which create a larger problem than it attempts to solve. First, in engaging one person, the pitcher must be extremely careful not to ignore the next person who also stops, otherwise they are likely to lose both potential customers. As Mack informed us:

'If someone else comes up on the side you've got to try to include them as well. Sometimes what happens is you talk to one person and then you see someone else and when you show that other person what you're selling, the first person goes away because they've lost interest. So you lose them both. You've got to try to include the two together and it's bloody difficult.'

Second, the underlying reasoning behind the 'pull-up' – that is, build your customer base one by one – is essentially narrow-minded and, as one pitcher put it, 'small time'. Consequently, it is ripe for failure. Many of the in-store demonstrators we studied spent so much effort trying to overcome the difficulty of getting their initial customer that it became an almost insurmountable barrier. They would try so hard to attract one particular person to the stall that when they eventually succeeded in doing so they would usually postpone any attempt to build a larger audience and try, instead, to win a sale from the individual who had stopped.

Most pitchers adopted another more radical solution – the 'grand gesture', the big risk. This enterprise, if it comes off, can reap major dividends.

THE BLIND START

The 'blind start' is one such risky grand gesture. It consists of the pitcher shouting and creating a commotion until a crowd has gathered, and it capitalizes on the fact that people, in this case passers-by, have a voracious appetite for witnessing a public incident. It was, you may remember from the Introduction, precisely such a commotion that first drew us to the world of market pitching. In one sense any loud words, any form of noise, will do. As Terry explained: 'If you collapsed in the high street grasping your throat and rolling around going

"Aaaargh!" one person might go and phone an ambulance. Another seventy-three would stand and look at you.'

This technique of creating a commotion to draw a crowd is perhaps one reason why they used to have race-day public hangings on the York Knavesmire, and it is regularly used today by street entertainers (see Chapter 9). For instance, a comedian we filmed on Venice Beach, Los Angeles employed the very effective technique of running up and down the sidewalk shouting like a madman, sounding off an excruciatingly loud klaxon and telling passers-by that he wouldn't stab them if they stopped to listen to him. Most pitchers, though, tend to prefer to blind-start by talking very loudly about what it is they will soon be selling. Terry elaborated on what a pitcher would actually do in this regard:

'You'll take a line, perhaps your favourite line – something you know a lot about. You look at the line – *you don't look at anybody*! – and you begin to talk about it, mention everything there is to know about it. You do that for three or four minutes and then look up, and then I guarantee that you'll have the beginnings of an edge.'

This strategy isn't as straightforward as it appears. It is high risk in the sense that it can lead to the embarrassing situation of the pitcher finding himself spieling into thin air. The key feature of this procedure is that the pitcher must never look up at the passers-by or at those people who have stopped at the stall. Instead, he or she strictly adopts a pose of solitary musing, pretending to busy himself or herself with rearranging the stock. Avoiding their eyes seems to encourage people to gather – they feel under less of a threat and more relaxed about stopping.

Of course, the type of patter used in the blind start is also important. The various features of the goods soon to be offered for sale are usually extolled in short, catchy, appetizing and often outrageous 'sales bites' which summarize the upcoming sales offer in a concise and highly dramatic way. The following examples are typical:

P   It'll be the *best* deal for *cash* you'll find *anywhere*. And we'll give you more value for money now, in the *next* two *minutes*, than them shops and stores will give you *there* in two *years*!

P   In fact, the man who owns this stock, he's in Spain with my wife right now. An' what he's doing to my wife right now, I'm gonna do to his business. *Now watch*.

P   BY THE WAY, if *you've paid* more money for them *don't* shout at me. I only apologize when I put my prices *up*, NOT when they're still going *down*, so look.

P   Ah'll tell you something. *Whoever* comes in possession of a pair of these, at the *ridiculous* amount of money I'm gonna charge you today, never mind a *customer*, you'll be a *friend for life*!

Each of these short sequences of patter are the pitchers' equivalent of fast food — a tasty snack created specifically to appeal to that fleeting moment of economic lust in the otherwise uninterested passer-by. What is likely to follow is made as clear as crystal. Anyone who cares to stop at the stall is soon likely to receive the chance of obtaining a major if not unparalleled bargain. Because each of these summary phrases lasts, at most, only a couple of seconds, every member of the public who passes within hearing range of the stall is provided with the opportunity to listen to at least one self-contained segment of sales patter.

KNOCKING OUT

Another strategy pitchers use to start a sale is called 'knocking out'. Rather than simply shouting about the bargains that are to come in the forthcoming sale, the pitcher holds a preliminary sale of goods at extremely low prices:

P   This is Loctite glue. It's little bits of odds and sods that I get from time to time. They're ninety pence each. There's one, two, three of them. [P stops and 'thinks to himself' for a short while] Go on, there's four, there's five, there's half a dozen of them. Somebody give me a POUND the price of *one*. Here you are. [Gives bags to PC]

PC [To a buyer] Got your pound?

P   In fact, COME BACK! What did I say? *A pound the price o' one?* Here you are, let's be bloody fair with them. *It's Christmas.* Ninety-nine pence each, there's six in a bag an' I said a pound. [BANG] I'll take *FIFTY PENCE* to get them out of the road.

The goods sold during 'knocking out' sales serve the same function as supermarket loss leaders. The expense of selling the items so cheaply will be recuperated later from the extra shoppers who gather. The stock offered is invariably cheap items such as tea-towels, playing cards or job-lot remnants such as the tubes of glue in the sale above. Passers-by are attracted to the stall because their expectations about what something is worth are speedily and dramatically subverted by a pitcher actually selling that item at a much-reduced price. In contrast to the blind start, which claims that bargains will soon be on offer, knocking out provides a more concrete and immediate proof that bargains are to be had. In the above example the pitcher undermines the audience's expectations of the price of the goods on offer by obtaining purchases of the six tubes of glue at a pound before finally halving his original asking price to fifty pence. By going lower than the price that some members of the audience were either expecting or were willing to pay, the pitcher manages to convey the impression (and perhaps thereby plant a precedent in the audience's minds) that he is selling major bargains and that he doesn't have a care in the world about effectively giving away his stock. This technique is likely to be more successful than the blind start because the movement created by people actually buying the goods often serves to attract passers-by who, seeing other people waiting to buy, become especially curious about what is happening.

FERMENTING THE EDGE:
BUILDING AN EXECUTION PITCH

Building a big edge takes time, so any pitcher worth his or her salt will not be satisfied with the number of people who have initially gathered at the stall and will go on to attempt to build an 'execution pitch'. This is a crowd of the size that would, as tradition holds, turn up to watch public executions. To build such a large crowd (with at least fifty potential customers), the pitcher employs the audience who have already congregated at the sales site to act unwittingly as sales representatives in order to attract even more people to the stall. This is achieved by getting the initial edge to respond positively (by raising their hands or laughing) which, in turn, advertises in an independent and thus more credible way the merits of the market trader and his or her stock to other people on the market. The louder and more ostentatious these displays of responsiveness are, the better for the pitcher's edge-building project:

P   Ladies an' gentlemen, the *next* time [CLAP] I clap my
     hands like that, the *FIRST* few buyers [P raises his right
     hand] to have their hands in the air like that can have one
     o' them bath towels. [P points to someone who already
     has a hand raised] I want *no* cheatin'. NOT three p, NOT
     two p, *NOT* for a penny (. . .) when I *clap* my hands, I'm
     watching who's first. I'll be the judge and I'll be the jury,
     it's the end of the day. NOT three p or two p, not for a
     penny, *who could* make use of any one o' them bath towels
     today?
P   [CLAP]

15

AS   [Many hands are rapidly raised]

P   For twenty pound?

AS   [LAUGHTER] [The vast majority of the audience who
     have raised their arms rapidly lower them]

P   *I'm only joking*! You ought to have seen your face— *your*
     hands then. *Your* hands went *like that* [P rapidly raises his
     hand] and bloody *like that*. [P rapidly lowers his hand] *Eh?*

AS   [LAUGHTER]

In this sequence the pitcher succeeds in getting practically every
person in his edge not only to raise and lower their hands in
unison, but also to laugh. These positive and collective signs of
responsiveness convince more passers-by to stop at the stall.
Pitchers often obtain extended sequences of this type of audience responsiveness under the guise of being unable to ascertain
who was the first person to raise their hand, or by claiming that
the crowd do not deserve the bargain on offer until they raise
their hands again and more quickly.

The audience act as unpaid 'opinion leaders', demonstrating
to others nearby that it is worth stopping at the stall. Street
entertainers use a similar technique when, early on in their
show, they get the audience to applaud loudly even though they
have done nothing to warrant the applause aside from explicitly
asking for it. This vociferous and apparently genuine display of
appreciation serves to attract other people to their performance
(see Chapter 9). In the gambling halls of Las Vegas the same
type of ploy is used. Casino owners make their slot machines as
noisy as possible when they pay out the jackpots so that other
potential slot-heads hear the sound of every winner and are
drawn to try their own luck on the machines.

Although nothing is sold during such edge-gathering antics,
the pitcher's audience usually treat what has transpired as a
mischievous joke at their own expense rather than as a cruel
deception. Terry told us: 'Now if you understand human
nature, they're not going to say "Oh what a bloody con" and

walk off. They don't, because people are people. They love it, and they laugh.'

Another method of building an execution pitch is to sell one or two items of regular stock at a drastically reduced price by playfully teasing an individual in the crowd:

P   OOOH, *look at this*. There's only one of these an' one of you can have it. Seven, six, five, four, three, couple o' quid, [BANG] A POUND, who's having it? *Sold*, that lady there. Lady down there. Give her a bag. *Are you married, love?*

A   Yes.

P   Fifty pence. *Do you swear?*

A   Sometimes.

P   Thirty p. *Do you go to church?*

A   No.

P   Ten pence.

AS   [LAUGHS]

P   *Got any kids?*

A   Yeah. Five.

P   [Smiling] *HOW MANY?*

AS   [LAUGHS]

P   I see you're back on your bloody feet again. [BANG] *Charge 'er five pence. An' do you believe in free love, yes or no?*

A   [Laughing self-consciously] Yes.

P   *Right*, we're off. [Pretends to climb over the front of the stall as if he was about to elope with A]

AS   [LAUGHS]

P   [Looks momentarily at his assistant] Here, give her the bugger for *nothing*.[PC puts the goods in a carrier bag and goes to hand it over to A].

P   *Hang on!* [P takes item back] I don't mind you having that for nowt [tears the handles off the bag]. You're *not* having *all* the bleedin' bag. Now then, here y' are.

AS   [LAUGHTER]

Throughout this sequence, as with the previous ones, we see that the pitcher accomplishes the desired outcome by lacing his performance with humour. In the sale above, which lasts no more than about thirty seconds, there are four separate instances where the audience are laughing and thereby producing exactly the kind of noise that attracts more people to the stall. This is not an accident. Humour is frequently used in everyday life as a means of dealing with problems. A crowd is far more likely to go along with a series of unorthodox actions if those actions are undertaken in the spirit of 'having a bit of a laugh and a giggle'. But just because what occurs is humorous does not, of course, prevent it from having a deadly serious purpose. By entertaining the crowd, a pitcher is more likely to get people to stay at the stall ('It's good fun. Free as well') and also put them in a relaxed frame of mind for buying.

Gathering a large number of people to a stall is not, in itself, sufficient to achieve sales. The crowd have to be constantly worked on by the pitcher in order to prepare them for the ensuing bargain offers. Yet people who stop to listen to a pitcher's spiel are not automatically going to buy goods. Many are intent upon enjoying some cheap entertainment and they sometimes go to enormous lengths to resist the various temptations which these sellers place in front of them. They display this resistance in a variety of often very subtle ways.

MANAGING THE PEOPLE WHO HAVE GATHERED

At first sight what could be more straightforward and unproblematic than gathering at a stall to listen to a pitcher? After all, it's a 'free country', the market is a public place, and one would think that no special obligations would follow from simply passing the time of day in the vicinity of someone's stall. Yet when we studied our videos of these types of crowds we found a surprisingly large number of features suggesting that people in crowds follow unspoken social rules that govern the organization of such public behaviour. Pitchers have no need of videos to learn about these subtle rules of social organization – their very livelihood depends upon recognizing and overcoming them.

Of greatest importance to the pitchers are the various protective measures that some shoppers use to avoid being placed under any obligation to buy the goods on offer. These are evident right from the moment when people begin to gather at the stall. For instance, they tend not to stand just anywhere, but to place themselves so that they are shielded and protected by someone else who has stopped before them.

Once at the stall, many individuals adopt body postures that indicate a lack of interest in making a purchase, sometimes regardless of whether or not they intend to or actually do eventually buy. These include transient stances such as standing sideways on to the pitcher (as if to emphasize that they have stopped only for a moment), and 'closed' body positionings such as standing with their arms akimbo, keeping their hands in their pockets and avoiding eye contact with the pitcher.

The further you go back in a pitcher's audience the less likelihood there is of finding an individual adopting these types of stances. Also, when a pitcher moves towards a section of the crowd you can sometimes see the audience quickly adopting one or more of these defensive postures. More generally, people also exhibit a reluctance to stand near the front of the stall. This creates a sort of 'no-man's land' between the pitcher and the front of the crowd.

Pitchers take distance to equal disinterest. The further away people are from the pitcher, the more protected people feel. They will attempt to remain in earshot of the sales patter while at the same time standing at a symbolic as well as a literal arm's length away from the pitcher.

This can create major problems for a pitcher, especially in

terms of maintaining the interest and attention of the people who have gathered at the stall. For example, passers-by will often walk idly through the no-man's land space. This can distract those who have gathered at the stall and, indeed, may also encourage those individuals standing at the front to follow suit by peeling off and walking away, too.

Furthermore, any objects situated between the front of the stall and the audience may be used by those people standing at the front as an excuse to avoid standing closer to the pitcher. Mack puts it like this:

'If you have your stall canopy low – like at hat high – the punters will stand behind it. It's a psychological barrier. Here's another thing: I was working one market where if you wanted to demonstrate you had to move your stall three feet back from the front of this line – in the tiles on the ground was a white line. I *couldn't* fucking get them to stand over that white line! So I had to paint black spots over it to make it look like the rest of the ground before they'd come closer. It's *amazing*! Another thing: sometimes you'll get a sheet of paper, like a newspaper, right in front of your pitch. They'll stand behind the newspaper! Why not stand *on* it? So, to get them close, I'll have to pick up the newspaper and sling it under the stall. *Mental, isn't it?*'

Mack obviously has enough experience of this type of problem to write a PhD thesis on it:

'When I'm looking down at the edge I look at feet. And if I see any that are pointing away from me it bugs me. I'd rather they pissed off immediately because I know they're gonna do it eventually, and I don't want them to do it just as I announce the price. If you pull them in right close to you, people like that are no longer noticeable to other members in the edge. Then he's not so much a threat to me because I can nail him with my eyes so that he'll go when I want him to go.'

An edge is, in many respects, like the pupils in a school classroom – eager swots at the front, the disinterested skulking somewhere at the back. The trouble for the pitcher, as for the schoolteacher, is that the disinterested can spoil things for everyone else. The last thing any pitcher wants is for those less than committed members of the audience at the back to transmit their reservations to the relatively more eager participants at the front. Pitchers may adopt special tactics to get those standing at the back to stay and, if they do, to move forward. If successful, they score twice: the people moving closer from the back become more committed members of the crowd, and they force those who are standing at the front even closer to the stall. A more likely option, though, is for the pitcher simply to mock those standing at the back of the edge. This happens in the following sequence; the pitcher is attempting to sell towels:

P   What's wrong with all you at the back? *Don't you get washed or something?* You can't *all* be tax inspectors!

In this way the pitcher at least obtains laughter at the expense of a group of people who were probably never going to buy the goods anyway.

Mack elaborated on the disruptive effect the non-involved persons at the back of an edge can have on those standing in front of them:

'All this standing back or being at the back of the crowd is *bad news all round*. When the punters are relatively close to you the movement at the back doesn't appear to bother them. If they're stood back, and there's movement behind them, somehow it gets through to them and it makes them fidget. Once your front row starts doing that then you've got real problems. Have you ever been to a party where your buddy invited you but you don't know any of the others? You go into that party and feel uncomfortable from *minute one*! That's exactly how I think the people standing at the back of your audience feel. They feel that, really, they're not part and parcel of, like, what's happening.'

Getting closer to heaven

In view of this array of potential problems, many pitchers will try and close up the no-man's land. One way of bringing the audience and the pitcher physically closer together is for the pitcher to throw goods out into the no-man's land space so that the audience are obliged to move forward to catch them before they fall to the ground and get soiled or broken. In so persuading one or two individuals to move forward to sample the merchandise, the rest of the edge are encouraged to follow suit and are likely to be pulled closer too. This is often done when selling towels, bedding or clothing. Other, more widely used options are, firstly, to demonstrate the goods in the no-man's land space (particularly effective with remote-controlled toys which can be used to lure the audience slowly to the front of the stall), and secondly, for a pitcher to dangle items of stock in such a way that people at the stall have to move closer to inspect them. This happens in the following sale:

P   [Speaking to a woman at the front of the crowd] Have a feel of those, love.

A   [Steps forward to feel the towel]

P   *Don't bloody wear them out!*

AS   [Laughter]

P   Go on, have a good feel.

A   [Feels towels]

P   If you don't like the way they feel you can have your feel back. Are those all right, love?

A   Yes.

P   [Holding out his hand towards A] Now feel me and feel the difference.

A   [Steps forward to feel the pitcher]

P   She bloody is doing as well!

AS   [Laughter]

22

By far the most obvious solution to this problem is for the pitcher explicitly to instruct the audience to move in closer. Gary explains:

'What a lot of pitchers don't do is, they have people surrounding them, sure, but they *don't bring 'em in close*. Unless they move in close they won't buy. When they're stood away from the stall they're protecting themselves. They think that if they are standing away from you they can always walk away without buying, right? So what you've got to do is to ask them to move in. *You pull 'em in*.'

There are a variety of ways of making these requests, such as berating the crowd:

P   Can you come a bit closer, look? If you stand any further
    away he'll [PC] 'ave to 'ave a motorbike to come an'
    deliver the bloody stuff.

. . . or the pitcher claiming that he is only trying to be fair to everyone standing at the stall:

P   If you'd like to be in the sale, can you please do me a
    simple favour and take one step forward. *Thank you*. Will
    you *all* move in towards the stall because I want now to
    give everybody the same chance. I don't want people
    saying, '*Aye*, he's only serving his friends, *aye*, he's only
    serving her 'cos he's *married* to her.' I want *everybody* to
    have the *same equal opportunity*.

In the second of these examples the pitcher, to help ease the move forward, actually thanks the audience for moving forward before they have started to do so. It seems that the audience, upon hearing this expression of gratitude, are more likely to believe that other people have already started to move forward and, therefore, feel less reluctant about doing so themselves.

Pitchers will try to make their requests to move closer sound reasonable and utterly inconsequential and, as we have already seen with other edge-related problems, often they are phrased in an exaggerated and humorous manner. In the following two cases the pitchers' humour serves to make their requests appear trivial:

P Can you do me a favour? Look, close in just a little bit. You know, put one leg forward, the other one will follow. *It's called walking*!

AS [Titters and moves forward]

P Move right in. *Move right in*! The closer you get to me, love, the closer you'll get to heaven.

AS [Laughs and moves forward]

Reluctance to move forward

In order to maintain their protected position, people at the stall will not always comply with the pitcher's request for them to move forward. Some people will, instead, shuffle their feet without actually moving closer at all. In so doing, they politely respond to the pitcher's request while also, in effect, ignoring it. Furthermore, members of an audience can often be seen to be monitoring each other after a pitcher has requested them to move forward. In this way they surreptitiously check each other out to see if others are complying with the request before deciding whether or not to do so themselves.

What all these subtleties of crowd behaviour show is that an 'audience' is not simply made up of an isolated set of individuals. To stand in a crowd is to take part in a form of public and social activity with all its attendant shared social norms, benefits, constraints and sanctions. These vary from context to context. For instance, no one will tolerate a person in a crowd at the opera getting up and shouting. On the other hand, if you stand among the home fans in a large football crowd and fail to shout when the home team scores a goal, rather direct and sometimes physically painful sanctions can follow.

It is this social nature of crowd behaviour which is crucial to a pitcher's quest for sales success. When the edge-gathering work has been completed a successful pitcher will have transformed as many isolated individuals and small groups of friends and families as possible into a common entity who share only one goal – to stay at the stall and listen to the rest of the pitcher's spiel. It is only after expending all this time and effort in attracting and managing the initial crowd at his or her stall that a pitcher can really go to work and get on with the 'easiest' part of the sales routine – trying to sell the goods.

CHAPTER 2

Working a Line

We were sitting in Joe's market café gingerly eyeing up two bacon sandwiches floating in a plate of grease on the table in front of us. Slouched opposite was Gary and one of his grafting mates, Tonto, looking in charge of everything. All it took was an almost imperceptible flick of one of their hands for a waitress immediately to come scurrying over to replenish our half-empty tea mugs. This nonchalant gesturing on their part was no mean feat considering that both of them had enough Old Gold draped around their wrists and fingers to be able to make an offer for the place right there and then.

Joe's was the venue of our second interview with Gary and, this time, we'd come prepared for everything. Everything, that is, except the food. It was obvious to us that the only way we could prove to the pitchers that we were worthy confidants was by asking 'intelligent' questions. To do this we had to have at least a passable knowledge of what this type of selling was all about. Yet there was no hiding the fact that we were still rank novices; we were sociologists after all, not experts on street markets. We weren't even experts on marketing. Our lack of savvy was all too clear to us and, more to the point, it was all too clear to the pitchers themselves. In almost every interview they would playfully tease us by dropping indecipherable pitching terms into their answers. They would then mischievously grin at the perplexed expressions on our faces before putting us gently, but triumphantly, in our place with a translation in our own, 'outsiders" language.

This time we'd decided to do some more homework. For starters we scoured the first batch of pitching videos we'd collected to look for any general trends in the sales routines. It didn't take a genius to figure out that the second stage of a sales spiel consisted of a pitcher describing and demonstrating the goods. We also couldn't fail to notice that in a very short space of time – perhaps no longer than five or seven minutes – the pitchers could transform mundane things like pens, pottery, towels and toys into enticing, exotic and, above all, highly desirable products. Although this verbal and visual alchemy seemed to be accomplished with apparently little effort, the effect this patter had on the people at their stalls was both profound and dramatic. In this world of marketing, sales were the rule rather than the exception.

We'd even visited the library again to find some academic support for our observations. We soon found out that product descriptions are an important feature of most types of sales promotions and advertising campaigns. Although we appreciated that there were obvious differences between street market selling and other forms of retailing, we came up with a couple of key concepts that we felt confident enough about to raise during our interviews.

Nearly all the books on selling stressed the importance of 'product knowledge'. Salespeople were supposed to have an intimate understanding of the various properties of each of the different products they were attempting to sell. In one case we'd examined a reproduction of a company stock brochure. Displayed within it were pictures of each product, accompanied by a table listing the unique features and benefits of that particular item of stock. The salesperson's task was to memorize these tailor-made descriptions and to use them as 'deal clinchers' at the appropriate juncture in a sales negotiation.

Another idea we had come across was that of 'target marketing'. Instead of adopting a 'blanket approach' of trying to sell goods and services to everyone, this principle proposes that companies should gear their sales and advertising efforts towards a specific sector of the market. By matching the goods to the particular needs and requirements of only a 'targeted' segment of consumers, these goods could be sold more efficiently and effectively.

Armed with this new-found knowledge, we were looking forward to hearing more about these concepts from the pitchers themselves.

'Fire away, then. Ask us anything you like,' said Gary.

The sandwiches we had been nibbling at were hastily returned to their plate. We switched on the tape recorder.

'Right, let's say you've already got your edge. What's next?' we asked.

'That'll be the fanny,' replied Tonto with an almost perverted look of relish.

We were lost already, but kept quiet about it.

Almost inevitably, Gary had started grinning at us. We began to get an uneasy feeling that we might just have read the wrong type of book. Perhaps Freud had written something on this subject?

'You work your line,' Tonto continued.

'"Dem" your gear,' Gary chipped in.

We just bit our lips as both of them sat back, satisfied with these answers, waiting for our next question. Here was our chance to impress.

'How important is product knowledge, then?' one of us ventured bullishly.

Tonto averted his eyes out of what looked to us like embarrassment. The grin on Gary's face changed to a sympathetic smile. It was a look that said we were more to be pitied than scolded. 'You can't sell nothing with product knowledge,' he remarked ominously.

'Well, what do you need, then?' we asked, taken aback by his response.

'You of all people should know that one.' Gary leaned

forward, just to make sure that we weren't going to miss the answer. What came next was almost as unpalatable as our sandwiches, not only because his point should have been obvious to 'experts' on human behaviour, but because it challenged everything we'd read in the marketing and sales textbooks.

'It's not *product* knowledge you need.' He leaned even closer, then hit us with the punchline. 'It's *not product* knowledge you need, it's *people* knowledge!'

The way he delivered this nugget of information – so slowly and so precisely that we were forced to savour every syllable – gave it such an authority that neither of us felt that it required any further explanation. There was nothing left for us to do but ask our next question.

'All right, then, could you tell us something about the type of target market you're aiming at when you attempt to sell your gear.'

'*Target market*?' Gary threw his hands up in mock despair. Now he didn't even try to hide the pained expression on his face. 'We're salesmen, not snipers.' Tonto nodded in agreement at this revelation. '*Everybody's* our target.' Tonto nodded again.

'Um, right.' We nodded too, and tried to hide our disappointment at the way they had dismissed the gems of information we'd gleaned from impeccable sources at the library.

One question remained, however. 'By the way. Um—' – it was an embarrassing question to ask – 'where does the . . . the fa— fanny bit come in, then?'

Gary and Tonto smiled knowingly at each other. Tonto's answer contained none of the homespun, innuendo-strewn wisdom we'd anticipated; it was simply a pitching anthem. 'Fanny's all about providing the maximum.' Then he said it again for emphasis. 'The *maximum* amount of information for the largest number of people in the fewest possible words.'

. . . And Tonto was right, too. Later that night, in the lab back at the university, another inspection of our videos confirmed his description. Goods have to be treated by shoppers as being worth buying and, to achieve this, pitchers endeavour to make their descriptions comprehensive, economical and, above all, convincing.

We'd assumed that every product pitchers attempted to sell had its own unique tailor-made patter, just like the product descriptions in the company stock brochure we'd looked at in the library. We were wrong. Regardless of the price or type of goods offered for sale, or of the geographical location of the market, or of the sex of the person selling the goods, pitchers employed a set of *common* rhetorical devices to describe a wide variety of goods. The similarities in the structure of the descriptive techniques they used far outweighed any differences.

THE THEATRE OF DREAMS

Selling on a street market exercises a marked influence on the type of descriptive techniques pitchers use, as well as on the way the goods are displayed and demonstrated. For one thing, the words 'understatement' and 'restraint' do not appear to figure in the pitchers' lexicon of successful description. We were amazed at some of the astonishing powers claimed for the products offered for sale. We witnessed, for instance, the sale of a perfume that could guarantee sex:

P [Talking to a woman in the audience] And all you do with it, darling, when you get home, put one drop under your pillow, it's 'Touché l'amour', you know what that means?
A [Shakes her head shyly]
P It's French.
AS [Nervous laughter]
P It means *'Tonight for sure'*.
P2 [Laughs]
AS [Screams of laughter]

... socks that were apparently so durable they warranted being treated as family heirlooms:

P   You'll be able to keep them for ten years, maybe twenty years. You're gonna give them to your children and your children will give them to your grandchildren. Have a look, madam.

A   [Examines the socks]

P   [To A] Don't forget to see your solicitor after you buy these. Don't forget to see your solicitor about changing your inheritance.

... and another perfume whose scent was so powerful that the unfortunate pitcher continually had to fend off the sexual advances of his wife (unsuccessfully it seemed) whenever she wore it:

P   *Look. Watch*! This one's called Torment. My wife wears this and she torments me. We've got fifteen kids.

Hearing this type of patter, it is easy to conclude that pitchers are con artists, and that their sales 'fanny' is little more than a series of empty vaunts and false promises. Yet these outrageous and bizarre claims are far more subtle and sophisticated than first appearances suggest. Most of these descriptions, for example, are delivered tongue in cheek; they are meant to entertain the crowd as well as deal with the difficult task of trying to sell goods on a street market. Underneath all this humour and puffery, however, is a fine-grained analysis of what pitchers deem to be needed to stimulate people's interest in the goods in this type of sales setting.

WELCOME TO HYPER-REALITY

Pitchers go to extraordinary lengths to show that they can relate to the people who stand at their stall. One way in which they do this is by showing that they know the features and benefits of goods which market shoppers treat as important when deciding to buy. For example, they will take time talking about things such as what a cuddly toy should look like:

P   These two *look* like Teddy bears. It's not something that's gonna frighten the kids to death. I've seen some Teddy bears that look like *monkeys*! *They do*! They've got one eye over here [i.e. near its ear] and one in the middle. *They do*! And they frighten the kids to *death*. These are *British* -made. *Every one* is British-made.

. . . and the problems people face when cleaning cooking implements:

P   You might think, 'Oh well, we'll go an' spend a hundred an' twenty quid on a set o' those Swan pans, stainless steel.' 'Ave you *ever* tried to cook with stainless steel? [Laughing] It's an *absolute* bugger, ah'll tell you. Everything jams on the bottom, it scorches, an' it's *terrible*! These're *not* stainless steel.

. . . and what people take into consideration when buying jumpers:

P   Shall I tell you something else that certain customers have passed comment on? At several markets during the week they said, 'The difference is, Maggie, you go to any other stall selling jumpers, and they've *all* got a carbon copy of one another.' An' it's true, you know, *they have*. So what I'd like to do is give you something *really, really different*. You'll *love* these.

Pitchers also attempt to portray the world their audience inhabit in an authentic manner. In fact, the routine and mundane activities of market shoppers' everyday lives are often celebrated in a highly exaggerated and hyper-realistic fashion:

TOY CAR THAT HAS AN EXTREMELY NOISY
POLICE SIREN

P   *Night Rider! Night Rider! Here*, can you imagine that one
     coming round the bedroom door at 4 o'clock on Christ-
     mas morning? *Eh?* You've had a skinful the night before?
     You'll be thinking of me then, *won't you?*

PEN SET

P   [Breathless with excitement] An' look, *look at that*,
     ANYBODY 'oo's not used a fountain pen, any o' you
     youngsters, it's AN *ABSOLUTE* PLEASURE, it's an
     absolute pleasure to use. *Look at that.* You can sign
     your cheques with it,
A   Ooooh.
P   You can sign your Giros with it, an' you youngsters, when
     you get older, you'll be able to *sign on* with it.

PAN SET

P   It's turned on a lathe. An' without jokin' about it it's
     double an' treble the weight of ordinary pans. [To A]
     'Ave you had a look at it already? 'Ere y'are, look. [Hands
     A one of the pans] Anybody else? Jus' feel the weight of it.
     [To PC] Show the ladies over there. [To AS] Jus' feel the
     weight of it. If you hit the old man around the head with
     that he'd stay hit, I'll tell you. *Right?*

By depicting how, where or when the product might actually be employed, albeit in an often overstated and humorous way, pitchers situate the product in a mundanely realistic use context that is designed to appeal to people at their stall. In the above examples, the sales goods are tied in with the humdrum reality of having young children (a prime cause of headaches and lack of sleep), being a youth (the likelihood of unemployment), and marital disharmony (cooking utensils as potential weapons).

UNIQUENESS AND INCLUSIVENESS

The types of products pitchers sell are mainly personal and household wares, and this certainly helps in the task of describing the products in the context of people's domestic scenarios and everyday lifestyles. But the very ordinariness of these kinds of goods can present problems for pitchers. Items like socks, towels and pans are not exactly the most glamorous of products and, consequently, they are not tailor-made for showcase descriptions. Although such stock may look unremarkable to most people, a pitcher's eye will see them as being special and thereby worthy of very detailed description. For instance, it is not unusual for relatively ordinary items such as these to be invested with 'one of a kind' qualities:

RETRACTABLE BALL-POINT PEN

P WE'VE *ALL* USED THEM BEFORE. All you do, quite simply, is *press* the button at the top, the nib disappears, *press it again*, an' it reappears, *just like magic*.

TOY DOLLS

P *These* are dollies with a difference. There are no other dollies anywhere in the country that do what these do. *Watch, look* and *listen*.

FOUNTAIN PEN

P You *won't* find another pen that'll do this, now, just watch. Very simply, *it's the only one. Look, INSIDE* THE PEN, is that *unique*, high-tech cartridge.

TOMATO SLICER

P There is *no* electronic machine in the world which can do this job [i.e. finely slicing an entire tomato]. And if you do it with a knife, *correct me if I'm wrong*, you get halfway, and the other half collapses between your fingers.

There was rarely anything unique or peerless, though, about the people who were eligible to buy these goods. Almost without exception, pitchers included justifications as to why all the people gathered at their stalls should be interested in the product being offered for sale:

TOWELS

P Ah don't care *how many* towels you've got, *you can always* use some more, is that *right?*

AS [Yesses]

P It's the *best* value for money you'll see *today*. An' providin' you get washed you need *towels*.

FLOWER VASES

P They'll adorn anybody's house, from a council house to a mansion to a caravan.

PENS

P It's *all* the five of 'em. They'll make a *tremendous* stocking-filler, and for anybody 'oo can read or write, God bless 'em, they'll be an *absolute asset*. (. . .) *It doesn't matter if you're left-handed or right-handed!* It'll write equally as well.

'DESIGNER' JUMPERS

P My own daughter won't have anything, ladies, unless it's a little bit trendy, do you know what I mean? She's like *your* daughters, they like trendy things, don't they? If they're not trendy they won't have it at *all. Don't get me wrong* when ah say that, 'cos you could give this to a lady of *any* age.

TOWELS
P   An' what about these? Made for a firm called *Habitat*. Has anybody ever heard of that firm?
AS [No answer]
P   *Yes?*
AS [Yesses]
P   These will go with *anything*. Like me.
AS [Titters]

On those few occasions when a pitcher acknowledged that a particular group of people were not eligible to buy the goods, those people were, invariably, not present at the stall:

BEAN-BAGS
P   Now whether you live in a one-bedroomed flat, a bed-sitter, a council house or a bloody forty-bedroom mansion *I'm not bothered*. These will look nice in *anybody's* home. They are no good if you camp out with a dosser or live in a tent. I will tell you why . . .

LISTS

It may already be apparent from many of the examples above that pitchers routinely list the features and benefits of the goods they are describing. One would imagine that, within reason, the more features and benefits of a product that are itemized the greater a pitcher's chance of maximizing the number of people who will become interested in that product. But this is not the case. The most popular of these lists, by far, are those that contain only three items:

DOLLS

P   [1] The dolls are *hand-made*, [2] the dolls are *safety-tested*, [3] the dolls are *also vinyl*.

FELT-TIP PEN

P   It'll write [1] *upside down*, [2] *back to front* or [3] *from any angle*!

MEAT

P   There you are again. [1] *Completely boneless* they are, [2] *perfect* to freeze, [3] *beautiful ham*.

TOY KITCHEN

P   Can you imagine setting that down and a young child's imagination going to work on all that lot? Eh? *Lovely*, isn't it? [1] The cooker really lights up, [2] the pots really rattle and [3] the kettle really whistles.

TWIN DOLLS

P   Today I will sell you [1] dolls that *cry together*, [2] dolls that *sing together*, [3] dolls that *laugh together*.

This quality of pitching description does not appear to be a coincidence. It is certainly not the case that pitchers can think of no more than three good things to say about their products. When more than three things were announced in a list, these longer lists were, more often than not, broken down into two or more sequences of three parts:

CLIMBING TOY

P   For the little'n's. *My favourite range.* Watch this. [1.1] Hits a wall, [1.2] hits a chair, and [1.3] over it goes. [2.1] Climbs on the wallpaper, [2.2] climbs up the chair, an' [2.3] climbs over the carpet. It's what they call the 'Turn-over Buggy'.

BATH TOWELS
P   These're the *big wrap-round* bath sheets. Look at the size of these. There's enough room under here for [1.1] *you*, [1.2] *your husband*, and [1.3] *eight lodgers*. You can [2.1] *wriggle*, [2.2] giggle an' [2.3] do what the bloody 'ell you *like* underneath them.

In many non-sales situations, people often treat the third item in a list as marking the end of that list. Lists of three are, for instance, a common way of marking the appropriate starting point for group responses, such as when initiating a race with '[1] Ready, [2] Steady, [3] Go', or inviting cheering with '[1] Hip, [2] Hip, [3] Hurray'. Max Atkinson's research into the rhetorical devices used by politicians has shown that audiences at party political conferences, when searching for the right moment at which to applaud a political speech, will often begin to clap just after the third item in a list has been announced:

CONSERVATIVE PARTY CONFERENCE, 1980.
From Atkinson, 1984: 63
THATCHER   Soviet Marxism is [1] ideologically, [2] politically and [3] morally bankrupt.
AUDIENCE   [Nine seconds' applause]

The conversation analyst Gail Jefferson's study of recordings of real-life conversations has also shown that three-part lists are employed to co-ordinate the orderly transfer of speakership in a dialogue. People listening to a list in progress would recurrently start to speak immediately after a third (and usually final) item, thus effecting a smooth transfer of speakership:

A   God, I was practically falling asleep he was rabbiting on so much! He just went [1] on and [2] on and [3] on.
B   [Laughing] He's always like that with me too.

In these types of cases it seems almost as if the very rhythm of speech encourages people to hear a list as having been completed after the third item. In the case of pitching, though, the use of three-part lists is not designed to occasion a transfer of speakership or to obtain an immediate direct response from the audience. They are used mainly for emphasis and to indicate exhaustiveness. Three-part lists seem especially apposite devices for pitchers to employ when describing their goods because they have a tendency to sound comprehensive. They have an almost mystical aura of self-sufficiency, completeness and finality about them – as if the three items in the list are the only possible items that could be in that list. By comparison, two-part lists seem inadequately short and therefore incomplete, whereas lists containing four or more items can appear to be tediously long, repetitive, time-consuming, over-precise and banal.

Similarly, many formal speeches begin by announcing a list of three groups in the audience, such as in 'My [1] lords, [2] ladies and [3] gentlemen', and Shakespeare's celebrated '[1] Friends, [2] Romans, [3] countrymen'. Both of these lists are an efficient way of signalling that what follows concerns not only these three types of people but, in effect, everybody.

More generally, one of the most characteristic features of a pitching spiel is the persuasive rhythm and pacing of its delivery. Three-part segmentation, as well as shifts in intonation, stress and volume – often supplemented by liberal doses of back slang – all add to the poetic and sometimes almost hypnotic quality of pitchers' talk and lend an even greater air of conviction and authority to their descriptions and claims:

[P is talking to a Chinese woman]
P   These're by the Hi-Tech pen company, me old China.
     They're not made in [1] Hong Kong, [2] ding-dong [3]
     they go wrong – it's a British-made product.

DOLLS

P   I *have* got cheaper dollies on my stall. [Takes one of the dolls out of its box and holds it up in the air] *If*, however, you want the *best*, [1.1] watch, [1.2] look and [1.3] listen. [2.1] Have a look. [2.2] *OH LOOK!* [2.3] *OH LOOK!*

Even short phrases and simple three-word sequences, when delivered by a pitcher, can sound like and take on all the benefits of three-part lists:

PENS

P   You've five *fabulous* writing instruments, it's a [1] NEW CONCEPT, [2] *IN PEN TECHNOLOGY*, at [3] point of sale promotion.

FOOD SLICER

P   [1.1] Every [1.2] single [1.3] slice [2.1] *comes* [2.2] *out* [2.3] *perfectly*.

Pitchers, like other skilful orators, appreciate how to segment their descriptions in such a way that they do not jar on the listener's ear but rather help convey information in a concise, convincing and effective way. This is particularly important at this stage of a sales routine because the pitcher has a lot of information to get over quickly. By parsing that information into lists of three, the pitcher ensures increased rhetorical effectiveness as well as displaying an acute ear for the subtle rhythms of language and rules of persuasion. Indeed, if we add or subtract items from the lists above, or do the same with famous three-part lists such as 'A Mars a day helps you work, rest, think, shop, relax and play', they sound odd, less lyrical and much less persuasive, not only because we are used to hearing the original phrase, but also because they have not been delivered as a list of three.

CONTRASTS

One of the most commonly used rhetorical devices in a pitcher's repertoire of description is the contrast. Contrasts are 'loaded' comparisons. They are formed by juxtaposing two related pieces of information in such a way that they stand explicitly in a relation of opposition and contradiction to one another. Pitchers use contrasts because they are a highly efficient and very effective way of packaging the features and benefits of the goods being described. The following pitcher describes the qualities of a coffee pot by making a contrast between the thinness of the china and its strength:

P   It's as [1] *thin* as an eggshell, and as [2] *strong* as steel.

In the following case a contrast is made between two types of pen. The first (an ordinary fibre-tip pen) is the pen being offered for sale; the second is what this pen writes like (a more expensive, 'high quality' fountain pen):

P   [1] It's a fibre-tip pen, but when you write with it, [2] it writes just like a fountain pen.

These contrasts work by capitalizing on difference in order to persuade. On the street market in particular, issues such as whether one product is better, cheaper, or of a higher quality than another are often crucial factors in influencing people's decisions to buy. A contrast provides a parsimonious way of delivering and demonstrating this difference.

To strengthen and maximize the contrastive effect, one or both sides of a contrast can be unpacked and delivered in three-part list form:

CHINA ORNAMENT
P   Would one of you buy it out the way, *'oo would*? An' ah'll

41

tell you what ah'm prepared to do if one of you'll buy it, but ah'll tell you now, before we go any further, [A1] it's not 50p, [A2] or it's not a pound, [A3] *it's not a lump o' crap.* [B] There's something down there which is proper bone china an' absolutely perfect.

SET OF PENS
P   *Now watch.* An' ah don't care, *ah don't care* if you buy [A1] *Parker*, [A2] *Papermate*, or [A3] *Schaeffer*, [B] they *can't* and they *won't* do this.

SET OF PENS
P   [A] These're from a *British* company. *Not* [B1] Hong Kong, [B2] Taiwan or [B3] Japan, [A] *Altrincham* in Cheshire at the other end of the motorway.

Researchers have found contrasts in other situations where people are in the business of persuading each other to 'buy' things – not only goods and services, but also ideas, jokes, religion and the like. Similar devices are common in political speeches (used by politicians to win favour, applause and votes), in courtroom trials (used by lawyers to persuade jurors to return favourable verdicts), and by stand-up comedians to get an audience to laugh.

STRENGTHENING AND REINFORCING
A DESCRIPTION

To make the goods seem even more exotic and enticing, descriptions can be reinforced by assessing the qualities and benefits of these goods in the strongest possible way. The conversation analyst Anita Pomerantz calls this device 'maximization'. We heard the standard of workmanship of a glass decanter described not only as 'perfect' but as *'absolutely perfect'*;

a battery-operated remote-controlled car, equipped with flash-
ing headlights and a noisy siren, was portrayed not only as
being 'electronic', but as '*totally* electronic':

GLASS DECANTER
P   *Absolutely perfect*! Not a flaw or blemish the size of a
     pinhead.

PERFUMES
P   It's *ALL* fire-salvaged stock. In other words, look, one or
     two of the outer boxes as you can see are a little bit
     damaged, they're a little bit damp, but the contents inside,
     I do assure you, are *one hundred per cent*, they are
     ABSOLUTELY perfect. I'm going to clear 'em out of
     the way now.

HAND TOWELS
P   A little commercial now, if you *don't* like burgundy, ah've
     also got them in the navy blue, made by a firm called
     Christie. Has anybody ever heard o' that firm?
AS   [Yesses]
P   Right. *You can't get better than Christie*.

ALARM CLOCKS
P   . . . and if that one doesn't wake you up in the morning,
     it's *not* an alarm clock you need, it's an *undertaker*! *It rings
     like HELL!*

One particularly powerful way of producing a strong
description is by making a claim about the goods and then,
immediately afterwards, going beyond that claim. In doing this,
pitchers attempt not only to meet the audience's expectations of
the qualities the goods should possess, but also to subvert and
exceed these expectations. One way this is done is by extending
what appears to be an already completed description:

DINNER SERVICE
P   What about one of you buyin' that lovely service down there? It's *even* got the sugar and the cream.

SET OF THREE SAUCEPANS
P   They're suitable for gas, electricity or a ceramic hob. *You can even use them on a naked flame.*

CHINA ORNAMENT
P   It's got *proper* china hands, china face, china feet. An' ah'll tell you now, *the bugger's even musical.*

In these cases a description is split into two, the first part supplying what the pitcher assumes to be the essential features the audience expects or would like the product to possess. Pitchers often deliver this segment in such a way as to make it appear complete and exhaustive – as if every feature that could reasonably be expected to be stated *has* been stated. Hence the common use of three-part lists at this point, as happens in the last two examples above. The second part of the description provides something additional and unexpected, and the adverb 'even', which often links the two parts of the description, announces the upcoming extension of the expected range of the product's properties in a more explicit way. To say that something is 'even' X implies that many people believe that it is not X. It implies surprise on the part of the pitcher at yet another remarkable property of the goods on sale.

OVERCOMING AUDIENCE RESERVATIONS

Many shoppers, and not only those who gather at a pitcher's stall, are likely to be wary of the claims salespeople make about their goods. They presume that salespeople will say practically anything to make a sale because they have a vested interest in talking up their products to part people from their cash. Such cautiousness is more pronounced when the seller is a market pitcher as these traders are often seen as crooked 'wide boys' (an honour that most don't live up to but many play up to) who conduct their sales in an unorthodox fashion. This wariness manifests itself in a variety of ways, ranging from a reluctance to stop at a stall (see Chapter 1) to challenging the veracity of what a pitcher has claimed about the goods offered for sale. In the latter case, this negative responsiveness, while not being welcomed enthusiastically, provides pitchers with an opportunity to nip in the bud any negative opinions the crowd at large may harbour, but would usually not voice, about the goods on offer. In the following sequence, the pitcher undermines the suspicion that the Wedgwood pottery he is describing is not the genuine article:

P   DINNER *SET*, SOUP *SET*. 'Ere, one buy.
    Wedgwood.
A   I don't believe that.
P   DINNER S— [To A] *Pardon?*
A   I don't believe it.
P   [Takes one of the plates over to A and shows her the
    Wedgwood mark stamped on the base of the plate] Have a
    look.
A   [She and her friend A 2 have a look at the base of the
    plate] Yeah.
A 2 That's right.
A   *Yeah*.
P   [Smiling] Yes, *thank you!* There you are, *that's shut you
    bloody up!*
A   + A 2[Laughter]
P   [Still smiling] DINNER *SE*— [Turns back to A] *There
    you are*, you can't say nothing now, *can you?*
A   No.

When there is no objector present in the audience, pitchers are likely to invent one and to voice an objection themselves. One way of doing this is by referring to some earlier (though often fictitious) event where a member of a previous audience allegedly took issue with or raised some problem about the sales offer:

PERFUMES

P And a lady says a minute ago, she says, 'Are they empty boxes?' Well, there's only one man round here who sells empty boxes, do you know who that is?

AS [Shake their heads]

P That's Fred Parfitt, and he's the local undertaker.

AS [Laughter]

PERFUMES

P Just look at this! A lady come up a minute ago, she says, 'Young man,' she says, 'Is it stolen?' Well, here, I wish it was 'cos I wouldn't have to pay for it. Just look at this . . .

Far from fuelling the audience's reservations about buying goods from a market pitcher, these claims seem to have the opposite effect. By explicitly raising a likely objection, and by formulating the objection as coming from someone at the stall who is outside their patronage and control, pitchers seem able to undermine the legitimacy of the objection and also to reinforce their own credibility. There can be few traders in any other line of selling who spend so much time deliberately raising potential objections to the purchase of their goods. Rather than skirting round or avoiding problematic issues, pitchers tend to confront them head-on and to deal with them in terms that are, to be sure, always favourable to themselves.

Pitchers also display their sensitivity to shopper scepticism by undermining any reservations the audience may have before such objections are raised. For example, they may temper and moderate their descriptive claims to make them eminently reasonable and believable. This happens in the following sequences. In the first example, the strength of a contrast made between the pens manufactured by 'the competition' and the pens being offered by the pitcher is weakened by the pitcher acknowledging that 'the competition' make 'lovely' pens:

P   They make nice pens, they make lovely pens, but I don't think they make them in Altrincham in Cheshire like these, look, *this is a British product*, now watch.

In the next sequence the pitcher concedes that the electronic game he is trying to sell is only 'as good as' one of the most popular games sold in high-street stores:

P   . . . *better than* Scrabble, *better than* Word Making, *as good as* Monopoly, from M and B Games . . .

Pitchers may also add supportive explanations to account for and clarify the claims they have made:

PENS
D   There is no company in the world that would give you a guarantee on a fountain pen nib. The reason they won't is because they can't control what you do with it.

PERFUMES
P   Look. IT'S *ALL FIRE-SALVAGE* PERFUME. In other words, do you know what they do with fire salvage? They sell it *cheap*. Well, I've bought the full consignment. *Watch this*.

They may even draw attention to the expectation that their more outrageous descriptions are likely to be treated as outlandish and unbelievable:

CASSEROLE DISH

P   Bit o' nice gear, eh? You can't buy this from old 'Secret Squirrel' [another pitcher] down the bottom corner there. Beautiful stuff. Do you know, you can get a twenty-five pound turkey in there? [Silence] As long as you put it through a mincer first.

AS   [Laughter]

TOY CAR

P   It's like 'Night Rider', isn't it? Close your eyes and it's *exactly* the same!

SET OF REPLICA TOY CARS

P   'Ere, do you wanna buy one o' those? These are *scale models. Replica cars!* One-forty-third-scale die-cast metal. A Mercedes GHR2, sells at two pounds forty-nine (. . .) but by the way, they've got proper perspex windows, it's independent suspension, you might get one where the bonnet will open, or the boot or the doors, y'know, they're all different. But one thing they've all got is a cassette player, y'know, a stereo.

AS   [Laughter]

P   [Takes car to individuals in the audience] 'Ere, listen to that. Can you hear it playing?

AS   [Laughter and Yeahs!]

By showing their humorous scepticism towards some of their own descriptions, pitchers seem able to enhance their own credibility as purveyors of reliable information about their goods.

External confirmations and endorsements

Pitchers appeal to people and things outside their sphere of influence for independent and external support in order to lend further credence to their descriptive claims. Celebrities, TV programmes and institutions of standing are much-favoured sources for enhancing the credibility of a product. The endorsements proffered range from those that generate laughter because they are so beyond the bounds of belief:

SET OF PENS
P   *WHAT AN OFFER* for anybody who can read or
     write, or anyone who's got youngsters at school. They do
     use blue ink and it has been passed by the education
     authorities.

SILVER-PLATED TEA SERVICE
P   *The Queen uses these*!
AS [Laughs]
P   [Straight-faced] When I went round for tea the other day
     she had one of these on the table.

. . . to those that have a greater ring of plausibility about them:

CHILDREN'S COLOURING BOARD
D   If you wanna buy it, it's available in sixty-two major
     stores. It's been sold on demonstration in Barkers in
     Kensington, in Selfridges and Woolworth's, an' they
     don't allow you to demo rubbish in their store.

PAINT PADS
D   Now you may already have seen this on a programme on
     BBC television called 'Tomorrow's World'. That's the
     programme that shows you the latest in technical and
     scientific innovations.

TEDDY BEARS
P   They are not made a million miles from here. They are
     made on the outskirts of Leeds at a place called Pudsey.

TEDDY BEARS

And if anyone watched that programme about three weeks ago – 'Children in Need' with Terry Wogan – they called the bear 'The Pudsey Bear'. *These're* made by the *same* firm.

Of course, the most direct and convincing form of endorsement is when a pitcher persuades people in the crowd to endorse the product themselves. As one pitcher remarked: 'A word from one of my customers is worth more than a million from me.' Such attempts may range from a pitcher attempting to obtain a collective endorsement by getting people to laugh (another reason for pitchers making outrageous claims) or to raise their hands in response to a question about the goods:

SET OF PANS

P   'Ow many ladies 'ave 'ad saucepans, who've had a non-stick coat on 'em, they've lasted a year an' they've virtually 'ad it? *'Oo's 'ad some o' that?*

AS   [Hands raised]

P   *'Oo's 'ad some o' that?*

AS   [More hands are raised]

P   [Pointing to some of the audience who have raised their hands] *You've* 'ad it, you've 'ad it and so've you. It 'appens to *everybody*, right?

. . . to obtaining individual endorsements from selected members of the audience which answer and thus undermine objections that the pitcher has raised. In the following examples two pitchers raise the same types of problems about their goods (perfumes and chicken legs). Because these goods are boxed and therefore hidden from view, many people are liable to think that, if the goods exist at all, they are not likely to be of the same quality or size as the pitcher has claimed:

PERFUMES

P   [Apparently responding to a shout of criticism from

someone in the audience] *Who said that?* Who said 'empty boxes'? *Right. Watch.* There's *no* empty boxes. *Now look.* Take *any* box. Pick *any* box, ladies. [Points to a young girl in the crowd] Any one. *Any* box you like.

A   [Smiles shyly]

P   Any one, *any single one.*

A   [Points self-consciously to a box]

P   *That one there.* [P picks up the box A has selected and holds it high in the air] And *look*, and a lady said to me, 'Ah, they're all right, they're *big* boxes,' she said, 'but when you open 'em up they're only *tiny* perfumes inside.' *INSIDE EVERY ONE* of these boxes is a *FULL, fifty-six*-mill. spray. *Now watch.* Am I right, love? [P opens the box and shows the contents to another person]

A   [Nods]

P   Thank you. In other words, it's *value for money.* You're not buying a *big* box with a *tiny* bottle in.

CASES OF CHICKEN — THERE ARE ABOUT
FIFTEEN CASES OF CHICKEN PILED ON TOP OF
ONE ANOTHER ON THE COUNTER

P   Who— *who's* interested in a case of chicken first of all?

AS   [Hands are raised]

P   [Pointing to a woman at the back of the crowd who had raised her hand]. You are. Which box would you like us to open to show you a sample?

A   The bottom one.

P   [Feigns disgust because he has to remove all the boxes on top of the one that A selected] The bottom one. [To A] Watch my lips. [Through a smile, the pitcher mouths what appears to be a swear word]

AS   [Small laughs]

PC   [Struggling to get to the bottom box]

P   [Smiling at A] *See what you've done?* [To the man standing with A] Is that your missus?

MAN [Nods]

P   [Smiling] I feel sorry for you, pal! [Opens up the box and chops one of the chicken legs in half and holds it up in the air] *Look at that!* Look at the depth of that meat there. *Fabulous!*

In each case, the pitcher uses the specific item of stock that has been selected at random by an individual in the crowd to undermine any reservations the audience at large may have about all the goods offered for sale.

DISPLAYING AND DEMONSTRATING THE GOODS

The way goods are handled, displayed and demonstrated can be used to support and reinforce visually what a pitcher has said about those goods. An attachment for a power drill, for example, will be roughly manhandled to show its ruggedness and durability, whereas towels are caressed in a sensual way to encourage the audience to imagine them as something they would want to use on their bodies.

Bone china pots and cups are delicately held underneath light-bulbs to show they are evenly translucent and thus of a high quality.

Clothing pitchers sometimes employ female assistants as models so that the audience can get a better idea of the style, cut and fit of each garment offered for sale.

Visual displays are also used to enhance and maximize verbal contrasts. Towel-sellers do this when they contrast the thickness of their own stock with an inferior product, holding each item up so that the audience can see this difference for themselves. To add to the visual effectiveness, members of the audience may be invited to feel and compare the thickness of the towels. In the following example the towel-seller frames an endorsement about the quality of his towels as a contrast between the feel of the towel and the supposed 'feel' of himself, thereby adding to the rhetorical effect of the endorsement:

P   Darlin', do me a favour, 'ave a feel of those.

A   [Feels towels]

P   Right, *don't bloody wear 'em out*. Go on, 'ave a good feel. If you don't like the way they feel then you can 'ave your feel back. Are those all right, love?

A   Yeah.

P   Now feel me an' feel the difference.

AS   [Laughter]

P   *She is doing as well*.

AS   [Laughter]

Goods are unpacked to prove what the audience will get. As Gary told us:

'A lot of people think that when you display something to them that you are going to show them one thing and sell them another. I've found that if you don't give them exactly what's in front of their eyes then they'll start to walk away. So you have to spend a little bit more time taking each item out of their packet or box, lay it on the counter, displaying them, showing them that it's okay.'

Collections of goods are stacked high, one on top of the other, or held aloft in a fanned formation to emphasize the quantity of items in the sale lot on offer. In this way the physical bulk of the collection is used to enhance the value of the goods.

Dinner sets are laid out in a vertical tier of baskets held up by an assistant so that the audience can see each individual plate, cup, bowl and saucer in the set.

Pitching butchers weigh each joint of meat on a giant set of scales so that the audience can see the exact weight of each joint (and the scale then return to zero) before they decide whether to buy it.

Demonstrations of goods are not only employed to show things such as mechanical toys, home improvement items and the like 'in action'. They are a further and crucial way in which verbal claims can be visually confirmed and authenticated. One grafter, when talking about the beauty of a good visual demonstration, told us that 'What can't speak can't lie'. In effect, it seems that what people are asked to believe with their ears is treated as not as half as convincing as what they are shown to believe with their eyes:

VEGETABLE SLICER

D   The washing-up's simple. *Look.* [The demonstrator quickly and easily rinses out the implement in a basin of water]. We don't just *tell* you it's simple, we *show* you it's simple.

When a toy, mechanical gadget or DIY implement is being demonstrated, the pitcher must make sure it does what is claimed. A car with a siren as its selling point won't sell very many if the batteries are rundown and the siren doesn't work or the whole of the audience cannot hear it wail when it does work. Pitchers rehearse these demonstrations. But never too much. A 'dem' must always be competent, but should never appear to be too slick, otherwise people in the crowd are liable to think that the pitcher is using sleight of hand.

Pitchers often attempt to give added credibility to their outlandish claims by providing an equally outrageous practical demonstration of their products. If a dinner service is claimed to be strong and durable, the pitcher will often confirm this feature by throwing a plate high in the air and catching it on another plate, or by bashing the living daylights out of one of the plates on the stall counter.

One pitcher who portrayed a crystal decanter as having a glass stopper that was tailor-made to fit the neck of the bottle turned the decanter upside down and shook it violently to prove to everyone just how good a fit the stopper was.

A glass-cutter demonstrator routinely raked the edge of a newly cut pane of glass across his face to show just how smooth the cut from his implement was.

In the following example a demonstrator has been describing a fountain pen. Suddenly he grabs hold of an unopened can of Coke:

D   You've all seen these, the old ring-pull can. It's a marvell-ous invention. You pull that ring out to get the contents. If you pull the ring and it comes away in your hand you're left with a can you can't open. If you own one o' these fountain pens and you're desperate to get in there – and I say desperate, because no one in their right mind would treat a fountain pen like this – but you can always open that can with your fountain pen, ladies and gentlemen. [Pierces the side of the can with the nib of the pen. The liquid squirts out of the hole] You'll spill the contents of that can [starts writing with the pen used to pierce the can], but you won't damage that nib unit in any way whatsoever. [Holds up a page of writing] It'll still write for you, absolutely perfectly.

These types of visual and demonstrational overkill serve as an especially convincing guarantee of factors like the quality and durability of the product on offer. As well as serving to demon-strate additional features of the goods (in the case above, the sturdiness of the fountain-pen nib), such unexpected and dra-matic demonstrations apparently help to keep the audience attentive. This is no mean feat when salespeople are attempting to sell products as mundane as pens which can be bought in any corner shop.

Because demonstrators usually ply some life-enhancing, home-improving or time-saving DIY implement, they have the added advantage of being able to employ a very direct form of visual endorsement – selecting someone from the audience to demonstrate the product in use for the benefit of others in the crowd. The main reason for doing this is that many people have reservations about whether the products demonstrated are as easy to use in real life as the demonstrator claims. The following paint pad demonstrator does this:

D   The very last nagging doubt going through your mind
        at the moment: will it work for you like it does for me?
        How many of you have ever stood an' watched a
        demonstration – usually kitchen gadgets – an' thought
        how marvellous it looked till you got it home?
AS   [Nods and sounds of agreement]
D   An' has it ever worked as easy for you as it did for the
        fellow showing you? They don't, do they? Am I right?
AS   [Some people are nodding their heads]
D   I know I'm right, I've got a kitchen full of them. I can't
        make them work either. In just two seconds I'll
        PROVE everybody can use 'em, an' you can all try it
        for yourselves. Ah'm gonna put it in the hands of
        someone who's never used one, never done any decor-
        ating [points to a board that has a rough, Artexed
        finish], and there's a surface a professional calls a night-
        mare. Let's have a look. [Looks in the audience for a
        suitable person; he finds a young boy] Are you a
        professional decorator?
BOY   [Smiles and shakes his head]
D   You're not on the dole or in the union or anything?
        You're not Arthur Scargill in disguise, are you?
BOY   [Smiles and shakes his head]
D   Have you ever used one o' these?
BOY   [Smiles and shakes his head]
D   Have you ever done any decorating?
BOY   [Smiles and shakes his head]
D   Go on, have a go. What's your name, by the way?
BOY   Neil.

D   Neil. How old are you Neil?

BOY   Nine.

D   Nine. Go on, then. [Neil tries the paint pad on the
       Artexed board] Who'd let a nine-year-old loose with
       one o' those? [To Neil] Can you go a bit faster,
       otherwise they'll think you're working for British
       Railways. [Holds up a six-inch paintbrush] Who'd let a
       nine-year-old loose with one o' those or a roller full of
       paint? *What a thought*! As a nine-year-old, Neil, just
       answer me one question, in a loud voice so that every-
       one can hear. Is that easy to do? [Stage whisper] Say yes
       if you wanna be ten.

AS   [Laughter]

BOY   [Nods]

D   Solved that problem, haven't you? Thanks very much
       indeed. Ladies and gentlemen [starts painting the other
       side of the board], nine-year-old Neil's just done that.
       Ah'm gonna hold it up an' show you. Before we do,
       ah'm gonna finish off that bit that Neil didn't do,
       because my company, Brushgenius, says this: You show
       me where nine-year-old Neil stopped, and where I've
       started, and we'll donate ten thousand pounds to your
       favourite charity. There's the proof. Part of it was done
       by Neil, the other bit was done by me. There is no
       difference whatsoever. Mums and dads, get a set, go
       home, sit with your feet up, watch television, let your
       kids get on with the decorating.

AS   [Laughs]

D   They can do it! You haven't got any kids? Get Neil's
       address, he'll come round and do it for you.

AS   [Laughs]

This demonstrator is able to enhance the credibility of his
demonstration even further by choosing an individual from the
audience whom the rest of the crowd are likely to believe has no
prior decorating experience.

* * *

Descriptions, built out of sequences of carefully chosen and deftly delivered words and phrases, supplemented with elaborate visual gestures and sometimes outlandish visual demonstrations, are one of the hallmarks of the pitcher's craft. They are the main way in which people's perceptions about the goods offered for sale can be addressed and altered to suit the pitcher's sales quest. The biggest problem for pitchers at this stage in the sales routine is that of convincing shoppers that they are speaking with an impartial voice. The various claims they make for the goods they are describing must be shown to be sustainable. This is especially important in this type of market selling because of the scepticism some shoppers have about salespeople in general and market traders in particular. What compounds this problem is that the people who gather at a stall are not often able to see the goods close up or to inspect them on an individual basis.

The verbal and visual skills pitchers employ to describe their goods are not based upon some kind of linguistic trickery; they are nothing more or less than a series of common rhetorical and communicative skills that can be found in many other types of persuasive situations. Each and every one of these rhetorical devices is designed to tap into and feed off the various cultural assumptions that shoppers hold about what comprises a product in which it is worth taking more than a passing interest, and the evidence people usually rely upon to satisfy themselves of the validity and credibility of a descriptive claim or product demonstration.

When pitchers have finished describing the goods, and have transformed their mundane and everyday products into something of interest and value, they are still only part of the way along the road to convincing shoppers that they are offering bargains worth buying.

CHAPTER 3

Building Bargains

Practically all you could see of him was his head, poking out from behind hundreds of boxes of toys, on top of a pantechnicon lorry, shouting for all it was worth at the crowd below. Clutched to his chest was a pair of life-sized baby dolls – the 'Love Me Twins'.

By some miracle of microchip technology the dolls actually behaved as if they shared that uncanny telepathic bond that human twins are reputed to possess. The pitcher lifted the boy out of his box and moved him away from his sister – they both started crying. He put them back together again, side by side – they both stopped crying. 'No wires attached!' he shouted proudly. He took the dummy out of one baby's mouth – it started crying. He took the dummy out of the other baby's mouth – they both stopped crying. '*Why?*' he asked everyone, but before they had a chance to respond he provided the answer for them: 'That baby's only crying because that baby had a bottle and this one didn't. *It's jealousy!*'

When he'd finished this tearful demonstration, he moved on to deal with far more serious matters – the business of how much these little miracles cost. He was obviously feeling generous today: 'Forget about money because *it's Christmas*,' he yelled. '*Forget* about the price.' To prove just how generous he was willing to be, he struck a bargain with the crowd: 'The more hands that I see the cheaper they'll be. Who might be interested in a set if I did you a deal?'

He pointed out a few of the raised hands. 'You might, you

might, you might. *Who else might?* You might. SAY YES! You might. *'Ere, THE PRICE.'*

There was a silence. Those people who were expecting a simple announcement of what he was going to charge for the twins were in for a very big surprise. What they got, instead, was something like a back-to-front auction. He started to reduce the price, step by step, and also began pointing out or nodding at individual members of the crowd, as if he were taking bids from them: *'Ere, LADIES AND GENTLE-MEN, THE PAIR* would cost you sixty. If you'll have a deal with me 'ere today ah'll charge you on the pair, dolls that *think* together.'

He bashed his stick against the stall. *'Not* fifty, *forty*-five or *forty*-two.' Then again – 'BANG' – just to make sure that everybody was still listening.

'WON'T CHARGE YOU *forty, THIRTY-NINE* or *THIRTY-EIGHT, THIRTY-SEVEN FIFTY.* In fact, ladies, you *all* go shopping in toy shops, yes?'

People nodded back.

'If *I* said thirty-five pounds the pair, *be fair*, it works out at seventeen pounds fifty for a hand-made doll. Is that dear?' he asked the crowd. *'No!* That's what it works out at. *Seventeen pound* fifty a piece, thirty-five pound a *pair.* And they *think* together. *No wires attached!'* He began to go even cheaper. 'Ah'll charge you *not* thirty-five, *TAKE THEM, the pair.* "Love Me Twins". Ah won't even charge you thirty-four.' He raised his stick again – 'BANG' – 'gimme thirty pound *the pair* to clear them outta the way.'

Nobody moved.

Although it was nearly Christmas (as it often is in the vicinity of many a pitching stall), not a single person was interested in buying the twins. The pitcher seemed surprised; he was certainly disappointed. *'AREN'T YOUR KIDS WORTH THIRTY QUID?'* he chided the crowd. 'I wish *mine* were. I'd sell all *eight* of the buggers.'

People started laughing. At least he'd got some kind of response. Then, true to his word, he made them even cheaper: 'Listen, *'ERE, an' NOW*! *Dolls that* THINK *together, dolls that* LAUGH *together, dolls that* CRY *together*, dolls that *DRINK* together. NOT *sixty* – ah'll give you your bus fare home if it helps you. *NOT fifty, NOT forty, THIRTY-FIVE* IS CHEAP, *NOT* thirty-two fifty, 'ere, *an'* to *CLEAR 'EM*, ah won't even charge you *thirty*.'

Finally, to make the goods into a bargain that demanded a buying response, he didn't just reduce the price further, he turned it into a favour. Up went his stick again and, as he brought it crashing down on to the stall, he split the price in two: *'HALF THAT!'* – BANG – *'FIFTEEN POUND* THE *PAIR*.'

Now the response wasn't enthusiastic; it was overwhelming. Less than seventy-five seconds later he had sold nineteen sets of twins.

When we first saw this pitcher in action we assumed that we'd just witnessed a classic example of a salesman coming up against the hard-edged reality of what economists call the 'normal demand curve'. When the price was too high no one wanted to buy. Sales occurred only when the price of the goods was reduced in line with what people were willing or able to pay. The skill of the pitcher, we surmised, was in judging the precise point at which he could maximize his profit by selling the most goods at the highest possible price.

But when we got back to the lab and studied this sale in greater detail it became obvious that he had never been serious about the price of £30 or, indeed, any price other than his final price. Fifteen pounds was always going to be the actual selling price and it had been as pre-planned as an ambush. We found that the pitcher used this same tactic of pretending to offer the goods at a higher price in every one of the four of his routines we had recorded. Moreover, during the 'Love Me Twins' sale, one of the pitcher's assistants – who had been standing at the front of the stall – had, during the early stages of these price reductions, been mooching around looking bored, but it didn't seem to be a coincidence that he suddenly perked up and quickly put out his cigarette just before the final selling price was mentioned.

This pitcher was working with a pre-existing selling price. In fact, all pitchers do. By going lower than what, for all intents and purposes, seemed to be the final selling price of £30, he had managed to convey the impression that he had failed at his usual or favoured price and was then forced to go lower because of the crowd's lack of interest. In this way he was able to build up the value of the goods and to demonstrate to the audience in a highly dramatic way that he was giving them an exceptional bargain.

THE GRAFTER'S RAMP

Pitchers sell their goods by creating deals that are viewed by shoppers as bargains. Bargains are built primarily by charging less than the goods are said to be worth. 'Before you can sell something cheap,' Tonto once told us, 'you've first gotta make it seem expensive.' The business of making something seem expensive is known as 'ramping'. The bargain is then completed by offering a selling price that seems cheap and value for money. Pitchers call this latter part of bargain creation 'auctioneering', or 'batting down the price', or 'coming to the bat'.

The techniques for bargain creation are various, and some of them are more complex than others. At the heart of all these techniques, however, lies a contrast between the high worth of the goods and their low selling price.

THE PRICE CONTRAST

The most elementary form of worth-selling price contrast is a straightforward comparison between a monetary value placed on the goods by the pitcher and a lower selling price:

MEAT

P   'Ere, ah've gotta piece of braising beef 'ere, or roastin' beef – whatever you want. Can anybody use that?

AS   [Some people raise their hands]

P   Here you are. Quick. Just 'ave a look at that. Not an ounce o' waste on it. Look at that. *Beautiful*. Braisin' or roastin' beef. *'Ere*, that little lot there, twenty-one fifty. One hand sharp, quickly. *Gimme a tenner for the lot*.

In this sale, the pitcher uses the difference between the price of what the meat is said to be worth ('twenty-one fifty') and the lower selling price (a 'tenner') to establish that the meat is a bargain and thus worth buying.

The implied contrast

Sometimes, pitchers only allude to what their goods are worth:

MEAT

P   Does anybody fancy that one there for Christmas? *Look at that*. Top rump steak an' *no waste*. An' that is a *beauty*. Go on, ah'll take *fourteen* pound on that big'n'.

This pitcher describes the qualities of the meat before he announces its selling price. The rump steak is portrayed as being 'top' rump steak with 'no waste' and as a 'beauty'. These qualities imply a high worth, but no monetary sum is attached to the worth of the meat. The contrast is implicit, and so the precise extent of the bargain being offered is less obvious.

The numerical contrast

On other occasions pitchers contrast their selling price with factors like the number of items they are selling in a collection:

BOOKS
P   It's all the five of 'em [BANG], *gimme two pound* the whole lot.

. . . or the weight of their goods:

BOXES OF CHICKEN PORTIONS
P   . They are A Grade, ladies and gentlemen. These boxes are thirty pound not twenty pound. I'll take fifteen pound a box.

. . . or the number of component parts of the product for sale:

TOY STABLE COMPLEX
P   *The lot*. 'Upstairs Downstairs', hundred and seventy working pieces, fifteen quid.

When a number such as this is mentioned just before the selling price, that number is invariably larger than the number of pounds mentioned as the selling price.

These forms of elementary contrast are, in fact, rather rare. Although they are obviously employed to indicate the bargain status of the goods, most often they are used primarily to summarize a deal that had already been offered in an attempt to generate further sales or to cope with a failed sale. More elaborate contrasts are generally favoured to build bargains. These contrasts build up and then break down, in a more detailed and explicit way, the worth of the goods and the cheapness of their selling price.

BUILDING UP THE WORTH

One way of building up and accentuating worth takes advantage of the fact that goods are often sold in collections. This enables a pitcher to underscore the value of the collection by, for example, listing separately each item on offer:

PENS

P   There's your retractable, your rollin' pen, your executive.
     There's the *fine liner*. An' I also put with it, look, that
     lovely fountain pen. *Look at that*, you must 'ave twenty
     pounds' worth. Ah want a *pound again* the whole jolly lot.

This pitcher lists each separate pen in the collection and then announces the price of what the whole set are worth ('twenty pounds'). He follows this by mentioning the lower (and contrasting) selling price of a pound.

Pitchers may also list the individual worth of each item on offer to emphasize the worth of the collection of goods as a whole. The total worth of the collection can then be contrasted with the selling price:

SAUSAGE AND BACON

P   'Ave a look. Amazin' bacon. *All* lean, not an ounce *o' fat*
     on it. [Places some bacon on the scales] *'Ere, that* little lot
     there'd cost you seven quid on your bacon. *Watch* this.
     [Places some sausages on the scales] *Clear the lot*. I'm
     gonna give you a *load o'* sausage on the top. *Three* packs o'
     bacon, 'ere, *four* packs o' sausage. *That* little lot there's
     worth over, what? *Nine an' a 'alf quid*? 'Ere, one hand.
     Gimme a fiver for the lot.

Here, after itemizing the collection, this pitcher summarizes the collective worth as a quantity ('three packs o' bacon', 'four packs o' sausage') and also announces a cumulative monetary worth of 'nine an' a 'alf quid'. This is then contrasted with the lower selling price of 'a fiver'. Although this type of listing may seem to be fairly innocuous — a way of reminding the audience of the different items on sale and showing the worth of the collection as a whole — the overall effect is to enhance the contrast with the final selling price.

Those pitchers who choose not to sell goods in collections are not prevented from building up the worth in this manner. They can do so by using a series of increasing assessments of worth, such as 'It's in the sales at ten pounds, their normal selling price is fifteen pounds, and I've even seen them in the catalogue at seventeen ninety-nine.' The worth of a collection can also be enhanced by pitchers displaying the goods in a fanned formation, thereby accentuating visually the number of items being offered for sale.

Embedded contrasts

Selling goods in collections gives pitchers added degrees of freedom in their pricing structures and provides them with yet further ways of building up the value of their goods. It enables them, for instance, to create further contrasts *within* the basic worth-selling price contrast format. One type of embedded contrast made possible by selling items in this way is the contrast between the selling price of the collection *as a whole* and the worth of just *one item* in that collection. In the following example, a pitcher claims that the price he is asking for a complete set of five pens is less than what one of the pens alone is worth. This embedded contrast is used to increase the value of the whole collection:

P In Denton on Saturday we sold out. Genuine Papermate Replay. *Only today. Five*, cheaper than *one*. [CLAP] A POUND the five of 'em.

Another pen-seller we recorded built up the value of his goods in a more unorthodox way. Rather than straightforwardly selling sets of five pens for a fixed price, he claimed he was giving four of them away for free and only charging a nominal price (a pound) for the fifth pen. Of course, these pens were being sold in sets and so the 'free' pens could not be claimed without buying the complete set.

One of the reasons he adopted such an unusual and, judging from the large number of sets he sold, highly successful selling strategy was because of the very low price of the set of pens – £1. If all five of the pens had simply been bundled together in an undifferentiated way the audience would probably have assumed that they were all of an equal value and concluded that pens costing twenty pence each were likely to be of very dubious quality. By claiming that he was only charging for one pen, he made it look as if at least that pen was of a high quality. In effect, the four pens he was giving away free were simply being used to enhance the worth of the other pen – a fountain pen:

P   I'm gonna do it like this, look, IF *AH GIVE* YOU
      THESE four pens for nothin', an' *AH CHARGED*
      you five ninety-five for the fountain pen, you'd have a
      bargain.

Having built up the worth of the star item in his collection, the pitcher then went on to contrast the worth of the collection as a whole, which he estimated, on this occasion, to be £15, with his selling price of £1:

P   FORGET the price of the four, *you get those for nothin'*.
      The *fifth* one, the *fountain pen*, ah *won't* charge you five
      ninety-five, *'ere's* what ah'll do with you. FIRST come
      first served. ALL the *five of 'em*. You must have *fifteen*
      pounds' worth of pens, [CLAP] ah'll take a *pound the*
      whole jolly lot.

Like other pitchers who engage in this type of activity, the contrast was visually affirmed, not simply by showing each new pen and adding it to the collection, but by holding the most valuable pen in one hand and the other four pens in a fanned formation in the other hand.

Maximizing the worth

Pitchers can make the monetary difference between the worth and the selling price seem even bigger by implying that their valuation of what the goods are worth is only a minimal assessment:

FOOD MIXER
P   An electric food mixer, in the shops an' stores, would cost you over forty pounds *at least*.

CUSHION COVERS
P   Ladies, ah'll tell you what, I promised you a bargain. They should be *at least* four ninety-nine each elsewhere.

Phrases such as 'worth at least . . .' and 'worth well over . . .' plant a seed in the audience's minds to the effect that the goods may, in fact, be really worth much more than has been stated. This enhances the bargain status of the goods even further by maximizing the contrast of the worth with the eventual selling price.

Validating the worth

It helps if pitchers can externally validate the worth of their goods. The most prized way of doing this is by selling stock that has a price already marked on it – that is, when the goods are already 'ramped and stamped'. In the following sequence we notice the pitcher's obvious delight in being able to sell such items:

DUNGAREES

P   Retails in British Home Stores. [Picks up a bag of dungarees and ostentatiously pulls off a label with the price marked on it – he now talks about his pitching associates working nearby] *Okay, lads,* you can compete with me now, if you *want* to. If you *can.* [Shows price tag to AS] *Twenty-two pound fifty.* It says: 'Co-ordinated leisure wear, *exclusive* to BHS'.

When the goods are not ramped and stamped, pitchers may use other types of independent sources to back up their claim about what the goods are worth, such as TV advertising:

TOY STABLE COMPLEX

P   *The price?* You've seen it on the telly, it's thirty-nine ninety-nine. I've got a *dozen.*

CARPET CLEANER

D   It's sold on Sky TV at nine ninety-nine.

. . . or by asking the audience themselves what the goods are worth:

TOY STABLE COMPLEX

P   Anybody seen the price of My Little Pony stables?

AS   [No response]

P   *Yeah?* [Still looking for a response from someone in the audience] How much is it? Anybody any idea? [To A] Twenty-eight? *I've* seen it at thirty-one. If you wanna take it off me *forget* twenty-eight . . .

The toy stable example above is more subtle than it first appears. The pitcher receives an estimation that the goods are worth £28 from someone in the audience. He claims he has seen the goods on sale at the higher price of £31, thus increasing the estimate of worth that the audience hear. But when he begins to reduce the price he starts from the more credible estimate which the audience member has provided rather than from his own higher and, perhaps, less believable estimate.

As with other potentially problematic events, such validations are often dealt with in a humorous fashion. In the following sequence the pitcher states that a famous toy store is also selling the 'Love Me Twins', but is charging a different price for each doll. He uses the price of each doll to build up the worth of the pair of dolls. He then accounts for their price difference by making a thinly veiled reference to the additional vinyl needed to manufacture the boy's 'private parts':

P   *There is only one other toy store, in the UK, apart from us,* that has got these and that is Hamleys in the West End of London. *THEY CHARGE*, for the *little girl*, twenty-eight ninety-nine. *THEY CHARGE*, for the *little boy*, twenty-*nine* ninety-nine.

AS   [Silence]

P   Well, you get a little bit *more* with the boys, *don't you*?

AS   [Laughter]

P   *Not a lot*, 'cos they're only *babies*.

THE BAT

Perhaps the most distinctive feature of market pitchers' spiel is the series of prices they say they are not going to charge for their goods:

CUSHION COVER SETS

P   Ladies, ah'll tell you what, I promised you a bargain. They should be *at least* four ninety-nine each elsewhere, so that's practically a tenner's worth of value. *If,* ladies, it does a little bit of good to you, such tasteful bargains sold at such a *give-away* price, *make* your *mind* up and tell us which you'd like to *have.* You've got a choice of two colours, remember. We're *not* gonna charge you ten your nine your eight your *seven.* Ah won't even turn round an' charge you six, an' ah'll tell you what, ladies, ah won't even turn round and charge you five. So you've got the most *handsome* pair of cushion covers, at a give-away price again [CLAP], give me *three ninety-five the pair.*

A   Thank you, ah'll have them. [Other hands are raised in the audience]

After mentioning what the cushion covers are worth ('practically a tenner's worth of value'), this pitcher lists five other increasingly lower prices that she is not going to charge. Only then does she announce the selling price of £3.95. She has opened a space between the declared worth and the selling price and then filled in this space and, as such, fleshed out the bargain with a series of other prices. Because each of these prices is lower than the previous one, and also lower than what the goods are said to be worth, they progressively build up a tension in the audience as to how low the pitcher is going to go and what the eventual selling price will be.

Indeed, to demonstrate unequivocally that they are about to offer a bargain, pitchers may make the first price drop a relatively large one:

FLOWERS

P   I'll do it one more time like this, thank you. This one'll cost you somethin' like twenty-five guilders. Twelve guilders, nine, EIGHT, seven, six guilders. I've only got five plants left. Give us five guilders for the big'n', who wants it?

PERFUMES

P   They're *not* twenty-three. Now when ah said ah were gonna make 'em *cheap*, I don't mean I'm gonna knock three quid off the price and charge you twenty pound. That'd be *discount*. *I'm not even gonna charge*, for all the four of them, a *tenner*.

The reasoning behind these series of declining price announcements is almost the mirror image of the techniques used to build up the worth of the goods by listing the amount and value of each item in a collection. Now, however, the pitcher is building up the value of the final price by making this price seem even more worthy, more tempting and more of a bargain than it would be if it was only mentioned on its own. Each price mentioned that will not be charged makes the goods sound more enticing than the previous price. By the time the final price is reached the deal has become overwhelmingly cheap, if not, in fact, irresistible.

The announcement of the final price must not fall flat. Because it is the main way in which a pitcher gets the buying to occur at one particular point, the final price has to drop like a bombshell and be as successful as a comedian's punchline. One way in which pitchers draw attention to the point where the audience are expected to make a purchase is by preceding the actual selling price with a loud noise. They usually do this by hitting a hard part of the stall with something like an auctioneer's gavel (the figurative 'bat') or by clapping their hands together. By following this noise with a long silence instead of a price, pitchers can create the impression that they are still thinking, even at this late stage in the sale, about how much they should charge for the goods. The longer the silence and the more thoughtful the look, the lower the price can appear to be.

We can see the effect this noise can have upon a crowd when we compare the price announcement in the cushion cover sale (see above) with a failed sale. In the following case the price is *not* telegraphed with a bang. Consequently, the point at which the audience are expected to buy is less clear than it could be:

CARPET CLEANER

D   It's sold on Sky TV at nine ninety-nine. Here we cut the price in half to a fiver, and whilst we're promoting and advertising, for the first five customers here, who buy one at a fiver, our promotion here is to give you another one absolutely free.

AS   [No response]

D   [Short silence] That's two for a fiver for the first five customers.

Another way of telegraphing the point where the audience are expected to buy is by making the monetary difference between each subsequent price drop in the series of possible selling prices progressively smaller:

JEDI SWORD AND OTHER TOYS

P   All the kids love Jedi an' Star Wars. 'Ere, ah don't want four pound, two pound, one fifty, an' not even one twenty. Ah've got two lads of me own, one's five months an' one is six on Wednesday. Ah know what kids go for. You can 'ave anything on the board. I call 'em stocking fillers. Whatever you like. [CLAP] A POUND a piece.

In this series of prices, each additional price reduction drops decrementally, both as an amount and a proportional difference. The drop from £4 to £2 is a drop with a ratio of 2:1; from £2 to £1.50 is a drop of 1.33:1; from £1.50 to £1.20 it is 1.25:1; and from £1.20 to £1 the drop is 1.2:1. Mathematicians call this type of reduction an exponential or logarithmic decline. It is the pitching equivalent of peeling the layers off a set of nested Russian baboushka dolls: each additional price not only whets the audience's appetite for what is in store for them, it also enables them to project and thus prepare for what the final 'gift' price is likely to be.

Telegraphing the wrong selling price

In spite of the points we have just made about the benefits of making it obvious when the selling price has been reached, there is also a strategic advantage to be gained by sometimes making it *difficult* for people to guess which price will be the actual selling price. For instance, by breaking away from a simple linear price reduction or an exponential reduction, pitchers can subvert the audience's expectations of what the next price will be and, as a result, can further enhance the bargain status of the actual selling price. One place where pitchers attempt to confound audience's expectations in this way is right at the end of their series of selling prices. This is the other main point in the sale where a larger than usual price reduction is often announced. This happened in the 'Love Me Twins' sale, where the selling price was cut by half. Here is another similar example:

CHINA FIGURINES

P   Instead of me sayin' it was fourteen or thirteen or twelve or a tenner. [BANG] Nine, [BANG] eight, [BANG] not even for seven. [BANG] An' not even for six. An' if one of you'd buy the first one [BANG], ah won't even say they're a fiver a piece. Fantastic Christmas presents ah would think. Ah'm gonna put these in level money. For half a dozen this time round. The first six of you to do it sharp. *Not* a fiver. The *first six buyers*. [BANG] Ah'll take two pounds a piece.

Here, the penultimate price is 'a fiver' and the final selling price is 'two pounds' – a difference of £3. The contrast between these two prices (and, indeed, with the number '6' which immediately precedes the selling price) is greater than all the previous differences between adjacent price announcements in the series of prices that are mentioned. This larger-than-anticipated drop at the end of the sale makes an 'already good bargain' even better than was anticipated at exactly the point where people are expected to make their purchase.

For this strategy to have any chance of succeeding, though, the pitcher must first provide information to enable and encourage a (wrong) prediction to be made. For instance, in the sequence above the previous five prices the pitcher announces are all reductions of one-pound units. This trend sets up a precedent that strongly encourages the audience to expect that the next price will follow suit and continue to be a reduction of the same order of magnitude.

Another way in which pitchers can exploit this expectation is to use the strategy employed by high-street stores of setting prices just below a rounded figure – for example, £3.99 or £3.95. This enables pitchers to announce a price that sounds lower than expected when, essentially, it is not. This happens at the end of the cushion cover sale above: 'give me three ninety-five the pair.' The difference between the penultimate price of £5 and the selling price is only five pence more than the difference between all the other adjacent prices. Yet, at first hearing, this difference seems much greater because the pound component in the final price – the measure most people seem to rely upon when making price decisions – declines by twice as much as before – from £5 to £3.

One other way in which pitchers can subvert an audience's expectations is by exploiting the noise of their gavel or the clap of their hands to misdirect the audience as to which price will be the actual selling price. This is evident in the china figurine example above. Of the nine prices mentioned before the selling price, five are preceded by a loud bang from the pitcher's gavel. We have already seen that this noise sets up an expectation that the next price announced will be the actual selling price. Here are some other examples:

TOWELS

P   On this occasion, [BANG] *forget* about seventeen pound. [BANG] Never mind sixteen ninety, [BANG] sixteen eighty or sixteen seventy, [BANG] and nothing like sixteen fifty. I am *prepared, on this occasion*, to charge you *nothing like* my *normal* price [BANG] of fourteen pound a pair of bath towels.

PLATES

P   And instead of saying they're twelve or eleven, [BANG] *ten*, [BANG] *nine*, [BANG] eight. [BANG] *Not even a fiver*. I'm not doing this the modern way by knocking you five or ten pence off, I'm gonna do it the *old-fashioned way*. And instead of four fifty [to PC] let's see if we can get a bit of a response from the crowd today. [To AS] *Ah'll take A POUND* the whole lot. *Put 'em in a bag*.

By making this noise *within* the downward series of possible selling prices, pitchers are able, again, to demonstrate that a good bargain is on offer because the selling price will be even lower.

Trading off audience responsiveness

One particularly convincing way of demonstrating that the selling price is a cheap one is by going lower than a price at which people in the audience have indicated they would be willing to buy the goods. Pitchers do not use this dramatic and somewhat bizarre way of announcing their prices simply to make them appear cheaper. It can be used to create the effect that an auction is being conducted and that the price at which the goods will be sold is being determined by what the audience are willing to pay for them. As Gary told us:

'You have to tempt people, don't you? You get them at it a little bit. You tempt them: "Never mind *five* pounds" – as if they're expecting you to say "five pounds". *"Never mind* 2.50" – as if someone in the edge has said "Oh, they're 2.50." It's all psychology, isn't it?'

Pitchers who are in the midst of declaring a series of possible selling prices are only rarely interested in serving people who have raised their hands 'prematurely'. They are much more likely to draw attention to them to show the rest of the audience that an independent and thus more credible source of opinion about the bargain status of their goods exists:

TOWELS

P   [CLAP] They're not eleven, [CLAP] they're *not even* the price you pay round the market of a tenner a pair. It's the end of the day, what pair would you like? *Not ten, not* nine, [CLAP] *not* eight, [CLAP] they're *not* seven, [CLAP] they're *not* six, [CLAP] *not* fi— [points to a member of the audience] Put your money away, ah *don't* want to sell one pair, ah want twelve customers to 'ave a pair, it's the end of the day and I don't want any of them left over tomorrow. [BANG] *Gimme four pound the pair.*

One pitcher took this principle to its extreme. In the following sale sixteen people have raised their hands to show that they are willing to buy his goods at £8. He then reduces the selling price further and uses these sixteen people to attract even more purchasers:

DUNGAREES

P   NOW I'VE *CHARGED* YOU EIGHT POUNDS, JUST TO *SHOW YOU* that I can get whatever money I want for stock like that. If I had *said* a

tenner we 'ad *three* shouts *there*. AH'M *NOT* GONNA
CHARGE YOU EIGHT POUNDS you'll be
pleased to hear. Ah'm gonna give you a little bit off, an'
for all those people who put their 'ands up and *would o'*
genuinely *paid* me eight pounds, AH'M *NOT GONNA
CON YOU*, like some *others* do, an' charge you seven
ninety-nine an' give you a free paper bag. I'll charge *all*
those people FIVE NINETY-NINE an' give you two
pounds in your pocket. An' *sixteen* times *two* is thirty-two
quid. An' I wonder how many people on this market
would *throw away* thirty-two quid. *I WILL*, because it
brings back *goodwill*.

We can also see that when he promises to reduce the price even
further he points out the madness of his deed. He refers
disparagingly to the same type of minimal price-reducing
strategy as was used in the cushion cover sale. Nevertheless, he
ends up using essentially the same tactic himself.

To enhance the impression that a price is the final price, a
member of the pitch crew may attempt to grab the goods from
the pitcher and move to serve someone before it transpires that
a 'wrong' price has been announced:

IRONING BOARD COVERS

P   *Not* a pound *seventy*, and not even sixty or fifty-five p or
anything like it. This is a *British* ironing board cover. We
'ave a laugh and a giggle but ah'm being serious. They're
all made in England, to fit any big ironing board . . .

PC   [Turning towards the audience with one of the ironing
board covers in his hand but speaking to P] A lady wants
one 'ere.

P   [To PC] *Will you wait a minute?*

PC   [To P] *They're sold!* A lady wants one here.

P   But I want to make them *cheaper*. [P continues to reduce
the price]

In the following sequence both of the pitcher's assistants act in unison, creating an even stronger impression that the final price has been reached and that people are already waiting to buy the goods:

CUPS

P [BANG] NEVER MIND twelve. [BANG] *Not even* eleven, [BANG] and not even a *tenner*.

PC1 [Pointing dramatically to a shopper with a hand in the air] *You're first, love*. [He then runs to the back of the stall as if to get the goods to serve this shopper]

PC2 [Who is standing to the left of the pitcher and holding the six cups in the air on a velvet board and nods in the direction of a customer who has raised a hand.] They're sold. Gone. [He then moves as if he is going to pack the cups away and give them to the customer he has just nodded to.]

P [To PC1] *Hold on, Paul. Hold on, hold on*. [Insistent, as if PC1 is not taking any notice of him] *Paul*! I want no bawling and shouting. I don't want to be unfair to the rest of my opposition [i.e. other pitchers working nearby].

PC1 I just wanted—

P [To PC1] *Hold on*. I don't wanna be standing up here shouting and screaming like a lunatic. I want to make my *PRICES* do the *talking*! [To AS] They're *not* nine fifty . . .

With this tactic the pitcher builds upon, and perhaps even manufactures, independent and thus more compelling evidence that some people in the audience were prepared to pay more for the goods than the pitcher plans to charge. By going even lower than this price, the pitcher creates a pretty persuasive impression of having temporarily lost his faculties of economic reasoning and having the best interests of the audience at heart. Of course, for this tactic to work successfully, the pitch crew must have colluded in advance with the pitcher and other crew members and know what the final price will be.

Maximizing the bargain

Just as the worth of the goods can be expressed as a minimal estimate to suggest that the real worth may be greater, similarly pitchers may claim that a selling price is extremely cheap. Indeed, they will sometimes announce that their price is actually the lowest selling price that could possibly be charged. This type of maximizing work almost always occurs during a series of downward selling price announcements, enabling pitchers to build up a bargain by following their reflections on a 'lowest possible' price with yet further announcements of even lower prices:

PERFUMES
P   Now 'ere's what ah'm gonna do with you. *AH DON'T EVEN WANT*, for all the four of them, A FIVER! FOUR POUND . . .
     [Silence]
PC   [Stage Whisper to P] Steady on.
     [More silence]
P   If ah go any lower ah'll go through the *floor*. [Continues to reduce the selling price]

In this case the pitcher, prompted no doubt by his assistant, reflects upon the cheapness of the selling price he has just mentioned. His comment 'If ah go any lower ah'll go through the floor' emphasizes that the price he has just announced – the one he is not going to charge – is an extremely low, 'bargain basement' price. But then he reduces the price further and thereby makes the bargain seem even better. Here are some other examples of these types of reflections on a possible selling price that is not the actual selling price:

TEDDY BEARS

P   And never mind a tenner. And if you've paid a tenner for them you'd not have paid too much, you'd have got a very good bargain.

ALARM CLOCKS

P   Forget seven or six. They are not even a fiver. And if I charged my own brother or sister a fiver for these I could go home tonight and sleep comfortably knowing I hadn't taken a liberty with anybody.

DUNGAREES

P   *Forget about eleven.* And *dammit*, [BANG] ah won't even charge you a *tenner*. And at a tenner you've got a *fabulous* deal, believe me, because they're over the road at twenty-two fifty.

CROCKERY

P   *Not even eleven*, [BANG] ah said ah'll make some of you the *envy* of the crowd. If you'll take it, the whole complete matching set, ah'll charge you *nothing like* ten fifty.

CUPS

P   [BANG] They're *not* six fifty. [To people in the crowd who have raised their hands to buy at this price] *Hold on, hold on*. Ah'll tell you here and now, the profit on these wouldn't buy our canary a set of garters.

In these examples the price following on from the pitcher's reflection was still not the final selling price. By going lower than a demonstrably cheap potential selling price, and even lower subsequent prices, the status of the actual selling price can be enhanced even further.

Other activity relating to the announcement of the selling price

At the point where the worth-selling price contrast reaches completion – when the selling price is announced – shoppers are presented with their first opportunity to purchase the goods. Pitchers deliberately structure their sales routines so that buying occurs only at this late point. By then the audience will have listened to the sales patter in its entirety and will have received all the information that the pitcher deems necessary to persuade them to buy. A number of additional devices can supplement and enhance the effect of the final price announcement further to increase the chances of obtaining mass sales.

Pitchers may, for instance, use short, catchy phrases immediately before stating the selling price to emphasize that buying is about to begin. These include phrases such as 'quickly and sharply', 'one hand sharp', 'first come first served', 'the whole jolly lot', and 'for level and silly money'. A mass of hands all raised in unison provides a pretty powerful advert to other shoppers and passers-by as to the merit of the price the pitcher is charging.

We have already encountered another device for shepherding audience responsiveness – the bang of the auctioneer's gavel or clap of the pitcher's hands. In a tightly packed crowd – especially when the pitcher is working near an audience and is at ground level – this noise can have a double-edged effect. According to Gary:

'You make that noise because it shakes people up. It gets some of the edge moving; they're startled, see? You get a big movement in front of you; *all the edge is moving*. Everybody starts to think that other people are reaching for their money and they think: "Well, I'd better reach for mine, I don't want to be left out of this."'

People standing at the back are then more likely to move forward to the front of the stall to try to get served. Those people at the front who haven't as yet made up their minds will feel the pressure of the people behind them moving forward and this, in turn, may be all it takes to convince them to seize the opportunity to make a purchase for themselves.

To enhance the influence that buyers can have on the rest of the crowd, a pitcher and pitch crew may also attempt to build on the commotion that often occurs at this point in the sale. The pitch crew will shout out the type of responses the pitcher has requested from the audience in order to sustain and even, on occasion, to initiate the buying responses. In the following sale, involving sets of pans, immediately after the selling price is announced one member of the pitch crew makes an exceptionally loud and high-pitched noise, indicative of exceptional buying enthusiasm. Another assistant shouts out 'YES PLEASE!' in response to the interest in the goods which the audience has shown. Overcome with excitement, both members of the pitch crew then continue to shout out, for the benefit of the crowd as well as the pitcher, the colour of the pans the buyers are preferring:

P   I *asked* you on the saucepan set *thirty-five*, I put the frying pan on the top, I *still* said thirty-five. The saucepans, the frying pan and the cookpot on top o' that, *the whole bloomin' lot together*, *not even* the thirty-five I said, [CLAP] GIMME TWENTY-FIVE POUND *THE LOT.*

PC1 *WHEEEEEEEEEEEEEEEEEEEE!*

PC2 *Twenty-five pound*, YES PLEASE!

P   Which colour do you want, *everybody*?

PC1 *A grey! A grey! A grey! A grey! A grey! A grey!*

P   *A grey one!*

PC2 A grey one!

The 'Love Me Twins'-seller also used a similar tactic. During the seventy-five seconds he took to sell his dolls he was continually shouting instructions to his floor crew as to where the willing buyers were standing and what these shoppers should do:

P   *Over there*, fifteen pound. And *again* fifteen pound.
    HAVE YOUR MONEY READY PLEASE!
    HAVE YOUR MONEY READY PLEASE! *Over*
    there fifteen pound. And *again* fifteen pound. HAVE
    YOUR MONEY READY PLEASE! *Over there*,
    fifteen pound. *Over there*, fifteen pound. *Over there*, fifteen
    pound. *Over there*, fifteen pound. *Over there*, fifteen
    pound. *Over there*, fifteen pound. *THE PAIR!*
PC THE *PAIR*.

He sold nineteen pairs of dolls, yet he shouted these types of announcements and instructions thirty-one different times.

THE PROBLEM WITH BARGAINS

Selling goods as bargains is not without its difficulties. The obvious question that arises is why are these goods being sold so cheaply? The discrepancy between the high worth and lower selling price can create a doubt in the audience's minds which, if left unchecked, can undermine all the work a pitcher has done to foster the impression that the goods are genuine bargains. People may start asking themselves questions such as: 'Are the goods of a sub-standard quality?' 'Were we naive to believe that the goods were really worth that much in the first place?' and so on.

Signs advertising a 'Closing Down Sale', 'End of Season Lines', and 'Liquidation Stock Clearance' in the windows of high-street retail stores address precisely this type of difficulty. They provide an explanation for why a sale is being conducted and why the goods have been reduced in price. The usual rationale for high-street price reductions is that stores clear out their stock at the end of a particular season, hence the familiar January and summer sales. Pitchers also use these types of supportive explanations to account for why the goods they are selling are so cheap:

DINNER PLATES

P   If you want 'em, love, I sell 'em *normally* for eighteen quid. But *again*, with something expensive like that I don't want it left over after Christmas. Is it any good to you? [BANG] You can 'ave 'em for a *tenner* the 'alf a dozen.

Other ways in which pitchers account for their low prices include having an 'advertising' sale:

DRESSES

P   So, ladies, when *I've* got professional dressmakers, who *come along* to *buy* these off me, *that's* the answer whether they're more than cheap or not. Ladies an' gentlemen, in *my case* they might be too cheap but it's an advertisement for me firm.

. . . adverse local 'economic' conditions:

MEAT

P   I call this me miners' deal because you get value for money on this one. [Puts turkey meat and chicken legs on the scales] Over nine twenty for the parcel, my normal price is six fifty, I've worked cost for the last four months because of the miners' strike, and this is the *only* line on the vehicle that I *don't* actually earn a profit.

. . . and also factors such as 'catalogue surplus', 'fire salvage', and 'It's the end of the day'. Not uncommonly, a pitcher will hint at the possibility that the goods were acquired in an unorthodox way:

PERFUME
P [Talking to a woman in the audience] They're not stolen, love, they just haven't been paid for.

TOWELS
P Every towel is *wrapped*, it is *sealed*. It has never *ever* seen *daylight, moonlight, gaslight*. I'll tell you what, the only things they've seen is torchlight.
AS [Couple of titters]
P An' that was the night the buggers were *knocked off*!

As already mentioned in the Introduction, in nearly all these cases the source of the goods is, in fact, a legitimate one – they are purchased wholesale. Yet many pitchers cultivate their reputation for being 'wide boys' because this identity provides shoppers with a feasible explanation as to why the goods are being sold so cheaply. However, pitchers have to walk a fine dividing line here. They must be careful that they don't sound too convincing when they proclaim that their goods are stolen or hint that they have been obtained by anything other than legitimate means, otherwise their whole selling project could be put in jeopardy. Indeed, to counter or temper this wide-boy image, pitchers often profess how honest they are and how long various members of their family have been serving the public. Sometimes this is said in the very same breath as their hint or claim that they are dodgy characters, or that they have obtained their goods in a less than orthodox way:

PENS
P I've been on this market every Saturday for the last ten years. Me father was 'ere before me. [Points over the top of the market buildings towards the heavens]. He's up

there now, God bless him. [Short silence] Getting the lead off that roof.

If there were such a thing as an encyclopaedia of successful selling, beneath the word 'bargain' there would surely be a photograph of a market pitcher caught in the extravagant verbal and visual act of 'coming to the bat'. Building bargains by 'ramping up' the goods and then 'auctioneering' them by 'batting down the price' is what many people, including most pitchers, deem this type of selling to be all about.

But, as we have seen, building convincing bargains is a pretty complex process involving a wide variety of price manipulation strategies and subtle rhetorical ploys, and no matter how much work pitchers do to build and manage a crowd, they cannot ever guarantee sales, let alone mass sales. People who are interested in purchasing their goods may decide either to look elsewhere before making a final decision, or to buy from the pitcher at some later date. One strategy often employed to prevent this type of prevarication involves a pitcher stating that the amount of goods he or she has available to sell is limited. Another, more complex and successful tactic entails pitchers obtaining expressions of interest from people in the audience *before* the selling price is announced which, in some way, commits and perhaps even obligates them to buy. We examine both of these tactics in the next chapter.

CHAPTER 4

Securing Sales

Whenever we saw him, 'Tattooed Doug' just wouldn't give up trying to sell everything on his lorry. Indeed, his sales team's motto was 'We won't be beaten'. Even when everyone at his stall who wanted to make a purchase had done so, if some stock still remained unsold he was always adamant that he was going to sell the rest. And he usually did.

We recorded Doug's sales patter to try to fathom out why he was so successful. In one routine he'd just finished selling several china vase sets for £2 each. Everybody who wanted to make a purchase had already done so. Searching at the back of his stall he found another vase set; a few moments later he'd found yet another – 'the very, very last one'. He then tried to sell these vases to the same people at his stall. As an incentive to the crowd he promised that the price would be less than their original price of £2:

P   [Having just found the first vase set] An' 'oo's gonna buy the other one an' ah'll make the bugger's cheaper than two quid? Come on.

AS   [No response]

P   *Come on!*

AS   [No response]

P   *'Oo's gonna buy the other set?*

A1   [After a pause, a lady raises a hand.]

P   [Pointing to A1] Lady here. [Picking up the second vase set from under the counter] An' 'oo's 'avin' the very, very –

A2   [A man raises a hand]

P   [Pointing to A2] Gentleman there. Knock 'em all the
       profit off. [BANG] One ninety-nine an' a 'alf. [Smiling]
       Now then, 'ere y'are.
AS   [Laughs]
P   [Smiling as he throws the goods down to his pitch crew.
       The goods are then exchanged for money from A1 and
       A2] There wasn't a lot of – there wasn't a lot of profit
       on them, ah'll tell you now!
AS   [Laughter]

So, Doug was again successful. Two more people in the audience eventually raised their hands, indicating their willingness to buy the remaining vase sets. Rather than receiving the substantial reduction they no doubt expected, however, all they received was a reduction of a mere halfpence. (The halfpenny coin was still legal tender when we recorded this routine.) Despite this minuscule discount, these two people still purchased the vases.

By not stating precisely what his final price would be, and by getting two people to indicate their willingness to buy the vases at a lower but unspecified price, Doug managed to accomplish two things. First, he was able to sell two additional items of stock which otherwise would not have been sold. Second, he was able to sell the vase sets at essentially the same price as he had originally charged.

What puzzled us about this sale, though, was why these two people bought the vases. After all, it was quite obvious that they didn't want to buy them earlier, when they had a chance to do so. Moreover, a reduction as small as half a penny – the smallest possible reduction – was not likely to convince anyone to revise their previous decision not to buy. Furthermore, the two buyers certainly didn't appear aggrieved at the minimal reduction they received. In fact, they were laughing along with everyone else, maybe not with the same gusto but, nevertheless, they were still laughing.

The main reason why these two individuals bought the vases is because they had earlier committed themselves to the purchase by raising their hands. Displays of interest such as this at a pitching stall are treated as obliging people to buy, not only by pitchers, but also by the hand-raisers themselves.

We might also ask ourselves why these two customers did not complain. But, really, there is little for them to complain about. Doug had fulfilled his side of the bargain. Although the price paid for the vases was almost certainly more than was expected, they were actually sold for a price 'cheaper' than £2. If Doug had been challenged he could always have maintained that the profit on this particular line was indeed only half a pence. After all, Doug is the only one who knows what the margin on this line of stock actually is.

More importantly, by not going significantly cheaper, Doug did not risk offending the other vase-buyers standing at the stall who had paid the full £2 for the same items. Indeed, by getting the audience to laugh along with him at the misfortune of the two buyers, Doug managed to do exactly the opposite. The laughter helped sell the two extra vases. Doug had created the conditions whereby these two individuals were cajoled into buying the goods and treating their experience as something which, although not wholly fair, could be 'laughed off'. The vase-buyers had taken a gamble and to complain would have entailed revealing themselves as being greedy or 'bad sports'.

Doug's strategy in this sale is known as 'back nailing'. It is a form of 'nailing' because the two vase-buyers' display of interest in making a purchase symbolically nails their feet to the sales site until they have actually concluded the purchase. It is 'back' nailing because it is a sales technique that refers back to an already successful sale. This strategy can only be used to sell one or two more items of goods already offered. The amount of money pitchers take while back nailing hardly covers the cost of their time and effort. It is more often used to bolster the ego of a male pitcher, or to get the audience to laugh in order to maintain a convivial mood conducive to attracting additional customers to the stall for a different line of stock which will be offered in the next sale.

Indeed, back nailing cannot work as a means of obtaining mass sales because it plays off the people who have already bought the goods at the 'higher' price against those individuals seeking an even cheaper bargain. Nevertheless, such commitment- and obligation-inducing tactics can, as we shall see below, also be used to ensure mass sales.

Techniques like these are needed by pitchers because sales can never be guaranteed. George put it this way:

'I can stand here shouting about this gear till I'm purple. I can fanny the stuff up so that they think it's manna from heaven. But that doesn't mean they're gonna part with their dough, does it? You've got to *push* them and *prod* them a little bit. That way, they'll punt.'

People who are interested in or even eager to buy the goods may nonetheless prevaricate. There are no techniques that actually guarantee sales success, short of extreme measures such as holding a gun to someone's head. Nevertheless, there is a range of techniques that pitchers use as a means of ensuring immediate sales success. One of the most common is the creation of scarcity.

SCARCITY

Because the harder goods are to come by, the more people seem to want them, pitchers will make the most of any occasion when their stock appears to be running low. Tattooed Doug did this when attempting to sell his 'last' and 'very, very last' vase sets. More generally, announcements by pitchers that they are short of stock may range from a gentle hint to the effect that the crowd should temper their buying enthusiasm so that as many people as possible can get served:

SOCKS

P   Would you do each other a little bit of a favour please? If you don't mind me asking you. Would you have one lot to a customer? And that gives every one of my customers a sporting chance.

. . . to a full-blooded announcement detailing precisely how many items of stock remain to be sold:

PERFUMES

P   [Counting out the items of stock on his sales counter] There's exact – there's one dozen left and that's it . . .

PC   That's it, when these have gone . . .

P   *That's it, there's no more.* It's your *last* chance to get them, 'cos here, I'll show you quickly now, the first dozen people, I'm going to make 'em look so cheap, you'll *swear blind* the buggers have been *stolen.*

A   Oh dear, don't say that.

P   [To A] They've *not* been stolen, love, they've just not been paid for.

By stating that there are only, say, twelve items left to sell, pitchers imply that their goods have been selling so well that they will soon have run out of stock. This information is designed to secure sales immediately. Stating that there are only a limited number of the goods left implies that not everyone who wants to make a purchase will be lucky enough to get served. The fostering of competition among those people at the stall who are interested in making a purchase helps in a small but significant way to ensure that buying responsiveness is both immediate and enthusiastic when the selling price is finally announced.

    Terry told us that raising the spectre of scarcity fosters fear in order to secure sales:

'In its simplest form it's done by pitchers saying: "I've only got three left." Now people are not going to be terrified, they're not going to be lying awake all night worrying – you're not frightening people to *death*. What you're doing, though, is invoking a fear – the fear of being fourth.'

But *stating* that the goods are in short supply and actually *convincing* shoppers that this is so can be two entirely different things. Sometimes pitchers attempt to prove the veracity of their scarcity claims by counting out the goods for the benefit of the audience. They may then reinforce this message by letting the audience know that the number they have counted out is the number of goods left to be sold (as happened in the perfume sequence above). Sometimes a discussion will take place between a pitcher and an assistant about exactly how many items are left. This can enhance the credibility of the scarcity claim:

PERFUMES

P   I can serve exactly, I've got— [To PC] how many's left of them?

PC   Oh, a dozen, a dozen, no more.

P   [Pointing out some additional stock] And there's them there?

PC   Eighteen, eighteen of the Anytimes.

P   *There's eighteen lots left.*

To drive home the message and further to stimulate an atmosphere of anxiety and urgency, pitchers may remind people at the stall of what could happen if they don't buy now:

TOY DOLLS

P   Tell you what, don't come back up to me next Saturday and say, 'Big gob, ah'll have one of those dolls,' 'cos ah'll tell you now there'll be none left.

PENS

P   *JUST LOOK AT THESE!* THERE'S ONLY SO
MANY TO GIVE AWAY, AH'M SORRY. When
these've gone there'll be no more, and ah can't give you
them for nothing then, *even if you pay me!*

PENS

P   Who else wants some of these while we're 'ere?

AS   [Hands are raised]

P   [Holding a boxful of pens towards the people at the stall]
Anybody else? Anyb— D'YOU WANT SOME 'cos
THAT'S *ALL* THAT'S LEFT? IF YOU WANT
THEM, YOU'LL HAVE TO GET THEM *NOW*.
Ah'm *sorry*. If you— ah've only got so many to give away.
Ah *can't* stand here all day givin' 'em away.

[PERFUMES]

P   There's eighteen lots left.

PC   An' that's it.

P   Now watch, *and when it's gone it's gone— there's no more
of them*. If you— *I can't serve you*, the nineteenth person,
if he gives me a *hundred pounds*.

For some pitchers, scarcity appeals are used to secure sales of the
last few items of a particular range of stock. Odd items left over
from previous sales are, in effect, worthless. In the case of other
pitchers, though, the claimed scarcity is not always genuine. We
have seen pitchers counting out small numbers of goods to be
sold, proclaiming that they are unable to sell any more than this
number, and then going on to sell many more of these goods in
subsequent sales. In the perfume sale above, a claim of this type
was made even though there were piles of cardboard boxes full
of the very same goods stacked up at the back of the stall for
everyone to see. Indeed, some pitchers sell the exact same
'scarce' goods in the very next sale.

Gary cited an occasion when he was guilty of this type of caper:

'You were there,' he reminded us. '"Last dozen," we said, yet we had gear stacked up to the ceiling [i.e. the 'sky' – they were working outdoors]. *Ten foot high*! *In boxes*! There must have been a hundred and fifty dozen.'

'So why did you bother saying that, then?'

'Well, because they're stupid, and they think that shops clear things out when they get near the end of a consignment. *It's common sense, isn't it*? They feel better about the gear when we say that, and also it stops them saying: "Well, I'll come back later"; or "All right, I'll have a little look round and think about it." *We don't want them to think about it*!'

At first sight, it appears that it is the pitchers who are not thinking when they make these claims. For instance, in one pen sale we recorded, the pitcher stated that he had only fifteen sets of pens left. But in the very next sale, after he had already sold a good few of these 'final few' pen sets, he went on to claim that he had only twenty sets left. We figured initially that he couldn't even get his fictitious story straight. What this pitcher was doing, though, was rather more subtle than at first appeared. In general, it is of little use a pitcher stating that there are only twenty items of stock left to sell if there are only, say, ten people at the stall. In this type of situation the number of goods available for sale is liable to exceed demand and, in so doing, is likely actually to reduce demand. Thus, the number used in a scarcity claim is usually lower than the number of people present.

Given this point, it would seem that the smaller the number of items claimed to be left available for sale, the more convincing the scarcity claim will be. But this is true only up to a point. The lower the number used or, more specifically, the greater the difference between the number used and the number of people at the stall, the more likely it is that there will be some people who want to buy the goods but who feel that they have little chance of succeeding in doing so. Such people may become too discouraged to stay. Pitchers thus have to use a great deal of skill in judging the optimum figure, because if they underestimate the number of people who want to buy they are likely to lose custom rather than ensure it. This is perhaps one reason why you can sometimes hear pitchers and their assistants disputing the number of items of stock they have left to sell:

PERFUME

P   *Right then.* [Pause] Right, watch this quickly now, look, the first twenty-four people

PC There's not that, there's eighteen, there's—

P   I've got a, there's eighteen of – I'm—

PC There's eighteen now—

P   I'm gonna serve now [starts counting the stock again] two, four, six, eight, ten, twenty, *twenty lots,* the first *twenty people.* Now it's gonna be *first come, first served,* and I *can't* serve you, look, if you're the *twenty-first person,* if you give me a *thousand pound,* now watch. And we're talking now, [to his assistant] Waldo, count for me twenty carrier bags, and not one more than twenty.

. . . and why pitchers create restrictions on how many separate items of stock individuals are allowed to buy when it is never likely that those restrictions will be exceeded:

PENS

P   YOU CAN HAVE UP TO FIVE, UP TO FIVE SETS PER CUSTOMER. No more than five sets. Ah'm sorry, ah want to serve as many people as possible.

In this sale no one bought more than two sets of pens.

Scarcity in other selling situations

Scarcity claims such as these are often used as a sales resource in other types of selling and marketing contexts. High-street retail stores and advertisers use the same kind of strategies in order to encourage sales. Discounted goods are likely to be available only 'while stocks last' and special offers are often said to be available only to, say, the 'first 100 people' who respond to the promotion.

More generally, the fact that people attribute a higher value to items that are in short supply is one reason why many people are loath to dine in an empty restaurant (the food may be no good) or to walk into an empty retail store.

ESTABLISHING COMMITMENTS AND OBLIGATIONS TO BUY

One of the other most successful ways in which pitchers can secure sales is by getting some form of public expression of interest or intent to buy from the audience before they actually do buy. This was the technique used by Tattooed Doug in the vase sale at the beginning of this chapter.

Getting the forks up

The most common way of obtaining buying commitments before the final selling price is announced is by asking people to raise their hands ('forks') if they are interested in the goods on offer:

PENS
P   Ah *won't* charge you five ninety-five, ah WON'T charge
      you three ninety-five or one ninety-five, in fact, ah'm *not*

even chargin', look, a pound and ten pence for all the five
of 'em. Now who can use 'em if ah go a bit lower than a
pound ten pence? Raise an' 'and?

AS   [Many audience members raise hands]

P   [Counting the hands that are raised] One, two, three,
four. AH CAN ONLY DO IT FOR SO MANY.
Five, six, seven, eight, nine, anybody at the back? Ten,
eleven. Here's what ah'll do with you. FIRST come
first served. ALL the five of 'em, you *must 'ave fifteen
pounds' worth of pens, [CLAP] ah'll take *a pound the
whole jolly lot*.

Unlike what happens in Doug's back-nailing sale, here the
audience are not invited to express an explicit intention to buy.
Rather, the pitcher simply asks 'who can *use*' the pens. Those
people who raise their hands display only, at least officially, an
interest in the goods; they do not make a firm commitment to
buy them. Nevertheless, because there is a more specific reference to what the actual selling price is going to be in this
question – that is, 'who can use 'em if 'ah go a bit lower than a
pound ten pence?' – the hand-raisers also imply by their actions
that a purchase is imminent. In fact, those people who do raise
their hands at these points during a sale almost always do buy
the goods.

The display of interest obtained by the pitcher seems not only
to commit those people who have raised a hand, but can also
attract additional people to the stall and persuade others already
present to make a purchase. The pitcher's success is especially
obvious in the above case because many of the hand-raisers
were waving money in the air to attract the pitcher's attention.
We also note that in order to enhance his prospect of securing
sales this pitcher makes a scarcity appeal. He states that he can
give this bargain only to 'so many', and that he will sell the
goods on a 'first come first served' basis.

All this pitcher has obtained, so far, is a public expression of 'interest' in the goods from people who are likely to buy in any case. Nonetheless, this responsiveness can be consolidated into a firm commitment to buy by pointing to or counting out each person who has raised their hand. This reinforces, in public, the interest that has been expressed. As such, it places the hand-raisers under a more ineluctable obligation to make a purchase. The pitcher in the sale above does just this by counting out each of the individual hand-raisers in turn ('one', 'two', 'three', etc.). The extra time this process of counting takes has an additional benefit; it provides passers-by with a longer opportunity to see the eager and willing buyers at the stall.

Bag nailing

A more concrete way of placing people under an obligation to buy before the selling price is announced is to supply those people who display an interest in the goods with carrier bags (or wrapping paper and the like):

[Perfumes]
P   They've got to be cleared cheaply an' quickly. 'Oo can use *all the four of 'em, twenty-three pounds' worth*, at *less* than three fifty, raise an 'arm?
AS   [Many audience members raise hands.]
P   *Anybody else*? Now as— [To PC] Now listen, *Rick*, the first eighteen people wi' their 'and in the air, [to AS] will you please step forward. [To PC] Now look, give every one of these people with their 'and in the air a carrier. Ah'm givin' out *eighteen* carriers an' *that's it*.
PC   [Hands out bags to those people who have raised their hands]

The question this pitcher puts to the people at his stall – ''oo can use – 'em – at less than three fifty raise an 'arm' – is again designed to get those people who have an interest in the goods to raise a hand. By giving out carrier bags to these people, the display of interest (hand-raising) is transformed into a more tangible and thus more ineluctable obligation to buy. The acceptance of a bag or a piece of wrapping paper – that is, something that ordinarily would be used to carry away the goods – implies consent to the imminent transfer of ownership of those goods.

It is also more difficult for people who do accept a bag to walk away from the stall. Even though the bags are given away free of charge, the people who accept them treat them as still being the property of the pitcher. Scrunching the bag up and hiding it in their hand or dropping it on the ground before walking away from the stall without making a purchase are very rare occurrences. The noise such tactics are liable to generate is, after all, liable to attract the unwanted attention of the pitcher.

We can also see that the pitcher does nothing to indicate that taking the bag is anything less than is expected. Rather than asking the audience if they would like to accept a bag, he nonchalantly instructs an assistant to give the bags to the people who have raised a hand. In this way a potentially troublesome action becomes a straightforward and normal event.

Again, a scarcity claim is used as an additional inducement to get people to participate in the sale. The pitcher says he will give out only eighteen bags. Once more, he exploits the imitative basis of buying behaviour to attract additional people to his stall and to convince any others present, especially those who are as yet undecided, that they should also buy. In comparison with the pen sale above, the inevitably longer delay between handing over such imminent signs of ownership and shoppers receiving the perfumes in these bags provides even clearer evidence of the existence of 'willing' buyers to other people at the stall as well as to passers-by.

A more extreme version of this technique was employed by a Parisian pitcher who attracted people to his stall by offering them an empty carrier bag free of charge. As soon as any passer-by accepted the bag this pitcher proceeded to fill it slowly with his perfumes while he waited for the other passers-by who would soon invariably stop.

The proviso

Obtaining an expression of 'interest' in the goods on offer and converting that interest into an explicit obligation to buy is quite a difficult task. One of the most consistently successful ways of managing this transformation and thus obligating people to buy is with a strategy known as 'the proviso'. This strategy is similar to 'forking' and 'bag nailing' in that the people who are placed under an obligation may have only initially indicated an interest in the goods. There are, however, two basic differences which make the routine more dramatic and successful in its outcome. In 'the proviso', shoppers raise their hands to display an interest in the goods at a much earlier point in the sale (and well before they know the exact selling price of the goods); and now, instead of accepting something that implies ownership (such as a carrier bag), they accept something even more obligating – the goods themselves.

Because this technique is, of necessity, more elaborate and time-consuming, it is usually reserved for sales of relatively more expensive goods – those on offer for £10 and over. It is particularly popular with some towel-sellers. This is because these traders usually sell nothing else (unlike pot and toy pitchers, for example, who normally carry a variety of different items), and therefore do not have an alternative line of stock to switch to if the crowd does not seem particularly interested in buying what is currently being offered.

'The proviso' gets its name from the original sales offer which is posited as being conditional upon the goods being sold cheaper than a specified price (for example, 'Providing I make the goods cheaper than . . . £X'):

TOWELS

P   An' ah'll put it to you like this. *Providin'* this morning that
     I make any set that's caught your eye a *lot* less than Marks
     an' Spencer's price of twenty pound, this morning,
     [CLAP] *providing* I make them a *hell of a lot less* than
     twelve quid a set, an' when ah say a LOT less, ah
     DON'T mean fifty pence or a pound or two, I mean a
     HELL of a lot less than twelve quid, [CLAP] is there
     any lady or gentleman listenin' to me at the moment who
     fancies a set of these, if I make them a *lot* cheaper?

AS   [Hands are raised]

P   Now if you do, *don't* show me any money. I *'aven't* asked
     you for any money. If you've seen a set you like, [CLAP]
     can you just show me a sign here please?

AS   [Hands are raised again]

P   [Pointing to and acknowledging the people who have
     raised a hand] *You 'ave*, darlin', *you 'ave*, madam, you 'ave,
     sir, you 'ave, sir, *you have, you have, you have, an' so have
     you.* Well, *everybody* has. Now, just a second.

Again, we can see that the sales offer is phrased in such a way
that people at the stall are led to believe that they are merely
being asked for an expression of interest in, rather than a
commitment to buy, these goods (e.g. 'who fancies a set', and
'if you've seen a set you like'). Because the pitcher states that he
does not want to see any money at this point (a phrase alluding
to the possibility that some people are so interested in the goods
that they have already shown him their money), the audience
are encouraged to conclude that he is only conducting something like an opinion poll rather than an actual sale of his
towels. But, as happens in the previous sales, even such inno-
cent questions are loaded because they are attached to the
proviso; the towels people 'like' or 'fancy' are towels that are
going to be sold below a certain price. Although the hand-
raisers are not likely to be aware of it, expressing an interest in

the towels at this stage of the sale starts the process of obligating. For example, this pitcher goes on to affirm the displays of interest by pointing out the people who have raised their hands, as happened in the pen sale above.

This pitcher now prepares to give out the 'nailer' – the towels themselves. But these goods are not immediately handed over to everyone who has raised a hand. Because of the greater degree of difficulty in getting people to accept the actual goods (rather than something like an empty bag), he starts by handing the goods over to only one person. As is usual in this type of situation, the hand-raiser the pitcher selects is chosen on the basis of the likelihood of he or she producing a positive response. In this sale the pitcher has already had at least two previous opportunities (the hand-raisings) to monitor which individual in the crowd is most likely to respond first and most enthusiastically. He then uses this person as an opinion leader to help persuade the others who have raised their hands to accept the goods. This is what follows:

P   [To one of the audience members who has raised a hand] Now just a second, darlin', can I speak to you?

A   Yes.

P   I won't embarrass you. Just a minute, love. Which colour do you like best?

A   [Points to a set of towels]

P   You like the burgundy, now just a minute. [To AS] Ah'm gonna ask this lady one question. Then ah'll serve *everybody*. [To another A] Now they've gone [i.e. a couple who were standing at the front of the stall], just come in a little bit at the front 'ere. Thank you very much. [Holding the burgundy towels up to the A who raised her hand] Darlin', would you say at twelve quid that was fair value for your money?

A   Aye.

P   *Yes*? If I make them a lot cheaper, you won't get annoyed, will you?

A   [Small shake of head]

P   [Smiling] 'Cos if you swear at me ah'll bloody swear back! Ah know all the words! *Listen*, ah'm gonna put those into a bag. Ah hope you're all watchin' this. Ah'm gonna give them to you now, but you've got a very nice surprise in store for you. *Okay, darlin'*? [No answer] *Don't look so bloody worried*!

A   [Nervous laugh. The pitcher hands over the goods to this buyer]

The most important feature of the above exchange is the way in which the pitcher progressively leads the shopper into committing herself to buy. He starts this by narrowing down her interest. Having asked her, and the rest of the crowd, to raise a hand if they 'fancy' or 'like' a set – any set – this individual is then asked to express a *preference* for a particular colour of towels – the set she likes 'best'. Then he pins down her interest even further by asking her if the towels she has picked are value for money at £12. Her affirmative reply ('Aye') means that a colour preference is transformed into something even more specific and obligating – a price preference. By the time the pitcher has finished talking to this shopper she has effectively bought the towels, although nowhere along the line has she explicitly been asked for any money or even if she wants to make such a purchase. The towels are then wrapped up in a brown paper bag and handed over. This confirms their status as goods that have already been purchased.

The main point of this one-to-one interaction for the pitcher is that it displays to the other hand-raisers in the crowd that the first and only person he has spoken to is willing to accept the towels. This pressurizes them into appreciating that they too have already committed themselves to accepting a set of towels. (Notice his ominous remark to the other hand-raisers as he talks to the first buyer: 'I hope you are all watching this'.) Just in case anyone remains unconvinced by this single endorsement, before he hands over the remaining towel sets he provides yet further inducements to buy. He gives another hint as to what his final price will be and also a reminder about his money-back guarantee:

P   That lady's got the first set. Now listen. Just a minute.
     There's one gone, ah'd like to make it into *twenty*. For the
     people who can't decide, I'm gonna do it for you. At the
     next price I stop at, they cost *more money*, seven or eight
     years ago. Ah'm showin' you the *best*. You *can't* buy *better*.
     They *cost* twenty, I've just been *offered twelve*. *Another* hint,
     [CLAP] ah won' even charge you ten pound a set. Ah'm
     still coming cheaper. An' they've *all got* that money-back
     guarantee. In other words *you can't lose*. Ah'll say that once
     more to let the penny *drop*. [CLAP] At *less* than a tenner a
     set today, *who else* wants a set, now let me see?
AS   [Hands raised]
P   *Everybody*. I thought so. [Talking to a woman who has
     raised a hand.] What colour would you like, darlin'? [The
     pitcher and his assistants then hand out the towel bales to
     the rest of the people who had raised their hands]

The earlier interest solicited from the hand-raiser is now represented as having been an actual commitment to make a purchase ('that lady's got the first set') at a specific and higher price of £12 ('ah've just been offered twelve'). By promising to lower his price (although he still hasn't said what that final price will be), the towels are portrayed as being an even better bargain. When he starts to distribute the remaining towel sets he has little trouble in getting most of the hand-raisers to accept them.

Only after the pitcher has finished giving out the towels does he say exactly what the price is:

P   This is the price. For the two bath, the two hand. There's
     twenty pounds' worth there. Mine's a silly price, but it's

marvellous value for your money. Not twenty, [CLAP] I
want nine ninety-five a set. *OK*?

The promised reduction to £9.95 from 'less than a tenner a set'
turns out to be a reduction of only five pence. As in Tattooed
Doug's vase sale, the final price of the goods is higher than what
these hand-raisers had been led to expect. Recall what the
pitcher had said at the beginning of his towel sale:

P   . . . *providing* I make them a *hell of a lot less* than twelve
      quid a set, an' when ah say a LOT less, ah DON'T mean
      fifty pence or a pound or two, I mean a *HELL* of a lot less
      than twelve quid . . .

This minimal difference between £10 and £9.95 is camouflaged
by contrasting the selling price with the claimed worth of £20,
rather than with the immediately preceding price of £10.
Despite the lower than anticipated reduction, the sense of
obligation the pitcher has spent almost the entire routine creating is usually more than enough to convince people who have
towels in their possession to pay for them.

The proviso is a highly structured and successful technique
for securing multiple sales. While one or two people do occasionally attempt to escape from or 'jebb out' of making a
purchase by returning their goods or trying to walk away with
the goods without paying for them (they will find an assistant
waiting at the back of the crowd to ensure that they do pay),
these people are the exceptions. The fact that individuals who
have accepted the towels are likely to see other people paying
for them obviously helps to create a climate in which it is
believed that nothing untoward has taken place and, as such,
exerts additional influence on people to pay for their goods
without complaining.

The success of the proviso, like all the other obligating tactics
we have examined, rests upon people rationalizing their

preliminary responses to the pitcher as having committed them to buy. The beauty of the technique from the pitcher's viewpoint is that it places the onus on the 'buyers' to return the goods already in their possession if they do not wish to complete the purchase. The decision as to whether or not to buy has in effect been made for them because the hand-raisers effectively purchase the goods before they either possess or pay for them.

All the techniques of back nailing, forking, bagging out, and 'the proviso' share the same basic feature of turning a public expression of interest into an explicit commitment to buy. In the latter case, because the sales are at a higher price and are deemed to be more difficult to obtain, the shoppers unwittingly become increasingly obligated. Where these techniques differ is in the point where the initial interest is elicited and the type of commitment into which this interest is then transformed. The dramatic success such techniques can achieve is highlighted by the last example, where we saw many people 'purchasing' the goods even when they did not know the exact price they would eventually have to pay.

Obligation in other selling situations

The ambiguous nature of this response to the ownership of goods also occurs in more orthodox selling environments. James, the managing director of a company that manufactures cable for TVs, told us about a similar technique which retail salespeople often employ to obligate their prospective customers:

'One of the greatest "closes" I've ever heard is a salesman who used to sell TV sets in the early days of colour television. He designed his shop, he did all his advertising to get people to come to his shop, and then he let people look at the TVs and play around with them. Then he'd say to them: "Look, would you like to take it home with you? We'll come and put an aerial in or, if you've already got an aerial, we'll bring the TV round to your house and you can keep it for a week." So, at the end of the week he'd ring these people up and ask how the TV was working. They're expecting him to try and 'close' but he didn't. He just asked them if it was working well and then said, "Okay, we'll talk to you in about a week's time." Usually within that week the people were in to pay for that television, because the neighbours had all seen it and the neighbour's kids had been in to see it. What are they going to do? Tell them it had gone back? They've *got* to buy it.'

It seems that in selling, possession is nine-tenths of a sale. As James says: 'The best way to sell anything is to get it into someone's hands, get them to use it, if that's possible. They *don't* give it back.' In book and music mail-order clubs a similar type of obligation strategy is used. Here the onus is often placed on the individual to return the 'monthly selection' which is often sent unsolicited to the member's house. In France, the sale of Minitel terminals works on the same principle. Prospective users are given the first two months' use of the terminal rent-free. On many occasions people find it easier to pay for the terminals than go through all the hassle of returning them.

Yet on many occasions it isn't necessary for a shopper or prospective customer even actually to have possession of the goods. A simple touch can be enough to convince people that they have committed themselves to making a purchase. Touching, in some circumstances, implies 'ownership'. Likewise, if we see a stranger fiddling around with the handle of the driver's door on our car, we are likely to jump to the conclusion that we have stumbled upon somebody who is about to commit a theft.

We are socialized from an early age, usually by our parents, not to touch things when we go shopping. And this is why some supermarkets still place confectionery beside the check-outs. Children who lurk around the check-out waiting for a parent to pay for the shopping often start touching or even eating the sweets on display. This places pressure on the parent to pay for the confectionery, particularly when the child's behaviour has been witnessed by the check-out operator.

Many of the ways in which sales are conducted has to do with negotiating the transfer of ownership of goods through factors such as touch. Two sales interactions that we recorded simultaneously in a small retail store provide classic examples of this phenomenon. One of the two shoppers we recorded bought a camera, the other bought nothing. The non-buyer did not touch any of the three cameras that the salesman had brought out of the display cabinet for his benefit. Indeed, he passed over two possible opportunities the salesman provided to hold a camera. Even when the shopper pointed to one of the cameras he was careful to make sure that his finger didn't touch it. Furthermore, this shopper constantly looked at the salesman rather than the cameras lest his eyes were ever seen to betray any interest in the items.

In contrast, the shopper who eventually did buy a camera picked it up, uninvited, three times during the sales interaction. Not only did he hold the camera, he scrutinized it closely and went through all the motions of owning it – he operated the shutter, twiddled about with the dials, and closely inspected the lens and the viewfinder. Unlike the non-buyer, this shopper asked the salesman many questions about the camera and, when he did so, his attention always remained focused on the camera, even while he was listening to the salesman's answers. It also became quite obvious that this shopper was reluctant to give the camera back to the salesman, even though the latter wanted to continue with the demonstration. He relinquished possession of the camera only when the salesman, seemingly oblivious to the advantage of keeping it in the shopper's hands, almost yanked it away from him.

Indeed, the most innocuous public displays of shopper interest (such as a glance at a product on sale), especially those witnessed by salespeople, are sometimes all that is needed to persuade a shopper that they have thus committed themselves to buy. We've probably all had the following harrowing experience when browsing in a retail store: after entering, and carefully noticing that the only salesman in the vicinity is occupied with another shopper, we relax our guard and start to pay closer than usual attention to that new hi-fi system we've been promising ourselves. After looking round again to check that the salesman is still busy, we move closer to this hi-fi; we start to touch it, twiddle the knobs, flick the LEDs into action, and so on. Time passes as we become more absorbed. Then, in a fit of self-consciousness, we decide to take another look round to ensure that the salesman is still busy with that other shopper. But as we turn our head, there he is, standing less than two feet behind us. He's probably been there for the last ten minutes. We feel pressurized into buying and, what is worse, he knows it.

For the same reason, browsers in retail stores tend studiously to avoid touching the goods on display. They will also avoid hovering around any one section of the shop and even letting their eyes dwell on any item of stock for too long lest their attentions are treated by a salesperson as indicating an interest in the goods, thus warranting an approach.

The lengths to which browsers will sometimes go to avoid being seen displaying any interest in the goods can be quite startling. Not only do they avoid touching the goods and even looking at the salesman, they listen for noises that may signify that the salesman is about to be free and thus likely to establish contact. In one typical case, taken from a corpus of videos we collected from a major British retail store chain, as a salesman who is occupied with a purchaser at one end of the store closes the cash register and takes his leave of the customer, the following events took place: one browser suddenly displayed signs of stress and, as soon as the salesman started walking down the store towards him, turned his back so that he was facing away from the approaching employee. At this point, two other browsers also started to walk away from the salesman to a safer spot in the store. After the salesman had asked the first browser if he needed any help (which he didn't), a fourth browser, who had been standing only a few feet away from the first browser and obviously believed that he was going to be asked the same question next, decided also to take evasive action by walking out of the store.

SOCIAL SKILLS IN THE SECURING OF SALES

Both of the skills we have examined in this chapter – scarcity claims and obligating strategies – show pitchers relying on social and interactional norms to generate and secure mass sales. Scarcity claims are employed by pitchers to create an immediate increased demand for their goods, and they work on the basis that people attribute a higher value to goods that are harder to come by or are observably in demand by other shoppers. As we have seen, pitchers make a special effort to ensure that their scarcity claims are held to be true. They also pay attention to creating the conditions where shoppers can see for themselves that the goods are in demand. Furthermore, because the demand at a pitching stall is almost always presented as outstripping the number of goods left to sell, an immediate response is deemed to be required by shoppers in order that they can be sure of purchasing what is on offer. In other words, in this type of real-life marketing there are no external measures of proof of scarcity in operation. Both the scarcity claim and the effect it has on shoppers are generated at the stall itself, by the use of speech and communication skills. Such skills play on the underlying cultural norms relating to product value determination which all these participants implicitly hold.

The same is also true for the process of obligation. The social norms that underpin the behaviour of buyers and sellers in more orthodox sales situations are brought to bear to enhance the pitcher's chances of securing sales success. Although what takes place at a pitching stall during back nailing, getting the forks up, bag nailing, and the proviso is, for many people, unorthodox, the same norms are in operation. The primary difference is that pitchers who employ these techniques do so strategically and, as such, seem to be relying on shoppers not being able to determine the full implications of their actions (such as raising a hand) until it is too late. Although pitchers never force people to buy their goods, what they often are doing, to varying degrees, is creating the social and interactional conditions where shoppers simply have little option but to persuade themselves to pay for the goods they have already, or at least symbolically, purchased.

CHAPTER 5

'Working the Edge':
the Subtle Art of Crowd Control

At about the same time as Bob Geldof organized the 'Live Aid' concert at London's Wembley Stadium to raise money for Ethiopian famine relief, and the film star Rock Hudson was dying, another kind of monumental and equally unexpected event took place on a street market in the south of England. Tonto had again gathered an execution pitch around his stall, but when he revealed the price of the bargains he thought he was offering, absolutely nobody wanted to buy anything.

The crowd just stood there, mute and motionless. All the hard work Tonto had put into building his edge and eloquently describing his stock, never mind the show-stopping run-down of the various prices he was not going to charge, had come to nothing.

Although the shock and astonishment must surely have been welling up inside him, Tonto kept his feelings hidden. He coolly surveyed his audience one by one. Suddenly, the expression on his face changed. He'd had an idea. 'Whoever buys any of these glasses from me and isn't *fully satisfied* with their purchase,' he shouted, 'not only will I give you your money back *in full*, I will also donate *one thousand pounds* to "Live Aids".'

He paused a moment for this unbelievable offer to sink in, but it was obvious that the crowd still wasn't interested. If there was anyone present who did want to buy his goods, they certainly didn't want to be seen, at this point in time, to be the first and perhaps the only one to do so.

Tonto, however, had it all under control. Instead of looking downhearted at all the non-buyers skulking in front of him, one of those all-knowing, Mona Lisa-type smiles lit his face. A second or so later he delivered his coup de grâce: 'YEAH!' he yelled. 'ROCK HUDSON'LL GET IT ALL!'

The crowd roared their approval of his 'sick joke'. More importantly, with this wave of merriment came their money. Many people chose this particular moment to make their purchase. The audience's laughter seemed to dispel all their previous reservations. Their laughter served, just as Tonto had intended it, as an independent and collective sign of appreciation that he was okay and that his goods were worth buying after all.

Many of the problems that pitchers run up against take the same form as that faced by Tonto in this sale – obtaining the desired responsiveness when something has gone awry. Sometimes, and for unfathomable reasons, audience responsiveness is absent altogether, or is of the wrong type or intensity or, worse still, is negative and disruptive. Getting responsiveness, keeping it, and dealing with it when it takes a negative and disruptive form, are seen by pitchers as being 'all in a day's work'. Certainly, if they are unable to do this, they cannot even begin to hope to obtain mass sales success.

OBTAINING COLLECTIVE RESPONSIVENESS

The appropriate buying response often depends on pitchers having received other forms of audience response before the selling price is announced (see, for example, Chapter 4). Because of this pitchers will usually try to get people to participate actively in the sale. Some people at a pitching stall, however, feel reticent about becoming involved. They are wary of expressing their interest in the goods on offer in any way that may put them 'on the spot' or oblige them to buy. Certain individuals show a marked reluctance even to look at, let alone respond to, a pitcher. One way in which pitchers try to minimize this is by conducting a humorous and entertaining sale. The appropriate reaction to humour – laughter – is a particularly infectious form of response. Laughter is usually shared – if anybody is laughing then everybody is likely to be laughing. Consequently, it is seen by those reluctant to get involved as a safe form of response.

Although pitchers often attempt to make a crowd laugh, they rarely tell jokes. Their humour is almost always directly tied to the serious business of selling. For example, it tends to be deployed when describing the goods:

TOWELS WITH PRINTED PARROTS
P   [Holding the towels up in the air] Does anybody like a cockatoo? The wife does! When I'm not there the milkman's always giving her one.
AS [Laughter]

. . . or when abusing an assistant:

CLOTHES
P   [Talking to PC] Eric, my lovely, just hand me over those sizes there, will you?
PC [Moves to get clothes]
P   [Talking about PC to AS] Ah'm only calling you lovely 'cos the camera's on us.
AS [Laughter]
P   [Talking about the authors to AS] I hate to tell these lads what I call him when the camera *isn't* on us.
AS [Laughter]

. . . or when playfully teasing a shopper:

CHICKEN-SHAPED CASSEROLE DISH

P   [Shouting to a woman who has just bought a casserole dish] *OY! OY! Come back and get a bag!* I can't have you walking all around this market with a *cock in your hand!*

AS   [Laughter]

Humour is usually used by pitchers 'in passing'; it is an important means to an end rather than an end in itself. Even so, some pitchers view audience laughter as being so important to their sales quest that they do not leave the potential for laughter entirely to chance. This can be seen in the following sequence. The audience's laughter is triggered and encouraged by the pitcher's assistant, who is the first to laugh at the punchline even though he has heard the same humorous remark many times before and, in fact, had used the joke himself earlier the same day when he was pitching:

PERFUME

P   [Talking to a woman] When you get home, put one drop under your pillow, it's 'Touché l'amour', do you know what that means?

A   [Shakes head]

P   It's *French*.

AS   [Titters]

P   It means *'Tonight for sure'*.

PC   [Loud guffaw coupled with rocking motion of head and upper body]

AS   [Laughter]

P   Now, it sells at [Pauses]

PC   [To P but for the benefit of AS] What a card.

When this assistant had made the same humorous comment earlier, while working on his own, he had had no one to initiate the laughter for him. On that occasion the audience's responsiveness had been far less enthusiastic.

As we have seen in previous chapters, humour is employed by pitchers at every stage of their pitching routines. Given that the amount of time people spend listening to pitchers selling mundane items such as pens or pans is often liable to exceed the attention span and boredom threshold of even a shopaholic, an almost constant stream of humorous remarks can help to sustain audience attentiveness and interest. Such humour can also create the kind of atmosphere that may break down people's reluctance to respond individually.

OBTAINING INDIVIDUAL RESPONSES

A task far harder than invoking laughter and collective respon-siveness during a sale is that of obtaining individual responses. In order to convince people of the merits of the claims made about their goods, pitchers seek confirmations from individuals to the effect that the goods are worth buying, that the prices marked on them are fair, that the towels are thick and soft to the touch, and so on. But because people do not like being put on the spot, they tend to respond in a self-conscious manner when addressed individually. People are more willing to respond non-verbally by, for example, nodding their heads – a response which, however, is likely to be missed by others at the stall. To get round this problem, pitchers may phrase their questions in such a way that individuals have only to confirm something already stated by the pitcher, allowing the pitcher to go on and publicly acknowledge that response. Thus, even a nod can be heard as being a positive response:

PERFUME
P   *Now watch.* To go with it, look at this. I'll put on top, look, World of Beauty's 'Number Five'. Now this one retails in all the stores, look, from World of Beauty. [Thrusting the

price tag under the nose of someone in the audience] It's
exactly six pounds, am I right, love?

A   [Nods]

P   Thank you.

In this sequence, the pitcher provides the expected answer in his
own question – 'It's exactly six pounds'. He then acknowledges
the individual's nod with a 'Thank you'. This expression of
gratification confirms verbally, for the benefit of others at the
stall, that the silent response provided was an affirmative one.

  Even when someone does respond verbally to a direct question, the work the pitcher has undertaken to receive that
response may end up being wasted. In a large, tightly packed
crowd many people will not be able even to see the individual
selected to endorse the goods, never mind hear their response.
To boost the number of people who do hear, the pitcher may
repeat the response in a louder voice. Occasionally, the pitcher
will even upgrade the response provided, especially if that
response is non-verbal. This happens in the following
sequence:

[Towels]

P   Have you felt the quality of those towels, love? Go on,
have a feel, you're nearest to me. [P holds the towel out so
that A can feel it]

A   [Feels the towel]

P   Don't wear them out, will you?

AS   [Laughter]

By saying 'Don't wear them out, will you?', this pitcher gives
the audience the impression that the person he has asked to feel
the towels has reacted very enthusiastically and that her opinion
of the towels is an overwhelmingly positive one.

  The obvious way of getting round the reluctance of some
people to speak is for pitchers to talk only to those people who

are most likely to talk back. This is another reason why pitchers use humour throughout their routines – they can monitor the audience's laughter to see who laughs first or most enthusiastically and choose these individuals to answer a question on the grounds that they are far more likely to respond verbally and positively when addressed individually.

In case the audience suspect that a confederate has been selected, pitchers usually ask two or three individuals at different places around the stall the same question. This strategy has another advantage. The different responses enable a pitcher to judge which of these people, if any, would be inclined to produce a more important type of response – an endorsement – later on in the routine. In one sale a pitcher asked three people to confirm the price marked on his goods. The first person responded by whispering the price and then giggling self-consciously at her friend. The second simply nodded her agreement with the pitcher's announcement of what the goods normally cost. The third person – a young woman – said 'Yes' twice in an enthusiastic and loud (though not suspiciously loud) voice. It may not have been coincidence that this young woman was the only one subsequently asked to endorse the goods.

CLOCKING THE DIVVY

When pitchers invite people to endorse their goods they cannot guarantee that the response they receive will be a positive one – unless, that is, they employ a confederate. Yet, as we have mentioned before, the vast majority of pitchers do not employ confederates. There are ways, nevertheless, in which pitchers minimize the danger of receiving a negative response. One strategy is to lower audience expectations about the strength of the positive response required. For example, more people are likely to agree with a pitcher that an item of stock is, say, 'nice' rather than that it is 'fabulous'. But we have already seen that pitchers often maximize the strength of their own assessments of their sales stock (see Chapter 2) and, therefore, that this strategy can create more problems than it attempts to solve. An endorsement from someone at the stall to the effect that the goods are only 'nice' is liable to stand in marked contrast to, and thus undermine the credibility of, what the pitcher is already likely to have said about that product.

We asked Gary how he overcame this problem when selling perfume. He reckoned he had the ability to find the individual who was likely to produce the most positive response – a procedure he somewhat cynically called 'Clocking the Divvy':

'You try and find a divvy, and you can clock her,' he assured us. '"Right, you be the model. Have you been a model before? Come here and try it." You spray a little bit on them, you hold their hand while you're doing it, and you rub the perfume in the back of their wrist. Then you say "Are you married?" "Course I'm married," they'll answer. "Well, this'll keep you married. If you're not married it'll get you married. If you put one drop under your pillow it's 'Touché l'amour', do you know what that means?" They don't 'cos it's French, so we tell them: "Tonight for sure." Then they all laugh. Then you say: "Is it nice?" And they'll say: "Oh, it is nice."'

'So what type of person do you reckon is the divvy?'

'You can tell by their own personal taste. Like, if they don't look like a million dollars, you know? If some old paraffin-lamp woman comes past and she hasn't got two bob to rub together, she's going to say it is nice because she doesn't know any better. But you're not going to pick somebody who's all dressed up, are you? She might have Yves St Laurent or Chanel or Estée Lauder on, she's going to tell you what is wrong with it.'

Our video of Gary and Tonto selling perfumes showed that this tactic was far more subtle than even they seemed to appreciate or were willing to reveal. They got round the difficulty of not being able to guarantee a positive endorsement from a bona fide individual by building a stairway of positive responsiveness. The person chosen to make the endorsement was, first of all, asked to confirm only a minimal estimation of the quality of the perfume's odour – that it was 'nice' – as Gary had told us in the interview. This response was then built upon, and the person chosen was encouraged to elaborate upon it in such a way that it became progressively stronger:

P   Now a lady's come up to me, she says, 'Is it *any good*?'

A   [Laughs]

P   Well, here, if you pay a tenner it should be *nice*. Now look, you be the judge, lovie, and just tell me if that one's nice. [Sprays some perfume onto the wrists of two women – A1 and A2 – as well as two other women at the stall]

A1 *Oh*. Nice –

A2 Ohhhhh – [To her friend] Come on, Eileen!

P   Is that nice?

A2 Lovely, *lovely*.

PC [Holds A1's arm, sniffs the perfume on her wrist and nods at her in an approving fashion.] It's lovely, is that.

P   It's lovely, am I – Is it *beautiful*?

A2 Yes, yes.

P   It's – Am I right? *Lovely. Beautiful*, am I right, love?

A1 Yeah –

P   It's *fabulous*.

PC [Nods and smiles at the crowd]

A1 *Yeah*.

Each of the assessments in this sequence – 'nice', 'lovely', 'beautiful' and 'fabulous' – is progressively stronger. The pitcher and his assistant – who busies himself with nodding his head and reacting positively to these endorsements for the benefit of the rest of the audience – act as a team to manufacture the strongest possible endorsement. In the above sequence the final assessment with which the 'divvy' agrees is all the more impressive because it contrasts with and is much stronger than the 'nice' assessment originally provided by the pitcher himself.

THE POWER OF AUDIENCE ENDORSEMENT:
THE CASE OF THE LILAC BEADS

When pitchers offer a choice of goods in a sale – like a range of different colours or sizes of towels, or a selection of, say, different types of toys or china figurines – the influence the first person's stated preference can have on the choices then made by other people at the stall can be very significant. Pitchers kept telling us that many shoppers relied upon the preferences of others before deciding whether and what to buy. Gentleman John was certain that this happened at his stall:

'People follow one another like sheep, you know. I mean, you must have noticed this when you are watching pitchers. *It's incredible*, not only from the point of view of them waiting for somebody else to make their mind up before buying, they follow colour-wise as well.'

'How does this happen?'

'Well, if I've got a choice of a pink and a blue and the first person picks pink, if you sell six of them I bet five of them are pink. If the first person picks blue I bet five of them are blue. Now that's the public being just like sheep. And they *are* like that. *It's incredible!*'

Such copy-cat buying is not always welcomed by pitchers. It can result in them being left with an unbalanced range of stock. Gary and Tonto had been suffering from the effects of this type of imitative buying behaviour when selling sets of plastic jewellery which came in a variety of colours:

'When we were working in the summer with costume jewellery – beads and bangles – we'd bought a lot of these beads. They came in packs of twelve and there would be, like, six different colours in each. One of the colours was lilac. *Nobody* wanted it. When we emptied our stock at the end of the day we were literally left with a big box full of lilac. And no wonder, it's a *horrible* colour!'

They decided that the solution to their difficulty was to change the way they were describing the goods:

'We fannied the lilac up: "*This* is the one that *everybody* likes, they're *all* wearing them with white" – because in the summer people wear white clothes. And *time* and *time* again all these people said: "Oh, I'll have the lilac," because they were scared to think that they're not fashionable or that they were going to be left out.'

'So did you get rid of it all then?

'We *had* to. We had no other choice.'

'Why's that?'

'We'd already paid for it.'

We had already videoed seven consecutive pitching routines where Gary and Tonto had attempted to sell these different-coloured sets of beads, bangles and earrings, and so we had some evidence that would enable us to judge precisely how effective they had been in 'fannying up the lilac'. It transpired that their claim was only partly true. Still, we learned something about how pitchers attempt to deal with the power of audience endorsement and how they attempt to forestall the difficulties associated with having an unbalanced range of stock.

During these seven sales, which lasted about an hour altogether, Gary and Tonto sold eighty-six sets of beads in all nine of the separate colours available. (In a whole morning on the same day a shop that was offering the same selection of beads in a covered market only fifty yards away from their pitching stall sold only two sets. Needless to say, neither of these sets were lilac.) In most of these seven sales the lilac beads were given the biggest build-up:

P   [Laying out the various coloured bead sets on the sales counter] I've got them in the *shocking* pink, the *pastel* lemon, I've got them in the *pastel* pale blue, I've got them in— [Silence. Picks up a set of lilac beads] *There they are*! Now *everybody's* wearing lilac, look, with *white*. Now the lilac ones are *very* fashionable. *Look, watch*. I've got them here in the jet colour [i.e. black]. *There's* your jet. Which do you like, lovie?

A   The light blue.

P   You like the— *that's* the electric blue. [To another A] Which do you like, lovie?

A2 Pink.

P   The *pink*. [To third A] Which do you like, love?

A3 [Hesitates before answering]

P   *If* you had a choice?

A3 [Points to the lilac beads]

P   You like the lilac. *Everybody's* wearin' lilac with— TOP SHOP are selling *nothing but lilac* with white. It's *fabulous*! [To fourth A] Which do *you* like?

A4 Lilac.

P   *Lilac*. [To fifth A] Which do you like?

A5 Pink.

P   *Pink*. [Points to another member of the audience]

A6 Pink.

P   *Pink*. [to A7] Which do you like, lovie?

A7 Lilac.

We had little doubt that people at the stall were influencing each other in their choice of bead colour, and they were doing so at two points in the sale – when individuals were asked which colour they liked (as happens in the above sequence) and, later, when they purchased the goods. In each case the colours selected or purchased would set off a trend in what the next person (and then the person after that, and so on) would select or purchase. Individual colours clustered together and, in different sales, certain colours were far more popular than others. These pitchers obtained selection sequences with a greater number of identical colours in adjacent positions than either chance or popularity would suggest. Here are two of the selection sequences: WHITE-LEMON-WHITE-WHITE-LILAC-LILAC-LILAC-WHITE-WHITE-BLUE-

BLUE-BLUE-LEMON-LEMON-WHITE; and
LILAC-LILAC-PINK-WHITE-WHITE-WHITE-
WHITE-RED-WHITE-WHITE-WHITE-WHITE-
BLUE-BLUE. Of course, different colours *were* chosen. Yet
even when this occurred it was not unusual to see the selection
cluster around only three or four of the nine available colours
during any single sale.

More interestingly, the colours people said they liked and
what they then actually bought were not always the same. But it
didn't appear to be the case that the people who made different
selections at these points were saying that they liked one colour
and then ended up buying the colour they 'really' liked. Rather,
the pressure to follow suit and to purchase the colour that other
people before them had bought seemed to replace the earlier
pressure to conform to other buyers' colour preferences.

Given the almost perverse reluctance most people had about
purchasing lilac, it appeared that 'fannying up' a particular
colour was effective; but only up to a point. In the sales we
recorded, this tactic did not lead to the runaway sales of lilac the
pitchers had claimed; Gary and Tonto were able only to sell an
average number of lilac beads – nine. As we had suspected all
along, their description of what they had achieved when selling
this costume jewellery was itself fannied.

AVOIDING OBLIGATION

The hidden cost of standing at a pitching stall, let alone
expressing an interest in the goods on offer – and thus being
more obliged to buy – may be alluded to by pitchers as a means
of securing sales. This happens in the following sequence. The
pitcher is knocking out tea-towels at a penny each:

P   [Throwing the tea-towels into the crowd] A young lady at
     the back wants one. A penny. *Right*, I'll tell you *something*.

If you *haven't* got a penny on you, you must have something drastically out of order with your *finances*. [Points to a woman who is walking past the back of the crowd] That lady's had three quid's worth, now she's *off*!

AS [Laughs]

Pitchers occasionally do what many people fear most – pick on someone at the stall and put them 'on the spot'. In the following case the pitcher suddenly stops selling his goods to talk to a young girl (A1) and her mother (A2), who have been standing at the side of the stall:

P   [To girl] Ah you buyin' or spyin'? [Silence]
A1 Spyin'.
A2 [Smiling] Er, spying.
P   Well, *Blake* got fifteen years for spyin', can you go— can you go spy round there, you schmuck.
AS [Laughs]
P   [Waving A1 and A2 away] *Go on! Off you go!* Anybody else want a lot? I wa— I want *buyers* not spyers. [A1 and A2 leave]

By publicly embarrassing one or two individuals in this fashion (although, as usual, with a degree of humour – in the above case the pitcher refers to the infamous double-agent George Blake), the other people in the audience are encouraged to realize the implications of standing at the stall – being obliged to buy. Of course, pitchers rarely turn custom away. In these cases they will try to pick only on those people who have been standing at the stall for a long time and look as if they are not likely to buy anything.

Sometimes, when the pitcher tells someone to leave, other people at the stall show that they feel under a heightened sense of obligation to buy. This happens in the following sale. The pitcher is asking two youths to move away from the stall:

126

PENS

P   I'm NOT bothered, if you want them from me, ah've so many to give away. [Pushes two youths standing at the side of the stall] Thank you. Are you waiting to be served?

A   No.

P   Well, move on and give somebody else a chance, 'cos a lot of these ladies like to buy their Christmas presents early, and their stocking fillers. *They've plenty to do.*

The only person who did not eventually buy anything from this pitcher was a woman whom the pitcher inadvertently pointed to when he said ' . . . a lot of these ladies like to buy their Christmas presents early'. At the exact moment when the pitcher's hand pointed to her she turned her head and upper body away from him, as if getting ready to move away from the stall, and then adopted a more defensive posture. It was as if this woman was trying to wriggle out of the heightened obligation to buy she believed she had been put under by virtue of being addressed and pointed at by the pitcher.

Avoiding being put on the spot

When a pitcher is asking a number of different people a question, other people at the stall start calculating whether it is likely that they will be asked a question next. If they think they will, and they feel uneasy about being singled out in this manner, they may take special steps (usually backward ones) to avoid being put under this form of obligation to buy. In one sale the pitcher was working his way up the stall asking people which colour beads they would pick if they had a choice. As he did so, a man stepped away from the stall and shielded himself from the approaching pitcher by standing behind another member of the audience. The pitcher passed him by and asked someone else further up the stall the same question. When the pitcher had moved back down the stall and was at a safe distance from where this man was standing, he moved back to his original, less-protected position. This individual did not buy the goods.

Mack the potato-peeler demonstrator claimed that it is not always necessary for a pitcher to obtain responsiveness or observe expressions of interest from individuals to keep them at the stall or oblige them to buy. A brief period of eye contact may be all that is needed:

'One of the problems with my dem is that you're looking down all the time. So what I do is, when I'm well into the middle of the sale I have two periods when I look at them all right in the eye with a smile on my face – "Honest John". Because if you don't, you'll not get a result.'

Sloping away from the stall

After all the special audience management and responsiveness-inducing work a pitcher has undertaken, those people who do not want to make a purchase may attempt to extricate themselves from the heightened obligation they feel they have been put under. They may, for instance, attempt to steal away from the stall without drawing attention to themselves. The most popular moment in the sale at which to do this is immediately after the pitcher has announced the selling price, because the pitcher is likely to be too busy serving customers to point them out or embarrass them in public. The buyers, who will be moving closer to the stall to make their purchases, also provide a protective screen or shield which makes it even more difficult for the pitcher to spot those people who are walking away. Furthermore, because other people are likely also to be leaving at this point, non-buyers can exploit the 'safety in numbers' principle; the more people leaving, the less likely it is that the pitcher will point them out and bring them to the public's attention.

Another popular time to leave is when the pitcher's back is

turned. In this way the leave-taker attempts to guarantee an unobserved exit. Many pitchers are aware of this tactic and will try, whenever possible, to avoid turning away from the crowd. This forces those individuals intent on leaving during a sale to adopt more sophisticated leave-taking strategies. Indeed, the intricate and self-conscious nature of the retreats such shoppers make during a sale show just how uneasy they feel about this type of all-too-obvious non-buying behaviour. Their retreats are typically managed, almost literally, step by step so as to avoid attracting the pitcher's attention.

Some shoppers even act as if they are going to buy the goods as a way of deflecting the pitcher's attention away from themselves in order that they can more easily leave the stall without making a purchase. In one sale, which was coming to a close, a woman who was standing right at the front of the stall opened her purse in readiness, it seemed, to make a purchase. However, as soon as the pitcher's back was turned, probably feeling confident that he had at least this one customer waiting to be served, she quickly left the stall.

It is not only non-buyers, though, who treat standing at a pitching stall as problematic. Shoppers who may be willing to buy goods may also act self-protectively. For instance, they may not want to make their intentions to buy obvious until they have seen other people doing the same. Some people seem embarrassed about buying from a pitcher. People like this may not want to be seen to be the only buyer, or may not want to be seen to be buying cheaper versions of prestige or aspirational-type goods from a market stall-holder. Buying goods 'cheap' may mean that they are taken by others to be cheapskates.

For example, in one sale the pitcher asked the people at his stall, 'Who could use them if I make them cheaper?' A man standing at the front of the stall was one of those who raised his hand. But he did not raise it above shoulder height, where it would be more easily spotted by others at the stall, and, indeed, he soon converted this hand-raising into a self-conscious nose-rubbing. Later on in the same sale the pitcher asked this question again and the man did exactly the same thing, apart from using his other hand and now rapidly converting the hand-raising into a nose-scratching. This individual eventually bought the goods.

PREVENTING HOLES IN THE EDGE

From a pitcher's point of view, the main problem created by people leaving during a sales routine is that they can generate an avalanche of leavers. The space that results when one person leaves can make the others who are left standing next to that space feel especially vulnerable. The odds on these people then moving away themselves are very high indeed.

One way of preventing such a hole developing is by having the crowd tightly packed. This makes exits negotiated without attracting the attention of the pitcher, particularly exits from the front of a stall, more difficult. 'Soft edges' – where people are not standing close to the stall, and are widely spaced one from the other – are especially difficult for the pitcher to control.

If someone who has been standing in a highly conspicuous position, such as right at the very front, leaves the stall, a sensitive pitcher is likely to take steps immediately to prevent others from following suit. In one sale, a woman who had adopted a sideways-on stance to the pitcher – a classic sign of non-interest – made her exit as soon as the pitcher turned his back. This left a space right at the front of the stall which others standing nearby seemed reluctant to fill. As soon as the pitcher saw this hole he got to work on closing it or at least ensuring that it did not get any bigger. He thrust a magazine under the nose of a woman who was standing to the immediate right of this space and asked her to confirm the price of the goods he was selling. This brief verbal contact seemed to be enough to oblige this woman to stay at the stall until the sale had ended.

During this episode there were two girls standing on the other side of the space. They also began to leave the stall. But as soon as they started to leave, they aborted their exit. At this point the pitcher had made his move towards the woman who was standing on the other side of the space. It looked as if these two girls thought that the pitcher was about to ask them to confirm the price of the goods rather than the woman standing on the other side of the space. They also stayed until the end of the sale, even though the pitcher had not spoken to or even looked at them.

Keeping willing buyers at the stall

Serving everyone who wants to buy the goods is not without its problems either. When a queue of willing buyers develops, any undue delay in serving can prompt those who are waiting to question whether their purchase is worth the extra wait involved. This happens in the following pen sale. As the pitcher hands over one set of pens to a customer, she asks for 'another set as well'. Upon hearing this, another lady, who has been waiting to be served, turns her head away in dismay and expresses her disappointment by tutting. The pitcher, recognizing that he may be about to lose a customer, is on to this woman straight away:

P   We *give* you those four for nothing, we charge you a
     pound for that lovely fountain pen. [Hands over a set of
     pens to A]
A   Can ah have another lot as well? [Upon hearing this
     another woman who has been waiting to be served tuts
     and turns her head slightly away from the pitcher]
P   [Talking to the lady who has just bought the set of pens]
     You want *two* sets, love? Right. [Talking to the woman
     who has tutted] And then *you* want some, love, *you're next*.
     [Talking to the audience at large] *Who else* wants some?
     'Cos ah'm running out.

AS [Some people raise their hands]
P   [Counting the hands that are raised] One— one, two, three, four, number five, an' you're number six.

Not only did the pitcher reassure this woman that she would be served next, he reinforced her obligation to stay and make a purchase by physically contacting her – he touched her on the arm. In seeming to recognize the problem he had created by taking too long to serve people, the pitcher then obliged other willing buyers to stay at the stall by getting them to indicate explicitly their buying interest and counting out each of their raised hands.

FAILED SALES

When pitchers announce the selling price of their goods, sometimes nothing happens. This was the case with Tonto at the start of this chapter. What emerges is a responsiveness 'blind spot'. This can be a very serious event for a pitcher. As Mack says: 'If nobody moves or buys anything, that's it; you'll take *nothing*.' It is here that a confederate planted in the audience will be used by fly pitchers to manufacture the audience response (see Chapter 7). Most pitchers, who do not employ a confederate, will try, like Tonto did, to use humour to overcome the problem. Another popular alternative is to simply and nonchalantly go on to the next sale:

[Meat]
P   Anybody want this big one? Quickly. You've got fifty quid. Ah'll take twenty-five pound for the big'n'.
AS [No response]
P   Quickly.
AS [No response]
P   Twenn'y five.

AS   [No response]
P   Anybody use it?
AS   [No response]
P   [Putting the meat back in the freezer] I ain't waitin' for
     you, it's staying down there.

In fact, the coolness on the part of pitchers at this point of the
sale is what usually separates them from fly pitchers, and why
many of them say that using confederates is a sign of bad
pitching technique. Rarely do pitchers publicly acknowledge
the problem, if a problem arises. This happens, though, in the
following example. When nobody responds to his sales offer,
the demonstrator starts to dig his own grave by talking about
guarantees and stating that 'there's no catch to it whatsoever'.
Rather than persuading people to buy, this type of information,
at this point in the sale, seems to provide people with the very
ammunition they need to convince themselves *not* to buy:

PEN SETS
D   I'll tell you what we do, we charge you a penny, for the
     refills, and someone give me a *fiver* for the complete set.
AS   [No response]
D   A written money-back guarantee for a *lifetime* from a
     British company for a *five*-pound note.
AS   [No response]
D   Does anybody want a set of those, ladies an' gentlemen?
     There's *no catch* to it whatsoever. If you wanna come an'
     try them, then be my guest. You get them *direct* from the
     factory, the *only* thing you *don't* get is any fancy boxes,
     cards or wrappers.
AS   [Nobody buys]

DEALING WITH UNSOLICITED AND
INAPPROPRIATE AUDIENCE RESPONSES

Notwithstanding what we have already said about people generally being reluctant to respond to a pitcher's questions, there are occasions, of course, when unsolicited responsiveness does occur. The least serious type is when the audience get carried away with the occasion and disrupt the sale unintentionally by, say, laughing a little longer than is appropriate. In these cases the laughter – rather than the sale itself – becomes the principal focus of the crowd's attention. Almost equally harmless are the occasions when individuals contribute humorous remarks of their own. This happens in the following sale of toy helicopters. This sale took place just after a leading British politician, Michael Heseltine, had resigned from the Cabinet over a policy difference with the then Prime Minister, Margaret Thatcher, over the running of the Westland helicopter company:

P   Here y'are. [Holds up a plastic helicopter] Heseltine Helicopters.

AS   [Laughter]

P   Hey? Yeah, Margaret Thatcher—

A   Yeah! Give her one.

P   *Give her one?*

A   Yeah!

AS   [Laughter]

P   *Do you mind, love?* This is a family bloody show! Will you stop it?

AS   [Laughter]

P   Margaret Thatcher and Heseltine, he chased her down the road. He chased her into 10 Downing Street, he got her in the kitchen and by 'ell 'e copped 'er!

A2   You've taken it far enough. [Laughs]

AS   [Laughter]

P   Ah'll tell you what ah'll do. For the kids . . .

The skill of the pitcher here is in being able to deflate the interruption by incorporating it seamlessly into his own spiel and then quickly moving on to the business in hand. In almost every other case, unsolicited responsiveness disrupts, and is sometimes intended to disrupt, the sale. Pitchers have to have their wits about them to restore order quickly and regain the floor.

OTHER DISRUPTIONS OF THE SALE

Unsolicited responsiveness can sometimes be very serious, especially when it is persistent enough to break the bond of attentiveness between the pitcher and the people at the stall. This happens when babies cry:

DUNGAREES
P   Okay, listen. *Shush*. [Pointing to a woman with a baby that is crying loudly] Keep him happy, love. Keep him happy. [To AS] The price is on 'em, the tab is on 'em . . . [Despairing stare at the mother as the baby continues to cry]

. . . and when people at the stall persist in talking loudly among themselves:

PANS
P   You can either have the set down there in the decoration they call— [To people making a noise in the crowd] *Oy! Drek. Excuse me.* If you're listening to me don't stand there with your back against me. It's *bad manners*. [To AS] If I could find one of you— [To the people who have been making a noise] During the last twenty minutes you three here have said more bloody words than *I have*! If you don't wanna listen to me, *go away*! Go an' see me Uncle

Rob [another pitcher working further up the market noted for his even sharper tongue] down the road and see how *he'll* treat you. [To AS] If I can tempt one of you, twenty, eighteen and sixteen centimetre. [The three talkers move away from the stall] They're going. It's the best place for 'em.

... and when a commotion breaks out as a result of some incident within the crowd:

MEAT

P [To a group of women in the audience who are obviously upset about something happening in the crowd] What's the problem, ladies?

A [Referring to a group of youths in the audience] They've been swearing.

P *Who's* been swearing?

A Them three here.

P Will you lads m – *move* yourself out of my crowd now? [The youths stand still] *Out of my crowd now. Go on!* [The youths slope away] You ought to be ashamed of yourself with a school tie on swearing. *Go on!* In front of these lovely ladies. *On yer bike!*

We note that in each of the above cases, as is typically the case, the pitcher ignores the incident until it is deemed to be disrupting others at the stall. In France, it seems almost impossible for pitchers to gather a large group of people at their stalls without these people splitting into smaller units and starting to talk among themselves. One enterprising demonstrator, who was obviously aware of the serious effect this type of disruption was having on his sales, employed an assistant whose sole task appeared to be that of keeping the audience quiet. The assistant would stand at the front of the stall – between the demonstrator and the crowd – and whenever anyone started talking he would quietly finish their sentences off for them or press his forefinger to his lips to discourage them from talking any further.

Nauses

Troublemakers and disgruntled buyers who 'make a scene' can be far more threatening. These people are usually making obvious and intentional attempts to prevent the pitcher from selling any further goods. Pitchers refer to such people as 'nauses', because they can induce a wave of nausea, in the form of a marked reluctance to buy, throughout the crowd. Practically every pitcher we spoke to had a tale to tell about nauses. Terry was no exception:

'I was working this vacuum flask with an automatic dispenser. At the time there were two types around – one had a silver glass container inside, the other was made out of plastic. The plastic ones were rubbish because they obviously didn't keep anything warm. The ones I was working with were glass. So I'd sold about thirty of these and I'm stood there working the next line and there's about thirty people with these airpots under their arms watching what I'm doing. And then there was a parting in the crowd – just like Moses – and a guy came forward with an airpot under his arm; *right to the front*. He was the same type of obnoxious guy as that old bloke in "Coronation Street" – Percy Sugden: "*You, you're a bloody liar*! Ah've heard all about you con-men and I want people to know you're a bloody *con-man*! Now I've bought this and you *said* to me – and you're all here, you all heard him, because I'm fetching the police in a minute – you *said* it was *glass, am I right?*" I said: "Yes." *I was dumbfounded*! I'd never seen anything like it before in my *whole life*! He opened it up and said: "I want you all to see now, it's *plastic*," he said, "it's bloody *misrepresentation*." So I said: "Have you finished?" "Aye, ah've finished. *For now*. What've you got to say? Admit that you're a liar in front of these people and we'll call it a day." So I took it off him, hit it and knackered it altogether. The inside shattered into a thousand pieces. It *was* glass. I then sprinkled it on the ground in front of him and said: "Is that glass or plastic?" He said: "Bloody hell, you're right. Sorry, mate." I said: "That's all right, don't worry about it. If you'd come quietly I'd have explained it to you, but you didn't give me any choice." I gave him a new airpot – a glass one – and his money back and told him that I was sorry for his trouble. He turned round and walked away and everyone just clapped.'

There are two aspects to Terry's story which are interesting. The first is that at the point where the alleged deception is being exposed, one would expect the other people at the stall at least to start having second thoughts about making a purchase. In Terry's airpot sale this was not the case: 'They were actually on *my* side, thinking: "Oh poor sod, look." They didn't want to be associated with him because he was a pain in the arse.' The second point of interest is the way in which Terry dealt with this complainer – not by taking him to one side and putting him right privately, but by using a 'grand gesture' undertaken in front of everyone at the stall, to prevent the complainer influencing the opinions of other members of the audience. Just as mass sales can develop as a result of the audience copying each other's behaviour, so a single complainant – acting as a negative opinion leader – can have the exact opposite effect. As Terry told us: 'When you're working, the edge becomes one person. If they're laughing they're all laughing or nobody's laughing. That's why you get mobs of vigilantes.' On the other hand, when such a person makes an unjustified complaint, a shrewd pitcher can turn it into an especially persuasive form of advertising.

Most complaints are not usually as serious or disruptive as this, and pitchers need only employ the same type of one-line 'put-downs' as those used by politicians and comedians to silence hecklers. On other occasions the experience can, for the pitcher, have a nightmarish quality, especially when the grievance aired by the complainer is a valid one. In the following sequence the pitcher stops his sales spiel to address a group of youths standing on the fringe of the crowd. One of these youths starts laughing at the pitcher:

PERFUME

P   Now watch what ah'm gonna do—

N   HA HA HA *HAAA*!

P   [Pointing to the group of youths but talking to the rest of the crowd] They're here. Shoplifters. Shoplifters and divs. [Pointing to the other end of the market while talking to the 'shoplifters'] The dole office is round there, lads, but they're not open on Saturdays so you can't sign on. [Talking to AS] Now look, you've got twenty-six pounds' worth of perfume, an' ah said I'll treat you, now look. This is perfume that all the ladies like, and its called Musk.

N   [To his friends, perhaps in response to one of them having said that the pitcher is likely to beat him up if he doesn't shut up] He's not strong enough.

P   Now Musk sells in all of your shops and stores at exactly four pound, look. Ah'll put that one on top, you've got thirty pounds' worth.

N   Ah think it's knocked-off gear.

P   [Pointing to the nause but talking to the rest of the crowd] He thinks it's knocked-off gear, Mr 'Big-shot'. *Mr 'Big-shot'*. HE HASN'T GOT TUPPENCE IN HIS POCKET, HE'S GOT A SCHNIDE GOLD CHAIN ROUND HIS NECK.

N   *I haven't*!

P   And he thinks it's knocked-off gear! [Points to nearby police headquarters] THAT IS THE HEAD-QUARTERS OF THE LOCAL POLICE. Can you read?

N   Yeah. I can read, y'know.

P   You don't look as if you can.

N   Ah can write too.

P [Beckoning N closer with his finger] *Come 'ere.*

N No.

P Watch. 'Ere, big shot. *Read this.* What's the price for Musk?

N Four pound bu—

P FOUR POUND. *WATCH!*

N It's Musk bottle, isn't it?

P And you'd know, *would you*? [Talking to AS] SPOTTY, PIMPLY YOUTH. STOOD THERE, AN' *I'M TRYIN' TO GET A LIVIN'*, AN' I HAVE TO STAND WITH A *SPOTTY, HORRIBLE*, PIMPLY YOUTH.

N HA HA *HAAA!*

P [To AS] LOOK AT THE CHAIN ROUND HIS NECK. IT'S MADE O' *PLASTIC.*

N *It isn't!*

P AN' 'E'S STOOD THERE TELLING ME MY PERFUME ISN'T REAL. [Talking to Clark] 'Ave you got this, Colin? [i.e. 'Is the video camera still running?']

CC [Nods]

N It's not plastic.

P [It suddenly (and miraculously) starts to pour down with rain and the youths leave to seek some shelter] Now watch. [Starts piling the boxes of perfumes on top of one another] One, two, three, four. There's four nice perfumes there, ladies. [To the authors] Ah'm blowin' this one out, all right? [The sale ends]

Because the allegation this youth makes – that the perfume named 'Musk' is not the same as the genuine musk-*style* perfume – is a legitimate one, this pitcher is prevented from using a 'grand gesture' to put him straight and to convince others at the stall that the perfumes are still worth buying. Instead, he attempts publicly to humiliate the troublemaker. He tries to get the rest of the audience on his side by pointing out that the youth is wearing a fake gold chain – a strategy designed to make it absolutely clear to the audience that the youth's judgement as to what is or is not genuine is questionable. Perhaps this is all the pitcher can do under these circumstances, but this strategy is a weak one. As we saw in Terry's example, the people at the stall are likely to side not with the person who is in the right but, rather, with the person who is losing face. In this case, and in contrast to the example Terry gave, it is the complainer, not the pitcher, who is losing face.

An interesting footnote to this incident is that even though the youth's objections were not overturned and the sale was brought to a premature but fortuitous end with the sudden onset of heavy rain, there was still a handful of people standing at the stall who wanted to buy the goods.

THE SUBTLE ART OF CONTROL

In learning about the dynamics of crowds on street markets and the subtle skills pitchers employ to deal with the various problems that can arise during the course of a sale, it becomes obvious that the term 'sales rhetoric' is both inappropriate and over-simplistic. This term implies that pitchers are using only broad, pre-scripted strokes to manage people at their stalls, and that the sales skills they require to persuade people to buy are little more than a mechanistic and simplistic set of crude stimulus-response sales tactics.

The sequences we have examined in this chapter demonstrate that although the sales patter of market pitchers may be structured, it is certainly not mechanistic or pre-scripted. For a pitcher, pulling off a successful sale routinely depends on very fine-grained, audience-sensitive social skills – especially when problems arise. Pitching is *not* only sales rhetoric, and those people who gather at a pitching stall are not by any means merely the passive recipients of a pitcher's spiel. Pitching can often be a sales negotiation and each individual who gathers at a stall has the capacity to disrupt the sale and influence others not to buy. Consequently, any pitcher wishing to obtain mass sales must be capable of adapting and varying their sales patter, sometimes moment by moment, in response to local contingencies.

It is when facing difficulties like this that 'paste-table' pitchers such as Gary and Tonto come into their own. By virtue of having only a basic stall – sometimes little more than a decorator's paste-table with a canopy over it – these pitchers may not always get the same execution pitches or always take as much money as their more elevated pantechnicon-owning colleagues. But because they are closer to, and at eye level with, the people at their stall, they often have to be more sensitive to, and more skilled at dealing with, these types of unexpected problems.

CHAPTER 6

If You're Not in 'Too Deep'
You're Not in Deep Enough

1.10 p.m.   First pitch: (I think I'm going to have a heart attack
             but I haven't even opened my mouth yet.) Too
             self-conscious. Far too quick. No one buys. Let's be
             honest: nobody even stopped at the stall, apart
             from some chip wrappers and a stray dog.

1.25 p.m.   Second pitch: Nothing and no one again. (Some-
             body laughed) Dog's left too. This is humiliating. I
             want out. My head is spinning with all the
             adrenalin.

1.45 p.m.   Third pitch: Slow it down! Remember the 'script'!
             Make some eye contact. Success at last – two sales!
             Dog's back now. But who was it that said: 'pitch
             and you'll get rich'?

Extracts from Clark's field notes on his first day at work as a
'market pitcher'

When sociologists venture out into 'the field' to do participant
observation it is usually to try to unearth some special insights
about the people they are studying by examining how these
people actually behave in the real world. Our own sudden
interest in this research method, though, was much more
straightforward. The grant for Clark's DPhil thesis had just run
out and all the other usual sources of temporary funds had dried

143

up long ago. His bank manager had begun to get visibly tired of him forever quoting statistics proving that a loan of another few hundred pounds would enable him to reap the rewards at some later date when he became a university lecturer.

The only marketable skill Clark possessed which gave him any hope of holding his head above water during this unexpected period of financial embarrassment was his newly acquired knowledge of the sales techniques of market pitchers. We talked it over between ourselves. Surely, as a way of making money it couldn't be all that difficult? After all, pitching was more or less the same type of public speaking enterprise as giving a lecture to students; also, by now, Clark knew dozens of sales 'spiels' off by heart. Indeed, one of the unexpected benefits of having spent all those hours in the social psychology lab studying pitching tapes was that we'd uncovered some sales ploys that even the pitchers themselves seemed to be unaware of using. All we needed to do was to find an appropriate sales script, garnish it with a couple of the more subtle techniques we'd discovered, and Clark would soon be rolling in the money.

What proved to be the deciding factor was an account Gary had given us in an earlier interview. He had opened our eyes to the power of pitching by recalling just how much money he had made in his first week as a spieler. Gary had come into this sales world for exactly the same reasons as Clark – to overcome sudden and unanticipated financial adversity. And, by his account, he had been a big success:

'I originally started working for Tonto because I had no money, and he said: "Well, if you want to come down and work I'll give you some gear and tell you where to go." So, at that time, the Rubik's Cube had just come out. Remember the Rubik's Cube? Anyway, he gave me a gross – a box of one hundred and forty-four – and I sold them within an hour. So I joined, really, at the best time. I thought: "It's always like this." We had so much money we didn't know what to do with it. The Rubik's Cube was in the shops at five pounds ninety-nine, made by "Ideal". We had copies from Taiwan that we knocked out at two ninety-nine. We got down to two pounds, and then they ended up at a quid for the last few weeks we were selling them. I worked a week and at the end of it Tonto said: "What do you want to do now?" I said: "I want a holiday," and we flew to the Canary Islands on a Monday and had a week off. I said to myself: "I *like* this game."'

Even taking into account the likelihood that Gary had probably gilded the lily when talking about his first experiences of pitching, we thought there was enough truth in what he'd said to convince us that we'd made the correct decision. The reality, however, proved to be somewhat different. Here is our intrepid participant observer's own account of what actually happened.

'I talked over the prospect of learning to pitch with Gary and Tonto and, after they'd had a good laugh about the thought of someone with a university education working on a street market ("You haven't the right qualifications to work for us"), they were willing to give it a go. Their decision certainly wasn't taken out of any respect for my persuasive abilities. The summer season was just starting and new markets were opening up. Grafters of any standard were suddenly in short supply. They warned me that making the move from the side of the stall, as "researcher", to behind the stall, as "pitcher", was going to be anything but easy. Nevertheless, they were generous enough to promise me some "on the job training" to compensate for my total lack of practical experience.'

THE PITCHING PEDIGREE

Many of the pitchers we'd met during our research seemed to have taken to spieling like a duck takes to water. And no wonder. They had learned the trade from their parents and grandparents; the secrets of pitching had been passed down from one generation to another. Some of these traders could probably build an edge before they could walk. Not all of them had learned this way, however. Some had come late to the game and had to learn from bitter experience. It was what these people had told us that had me worried. Daft Dicky, for example, claimed that the learning curve was a very long one:

'The way I started was to just stand all day long shouting: "Three for a pound your socks, three for a pound your socks." But then I started to get bored stiff with my own voice, you know? You build on your experience. It takes a number of years to have the confidence to have a big crowd of three hundred, four hundred, even five hundred people in front of you and actually tell a story, tell a gag and sell.'

Even those pitchers who had started off their sales careers as lurkers had nothing but bad news to tell us about their first experiences as grafters. Almost to a man they said that the transition from lurker to spieler was a difficult one. Terry recalled:

'It wasn't easy. There wasn't any training courses then, else I would have taken one. It was a question of watching, then doing; however simplistic that sounds, that's what happened. I stood on a box one particular week; set up slightly different – the stall was raised up a little bit and the stock wasn't priced. Then I went to work, started shouting, and died; died a *death*! As a lurker I'd been taking about a hundred and twenty pounds at that particular market and I think I took about forty quid the first time I pitched. I thought: "How can this be so wonderful?"'

As Clark contemplated what lay ahead, he was beginning to wish we'd never asked Terry to elaborate on the problems he'd experienced on his first day as a pitcher. We'd asked him how his fellow lurkers had reacted towards him when he'd started pitching:

'They took the piss,' he replied. 'The first couple of times I started, my edge consisted of eighty per cent traders stood there with their flat caps and money pinnies saying: "*Go on, Terry, you're all right. Go on, mate.*" As I got better they drifted away from me because they weren't involved any more.'

We'd also asked him to tell us about the type of spiel he had used in his first pitch. 'If you're a pitcher you pick something up, *anything*, and what you say tends to flow, yeah?'

We nodded quickly.

'Like: "We'll start the first sale now, an' instead o' me saying it's five, four, three, a couple of quid, thirty bob, a guinea, a pound, we'll place that to one side an' we'll call it lot number one, an' *'ere* . . . " – and it's like that. But when you're first starting – I remember this vividly – it's very much like: "*Roll up! Roll up! Come an' get it*, I've got, er, deep fryers today, I've got some, um, towels, um . . ."' He laughed. 'Although you know in your mind what you should be saying, when you've got to stand and do it something else actually takes over.'

Absolutely everyone we'd interviewed seemed to have some previous sales pedigree. Even those traders who had no directly relevant experience, such as Gary, who had been a DJ before he started pitching, could cite some benefit they had gained from their previous lines of work.

'Well, DJ-ing is the same sort of thing, isn't it?' Gary told us. 'I started off bingo calling which gave me a bit of confidence in front of people. Then I started to DJ for acquaintances. In fact, I still do DJ-ing now, but only once a week, and I cannot stop myself from using the same lines that I use when I'm selling. It's selling again, really.'

The only directly relevant experience Clark had ever had was three weeks in Tesco's stacking bags of sugar as a second-year undergraduate and two days the following Christmas as an assistant in a wine shop. This latter period of gainful employment had come to an abrupt and painful end when he had got drunk on one of the 'special offers' and injured himself falling down the cellar steps.

The longer we thought about this the more we realized that

relevant experience was not the only requirement. You also needed a particular sort of flamboyant personality. Clark certainly didn't have it. But who did? Terry had laughed his head off at us when we'd asked him if pitchers were born or made.

'How can you be born anything?' he replied, laughing at the very thought of it. 'Can you be born a prime minister? A born roadsweeper? What *can* you be born to be? I mean, are you in the maternity ward and you ask: "Is it a boy or a girl?" and the nurse says: "No, I'm sorry, it's a pitcher."'

Daft Dicky, one of the best pitchers we've ever seen, held out a ray of hope. When we'd put a tape recorder under his nose he went all quiet. And it wasn't because he was being evasive. He was one of the most sensitive, retiring and unassuming people you could ever hope to meet. Until you saw him pitch, that is. He seemed to have a penchant for doing his selling while naked from the waist up. And on more than one occasion, we'd witnessed him demonstrating women's lingerie and the like on his own body. He thought the issue of whether pitchers were born or made was 'A *very* hard question'. When we asked him why, he said:

'Because I know that as a kid I was *very shy*. There's no two ways about that. Even up to the age of twenty-five I used to keep myself to myself. I maybe played around a bit with my mates in the pub but, er, I don't know, I *really* don't know. I think it's the confidence of having sold something to the public. After a period of time, if you stick at the game, you tend to forget that you are talking to hundreds of people. Probably anybody could do it. Probably *anybody* could. But they need to have had a little bit of success. They need to have had about twenty people put their hands up at a fiver to make them feel confident, and take it from there.'

LEARNING TO PITCH

By the time Clark set off for his new line of employment, the thought of becoming a pitcher certainly wasn't looking as much of a cinch as it had previously. In fact, the whole idea began to seem unreal. For a start, it was still dark. Any normal person was still tucked up in bed. When he reached the railway station, he even phoned Gary to tell him that he was on his way. That, at least, was the pretext for calling; he really wanted to confirm that the previous meeting had actually taken place and to gain some final tips which would get him started off on the right foot. What he told him was hardly the most encouraging piece of advice to give a neophyte spieler: 'Remember,' Gary barked down the line, 'you're trying and learning in one of the hardest games in the world, with some of the hardest gear that you'll ever find to sell.'

Clark didn't want to believe this. 'How's it hard?' he asked.

'Cos they've seen them. *They've been knocking about for thirty years!* The only way you can do 'em again is if you do such a good pitch that they've *got* to punt up.'

Clark's vision of basking on foreign sands by Saturday, or any sands for that matter, was already beginning to fade. He asked Gary how long it had taken him to get the spiel off. 'Was it a season?' he suggested. This was a deliberate overestimate on Clark's part. Anything less would give him some hope that he'd soon be able to master pitching himself. '*A season?*' He had to ask it again.

'Longer. A couple of years, really.'

That wasn't the response Clark wanted to hear, and he let it show. 'Well, I can't be expected to get it off in just one day,' he muttered defensively.

'*Of course you can't*! But what you can do is learn a script. Then you can put your own personality into it.' Gary paused for a moment, thinking back in time. 'I was in the same position as you, and Tonto used to stand behind me and prompt me with

149

the first line. Once you get into a rhythm *then* you can deviate. You can come up with your own expressions, can't you?'

As Gary was saying all this, Clark was checking the change in his pockets just to make sure he'd brought enough money for the train fare home. Gary must have heard him starting to hyperventilate because he suddenly went all sympathetic:

'Well, I don't think it'll take a season. Not to get the basics. If you pitch for twenty solid days you should by then know exactly every sentence to say. After that, it's just experience, delivery and timing, that's all.' As the pips heralded the end of the call, Gary shouted one final piece of advice down the phone: 'Really, though, the easiest way of learning is just to fuckin' *do it*, so hurry yourself up, *okay*?'

On the train the panic attack started to subside. Clark managed to calm himself down by thinking of the basic sales script he'd learnt over the weekend. He began to repeat the various stages of a pitching routine under his breath, as if they were a Buddhist mantra: 'Pull the pitch, describe the gear, do the dem, get some interest, come to the bat. Pull the pitch, describe the gear, do the dem . . . ' Fifteen minutes later he was standing at the stall.

The first sale

Clark's first attempt at pitching was even more humiliating than he'd dreamt about: it was a nightmare. He had to suffer the indignity of receiving his 'on the job' training literally on the job – right in front of a crowd of prospective customers who had miraculously congregated at the stall. He was introduced as the 'new apprentice' and handed a microphone which was hung round his neck. It felt more like a noose. Tonto took up a position to one side of him and started telling him what to say, phrase by phrase, in stage whispers. The people at the stall were highly amused by all this. No doubt they were thinking that if Tonto's mouth had been any closer to Clark's left ear he would have been arrested for obscenity. When he eventually looked up at the crowd, Clark noticed that they were looking at Tonto, not at him. When he eventually announced the selling price, only two people decided to buy. One of these was an old lady who owned a nearby stall who sympathized with his plight.

Those few minutes of humiliation were the full extent of Clark's first day's 'on the job' training. After having the audacity to tell him to 'slow down else you'll have a heart attack before we get back', his mentors left to work another market. He was on his own and the stall was his for the rest of the day.

He surveyed the boxes of stock piled up at the back of the stall. There was enough to open a wholesaler's. The view of the front of the stall was equally depressing. Where were all those people who had been standing there a few moments ago? There was now only a bare patch of ground. He considered taking the next train home, and probably would have done if he could have figured out where to leave all the stock until Gary and Tonto returned. Now *he* was nailed. What excuse could he give Tonto that night? None. There was no other option but to start to pitch.

He decided to have a large cup of tea first, though. Then he had to visit the toilet. It took a while. After that he struck up a conversation with a neighbouring stall-holder. It was his fault, really. He wanted to talk about football and it seemed only decent to share a shot from his hip-flask and lament the demise of the England team. It was becoming obvious that Clark shouldn't rush into things. What was needed, before he finally got down to work, was at least a few minutes more of considered thought. After all, he mustn't be too selfish. He wasn't here only to make money. He'd been presented with the ideal opportunity to do some additional research. If he started lurking the goods for a while and did the pitching later on, like tomorrow, he'd be able to compare the money he'd taken from these two different types of selling to find out, once and for all, if pitching was more successful than lurking. On went his best 'eager to serve' face as he began his new sales career by trying to catch the eye of each and every passer-by.

The trouble was that there were no eyes to catch. No one bothered to look at him. The gaze of every passer-by seemed fixed hundreds of yards up the road – as a protection device, no doubt, to avoid the sales overtures of people like him. The longer he waited, the more obvious it became that nobody was interested in his wares. Lurking proved to be as exciting and as lucrative as the pitchers and demonstrators had told us in our interviews. When we'd asked one demonstrator if he took as much money lurking, he'd laughed at us. 'With this tool? [a drill attachment] No way. Impossible! When I'm on form I'll sell five times more grafting.' Indeed, the general consensus was that pitchers can take far more money by talking up their stock than by lurking it. Terry had agreed with this estimate:

'If I took my pitching joint and set it up for a day on a market that I usually pitch on, but instead I just lurk it – you know, price all the gear up. If I did that for one week and then pitched the same spot the next, then I'd imagine that I'd take six, seven, perhaps eight times more when I was pitching.'

Another demonstrator was even more emphatic about what would happen if he only lurked his goods:

'We wouldn't take *two bob*. It would be a *total* waste of time. We wouldn't get enough to pay our hotel costs. You could have that vegetable cutter in a hardware store and you would sell about four or five a week. Take it out and promote it the way we do and we would sell four hundred to four thousand a week, depending where we were selling them. It would be the same difference even if you put a video of our demonstration in the store right next to the product. I know because we've already tried that one.'

Lurking had become a waste of time for Clark too. He'd had one or two 'small enquiries' but had taken nothing. Out of boredom more than anything else he finally decided that it was time to pitch. He cleared his throat and launched into it, studiously avoiding telling people to 'Roll up, roll up'. That first spiel is one he will never forget – unfortunately. Whether it was embarrassment or self-consciousness about starting to shout when nobody was even in earshot of the stall, he kept his head down and only dared look up when he announced the selling price. Rather than the sea of outstretched arms waiting to part with their money which he'd convinced himself would be before him, there was no one – except a dog and some chip wrappings.

He tried again. Same thing, but now even the dog had left. What was particularly upsetting was that the dog was a stray. Its owner (and thus at least one potential buyer) was nowhere to be seen.

He tried again. This time he slowed the pace down a little because he was starting to feel dizzy. He tried to expand on what he had been saying about the stock and even made sure he looked up during the demonstration. There wasn't a sea of faces, but the seven or eight people who were standing there provided a massive incentive for him to make sure that they appreciated they were getting a bargain. Linda the iron-pad demonstrator had once told us:

'You can tell those people who are likely to buy because of the amount of questions that they ask at the beginning and by the expressions on their faces, sometimes. When they are not interested they back away and look down. When they are interested they look at me.'

There were at least three people looking at Clark. The dog was back too. He announced the price and was shocked to find that two of these people came forward with money in their hands. He looked around warily to see if Gary and Tonto had set him up. They hadn't. He had lost his sales virginity and become a 'pitcher'.

By the end of the day he'd taken £90. The look on Tonto's face when he returned betrayed a mixture of pleasure and surprise. 'You've passed your first test,' he said. 'You're in business.'

'What test was that?' Clark asked.

'You had the bottle to stand up and make a fool of yourself. You gave it a go.'

He instructed Clark to come back at the weekend.

GAINING EXPERIENCE

In a pub after work Gary and Clark held a post mortem. Clark's main problem was that he'd found it hard attracting anybody to the stall, let alone a crowd. He could manage to get five, six, maybe even seven people to stop at the start of the pitch, but he just couldn't get them to stay. He wanted to know exactly what he was doing wrong.

'What you've got to do,' Gary advised him, 'is to get six standard slogans off to a "T" in your mind, so as soon as you start there's your caption, "Never mind what they charge, they charge you x pounds, well I'm gonna do it now for a matter of pennies." *That's one.* "If you think I'm jokin'" – as if someone has said: "Aye, he's joking" – "If you think I'm jokin', when I tell you the price in a minute's time, you'll feel like chokin.'" *That's two.* They're standards. Just to get people round to watch. All you're doing is making a noise. If you could stand and bang a drum, people would stop to see what's happening. But some days you'll see just how hard it is, then you've got to be able to fire off dozens at them. You've got to be able to have, like, a continuous-tape loop of them running round your head, otherwise you'll keep repeating yourself which is no good. You've got to make everybody who is standing in front of you think that you're just about to start.'

What Gary was saying was that Clark was acting too mechanically. The amount of time pitchers spend building a crowd depends crucially upon the number of people who have already stopped at the stall. If only a few people stop at the beginning of a sale, then pitchers have to extend the time spent building the edge until they have attracted the number of people they require. The trick is never to repeat yourself. You have to become adept at varying the spiel, extending it and shortening it as necessary, in order to maintain the attention and interest of those people who have already stopped, at the same time as attracting additional passers-by. Pitchers always have to be on the look-out for subtle cues so they can ascertain what sort of edge is gathering and whether they are likely to co-operate. Judging this isn't easy. Assessing the composition of a crowd is a skill that can only be acquired by observing many different sorts of crowd.

In effect, where Clark was going wrong was in sticking too slavishly to a sales script. Learning what to say and repeating it mechanically was okay, as a first step, but it wasn't the way to make real money (or much money, in his case). Pitching, as we saw in Chapter 5, is not a matter of stimulus and response; nor is it ever only sales rhetoric. It is an interactive communication skill which depends upon pitchers being sensitive to what they are saying, how they are saying it, and the types of reactions and responses the audience are providing constantly during a sale.

From our videotapes we had failed to appreciate the manner in which pitchers change their routines to deal with any unanticipated problems that emerge during a sale. Part of the reason for this is that pitchers often avoid drawing attention to the fact that a problem has arisen. If they made it obvious that they were reacting to some unexpected event, then people at the stall would sense the trouble and the problem could be exacerbated.

At the start of Clark's second day's pitching, he asked Gary and Tonto to watch his first sale of the day so that they could give him a few more tips before they left him on his own again. But he found it hard to perform under the gaze of the experts. He was stuttering all the time; the words and phrases just wouldn't come out or flow properly. The pitch was a blow-out. His next question to Gary was the obvious one: 'What happens if you get stuck for something to say?'

155

'All I'm going to say to you is this.'

Clark waited a few moments, but Gary said nothing else. 'Say what?' he asked.

'*That*! You're stuck, right? So all you say is: "All I'm going to say to you is *this*!" That'll buy you about ten seconds of space to think, 'cos after you've said that you've got their attention too – they're waiting for you to say something to them.'

This advice seemed totally weird to Clark. But there was a kind of logic to it. When pitchers have a problem, if they don't try to mask it, they draw attention to it, flaunt it even, as Gary suggested. It was so counter-intuitive that Clark had never even thought about trying it for himself.

Clark's problem was obviously related to the fact that he was still talking too quickly. Gary had already assessed the speed of his spiel:

'You're the same as I was, still am sometimes – too fast. *Too fast*. And it's understandable because you get adrenalin running.' That was certainly true. 'You'll get to the point where you can just relax and you don't even think about what you're saying – then you can have a bit of fun. Otherwise your mind is overflowing thinking about what you should be saying. Now, I *know* what I'm saying. What else you've got to watch, though, is don't let people hustle you into doing it any faster. Like Bill says: "You only get two things if you rush – babies and fleas."' Gary went into another of his pitching flashbacks and was back, for a moment or two, selling in front of a large crowd: 'What do you mean you've had them both, you cheeky bugger. *Watch*!'

Being able to pace yourself is certainly one of the most undervalued skills of the successful pitcher. In this respect Clark was in good company. Gentleman John, a champion pitcher, had once told us that he'd suffered from talking too fast himself:

'When I started to pitch I probably used to talk far too quick because you imagine that the people are going to walk away. I mean, when you've got the confidence you take your time; if they go they go. And if there's somebody that moans and says:

"get on with it," you just ignore them and take no notice. But when you are first doing it you try to talk fast because you think they are going to go away if you don't. And it must come over to the public that you are inexperienced because you are doing that and this. It all builds up in your mind your lack of confidence, I think.'

Delivering the various elements of a sales spiel at a slightly slower tempo seems to have at least two benefits. First of all it allows pitchers that little bit more time to think about what they are going to have to say next. That way they are more likely to be able to deliver each piece of information fluently and effectively. Secondly, because they are not having continually to stop and think of what to say next, what they do say sounds far more authoritative.

Twirling the edge

The next few times Clark pitched there was a steady improvement in his performance but not, alas, in profit. No matter what he said, how loud he shouted or how big a crowd he managed to attract, he could only get about two or three people to buy from each pitch. Slowing the pace down to what he thought was a more authoritative crawl made matters worse – he still tended only to make the same number of sales each pitch; now, they just took longer to achieve. Some people even started shouting things like 'Get on with it, will you?' and 'I can't stand here all day, you know.' He took their advice and tried to conduct more pitches per hour – to take what little money he was getting with the minimal possible delay.

He turned to Gary again, whose advice, once more, was completely counter-intuitive. Gary told him that when he announced the selling price the last thing he was interested in was trying to serve everyone who wanted to buy the goods. Neither was he particularly bothered about taking the money as quickly as possible so that he could crack on with the next sale. He was more interested in using these willing buyers to attract even more customers to his stall:

'When you "bat" them, then they'll hopefully pull their money out. But you don't just take their money and let them run away. You have to take their money in such a way that you can keep them standing at the front of the stall. You can only make some people wait, mind you. You can tell who will wait and who won't.'

'How's that?' Clark asked.

'Just by looking at them, really. So, if somebody's in a hurry – they're "tut-tutting" while they're stood waiting for you to finish your spiel – then you serve them first and get rid of them [see Chapter 5]. But if they're not in such a rush you can serve one or two customers and then you start all over again: "You want some as well? Well, just watch. Have a look at what we give you . . ." As you do that more people come round. It's called "twirling the edge", and if you're lucky you can twirl it, and spin it, and keep it running. That way you can have a money pitch for half an hour.'

This was a complete revelation. We had, of course, recorded and watched many examples of pitchers 'twirling the edge', but because they never drew attention to what they were doing we had never fully appreciated what was actually going on. One of these sales, of sets of pens, was a classic example of this strategy. It lasted just over fourteen minutes. The first announcement of the selling price occurred three minutes into the sale. The rest of the time, in other words over three-quarters of the routine, was spent using the gathered purchasers as free advertising to attract additional customers to the stall. A total of twenty-seven sales took place during this routine. But at the first point where the audience was asked to buy the goods only five people had raised their arms or had otherwise indicated that they wanted to make a purchase. By twirling the edge, the pitcher had been able dramatically to increase his sales.

In twirling the edge, pitchers appeal to the imitative aspect of buying behaviour; people rely upon others at the stall before deciding whether to and what to buy. Pitchers, consequently, make use of those people who are prepared to buy to persuade others to do so. By restating the nature of the bargain and delaying the handing over of the goods, other people can be brought into the sale.

Working as an assistant

As Clark started to twirl the edge, his sales improved dramatically. Eventually, he was 'promoted' and worked with Gary, 'one up, one down' (one of them would pitch the goods while the other managed the stock). This gave him an opportunity to watch Gary in action directly, and also to learn more about what it was like being a pitcher's assistant. The first thing he learned was to control his facial expressions when he wasn't pitching. Sometimes, and usually for no other reason than to alleviate boredom, Gary would vaunt the goods in an exceptionally exaggerated manner. It was at such moments that Clark noticed that people would be looking at him – as the assistant – to gauge the plausibility of Gary's claims. Laughter and smirks on his part were, of course, out of order. What he was required to do was to stand motionless. Looking nonplussed was better; small nods and sounds of agreement were better still. Correcting what Gary said had an even more profound effect. In one sale we had recorded at the start of our research, a pitcher had claimed that someone from Huddersfield had bought five sets of the goods earlier in the day and said that she was 'putting them away for Christmas presents' (it was September). His assistant then responded with a correction: 'No, you're wrong. She was from Hull.' This correction traded off and subverted the expectation that the matter the assistant was dealing with was the number of items the shopper had allegedly bought. Rather, by positing the issue as being about where the shopper had come from, the veracity of the number of products bought is further amplified.

More generally, Clark was told he must never do anything to distract the audience's attention from a pitcher – even scratching his face during the sale was absolutely forbidden. In our interviews it was stressed to us that during a pitch an assistant must never break the bond being developed between the pitcher and people at the stall. Mack had told us:

'You *mustn't* divert attention away from the pitcher, otherwise you'll create an activity that isn't required, thank you very much. When I worked with my old man I didn't dare speak. If somebody said to me "How much are them cups?" I didn't dare answer. The most I would say to them – and only then if they were adamant – is: "That's the next lot up," even if it wasn't. You mustn't get into conversation with them. *Ever.*'

Nevertheless, as we saw in Chapter 3, floor workers, on occasion, can play a crucial part in enhancing and even creating the audience's response to the announcement of the selling price. Some pan-technicon pitchers send the goods offered for sale out into the audience before it is certain that anyone has actually indicated a willingness to buy those goods. Terry told us:

'Your floor worker can be important round the bat. For instance, if you're selling something for a fiver, as soon as you're saying "a fiver" – when you get to the "r" at the end of the word – he should have picked one of the goods up and be halfway into the edge with it. Eight times out of ten there'll be a hand up before he gets there. Mind you . . .' – he started laughing – 'he might have to change direction a little on his way. Every now and again he'll get halfway out and there'll still be nothing. Then, well, you've just got to cover it.'

Every extra sale Clark was making was further proof of his growing ability as a pitcher. The experience made him realize that pitching was not like giving a lecture at the university. If your spiel at a pitching stall is boring, then people don't just turn on their tape recorders and start to snooze; they will quickly walk away with your livelihood in their pockets and purses. Even if you have a hundred people or more standing less than three feet away from you, you find that you develop an extraordinary sensitivity to any whisper or shuffle in the crowd. To look up and view a sea of faces all hanging, somewhat disdainfully, on your every word was an experience Clark had encountered quite often during lecturing. To have such a crowd within touching distance, knowing that in a couple of minutes' time they will register their assessment of you either by giving you their money or by sloping away from the stall, was a very different prospect to the threat posed by the student appraisal forms at the end of term. The unequivocality of it all was staggering. In the world of market pitching there are no ways of rationalizing failure. You can't have a quiet word with the people at the stall and say you're not feeling on top form today. You can't use excuses – the moment you do, you start to lose sales.

Clark's growing confidence in his ability as a pitcher led him to seek an expert opinion on his newly acquired skills. 'So, look,' he said to Gary one day after work, 'I've been pitching with you for four days. What do you reckon?'

'You've got it! You know how to do it! You've got the bottle; and the front to go with it.'

He was quite shocked. So was Gary.

'It's surprising, really.'

Then came another grain of truth:

'The only thing you can't teach somebody is experience. *You can't*! There's no way, because until you've pitched for ages – it's like anything else – it comes then. Then it'll come to the point where you'll be better than the person who's taught you – like Tonto. I reckon I can blow him off now.' (Clark remembers nodding shamelessly at this point and saying: 'I've always thought that myself.') 'You see,' Gary continued, 'I've seen his mistakes, and you'll see mine. Then you won't do 'em, you see?'

Gary gave him more advice to help improve his skills:

'It's one thing just to learn a script – anyone can learn a script

– it's experience that learns you how to handle people heckling you or having a go at you. Something happens to you once and then you see another grafter working and somebody will say something – he'll have a reply – and you use that. Everybody pinches each other's lines. Certain grafters have their own particular style. You could give two people the same item to sell – the same script – but everybody has their own way of working. Some of them are very brutal – Tonto is very harsh, *aggressive*, whereas I find it pays off for me to be a little bit softer with the punters.'

The art of the rick

Another thing Clark learned when working with Gary was how to 'rick' – act as a confederate in the audience. As we have already mentioned, it is mainly fly pitchers who use this technique. As Terry said: 'You rick for yourself when you're pitching straight.' To relieve the boredom one day, Clark asked Gary if he would show him how to do it. Gary told him to try it out for himself first.

Clark did and, in doing so, soon discovered that he had committed two cardinal errors: first, he stood far too close to the front of the stall at the beginning of a sale; second, when it was time to lead the audience responsiveness, he shot his hand straight up in the air. Gary told him that everyone had known he had been working as a plant in the audience and that's why he hadn't made any sales. Why? Because he wasn't acting like a genuine member of the public. When responding to a pitcher's request for the audience to move closer to the stall, he was told that a good rick will, at first, ignore this request. It would be far more convincing if he were to move closer only after a second request. That way he would give the impression that he was acting just like everyone else – initially reluctant to move closer to the pitcher. It also gives the impression that even a doubter can be persuaded. He was also told never to shoot his hand up when a pitcher asked something like: 'Who'd like to buy the goods?' Just a shuffle was enough. That way his movement would pass through the crowd like a shock-wave and would have an even greater effect.

When Clark worked as a pitcher he began to see what it is that makes these traders different from other people who work on street markets. For instance, although pitchers have much in common with demonstrators, there is certainly a small but significant difference in attitude. The demonstrators we spoke to appeared to be more sensitive to and knowledgeable about the particular market conditions that may influence sales success. Their stress on the importance of antecedent variables would earn them high praise from some economists. Many demonstrators elaborated on features such as unemployment rates, regional variations and disposable incomes and their likely effect on the success or failure of a sales routine. Pitchers displayed a flagrant disregard of such factors. If they paid any attention to them at all, it was often in terms of them being opportunities for obtaining further sales. For example, the unemployment and general hardship produced by the 1985 British miners' strike was seen by pitchers working markets in the heart of the coalfields as an unprecedented opportunity to sell more of their goods to miners with special 'miner's deals'. Such factors were rarely treated as being a barrier to sales success. Pitchers treated a tendency to dwell on the merits and significance of these and similar phenomena as a sign of having a 'bad attitude'.

Clark once made the same type of 'mistake'. One evening, when Tonto and Gary were driving him to the railway station, he foolishly proffered the suggestion that it wasn't very likely that he would take much money tomorrow as it was Cup Final day. The torrent of verbal abuse they threw at him was unbelievable. They left him in no doubt that they expected him to take more money than he had the previous week because he had an extra seven days' worth of pitching experience.

Another meaning of the phrase 'hard sell'

One of the biggest lessons we learned from this participant observation study was just how physically demanding the job of pitching can be. Often pitchers get up at four or five o'clock in the morning to load their lorries and vans and then drive them sometimes hundreds of miles to be set up in time for a market starting at nine o'clock. The stock must be transferred from the van to the stall and each item of the flash carefully displayed. And, as if concentrating on the actual pitching routine were not enough, the seller must remember which customers want what, make sure the right money is taken and change given, and furthermore that no one is stealing gear from the stall. They spend the whole day shouting themselves hoarse, and then all the unsold stock must be loaded up in the van once more, the stall dismantled, the van driven home, and the gear unloaded again.

Nothing prepared Clark for the shock of having to shout continuously for hours on end. It is no wonder that since the beginning of our research some of the pitchers we studied have already suffered (and on two occasions died from) heart attacks and other stress-related illnesses.

Tacit knowledge

Perhaps the most important asset pitchers need, apart from a strong heart, is, as Gary had told Clark, experience. In order to pitch effectively you have to be able to pitch automatically – without thinking about what it is you are doing. Mack the potato-peeler demonstrator gave us an example:

'I was working with my older brother one day – *years ago*, this was. He was a real showman, Rolls-Royce, expensive suit, *the lot*. He was having a pitch one day. I'm holding a basket with this dinner set and he's giving it a big build-up: "It was made for the Maharajah of Morocco, but due to unforeseen circumstances . . ." – he's trying to create a real splendour effect, you see? And there's a woman at the side has picked a vase up and she's giving it all this with the vase [i.e. a close and suspicious inspection]. And I could see that it was irritating him because he had the attention of everyone except this woman. So he reached across and took this vase from her, wrapped it up and said: "Two pounds please." And she pulled her two pound out. She was embarrassed, he made her feel like a right schmuck. He went straight back to his pitch, straight back to one hundred per cent attention. At the end of the day, after we'd finished two hours later, I said to him, "That were clever, Jimmy." He said: "What were clever?" I said: "The way you stummed that woman up like." He said: "*What woman?*" He couldn't even remember it. It was automatic to him. Somewhere, hidden in his brain, he *knew* that this woman was no good to his pitch.'

The fact that most pitchers do their selling 'without thinking about it' was one of the greatest barriers we encountered in our quest to understand and appreciate what this type of selling was all about. Although it seems possible to study an activity and work out, in principle, precisely what is going on and why, in real life it is often not the abstract principles which are important but, rather, the subtle, taken-for-granted skills that are needed to do the job. There is a world of difference between having the formal knowledge how to do something and having the tacit knowledge required actually to do it. It's like learning to ride a bike. Knowledge of all the laws of physics and the mechanics of balancing on two wheels are of little help in mastering the act. You just learn to do it, and when you can do it it is very hard to explicate what it is exactly you've learnt.

Our participant observation taught us that pitching was a difficult and demanding skill. But we also began to realize that it was a skill that could be learned. There didn't seem to be any unique psychological profile that made someone into a pitcher. Neither did pitchers inherently possess a special 'gift of the gab'. If Clark had been able to become a halfway decent pitcher then, surely, anyone could. Whether they had the desire to do so was, of course, an entirely different matter.

The art of pitching is based on the seller employing a wide and diverse range of persuasive communication skills, each of which is, of necessity, grounded firmly in the way human beings think and act in this real economic world. Pitchers don't have to use these skills consciously to be able to sell effectively. On most occasions, as Mack had said, they don't even seem to give them a second thought. In fact, many of the skills revealed to us were so subtle, and so taken for granted, that the pitchers themselves were only dimly aware of their existence, let alone that they had been using them. Even when we had captured their skills on videotape and had studied them back in the lab, we, as academics, as 'experts' on market pitching in the academic world, had often lacked the experience and lay knowledge fully to appreciate what was going on between pitchers and shoppers at a market stall. And although we had undertaken participant observation in order to obtain additional insights about this sales world – insights which revealed that we had previously missed or not fully appreciated some significant aspect of pitching – they certainly didn't make us rich. Our experience made us realize that academics like ourselves are usually only humble tourists in the worlds we seek to understand.

After all, we could always go home to another life. The genuine pitcher does not. There were, of course, days when the self-consciousness involved in selling goods on a street market took a back seat and Clark felt that he had pitched on autopilot and truly adapted to the task. These were the days when he could make fun of individual members of the audience without the usual fear that they would turn round and hit him, and when all the unexpected problems that emerged did so seemingly in slow motion, allowing him to deal with them in a nonchalant, 'seen it all before' manner, even if he hadn't seen it before, even once. These were the days when everything was 'sweet'. It was on one such day that Clark received what every participant observer dreams of – an independent confirmation that he had 'gone native'.

THE PRICE OF GOING NATIVE

It was raining heavily and Gary and Clark had spent most of the morning struggling to sell the only line of stock they had brought with them – sunglasses. They'd managed to get rid of some of them by claiming that the low selling price was a direct result of 'the inclemencies of the weather', adding, for good measure, that 'as soon as the sun comes out our prices go up.' There must have been nearly three hundred pairs left unsold, however. Because there were so few people on the market they had to use the 'pull-up' – that method of building a crowd by, first of all, attracting one person to the stall and conducting the sale round him or her as a way of convincing other passers-by to stop (see Chapter 1). Gary had noticed that when he started to pitch, this exceptionally attractive Scottish woman with a young baby in her pram had been only too willing to be the first to stop. But more than that, she was willing to stay at their stall for more than one pitch. They built edge after edge around her. Gary had the answer: it was obvious that she had designs on Clark. There was no doubt that she was a stunner. There was also no doubt that, because many of the younger pitchers are seen as 'likely lads', he was going to have to give her some gross chat-up. But, in fact, he didn't have to do anything. Being a spieler was all that seemed to be required. She invited him out for a drink that very evening.

Clark was whipping himself up into a right state of trauma. He was, undoubtedly, in that classic dilemma – what sociologists call a 'role conflict situation'. There was only one way out – he was going to have to tell her the truth. Fortunately, he'd remembered that when he went home at weekends and hung out at the local nightclubs and told women that he was at university, the result had been, without exception, quite cata-strophic. The young women he met were certainly pleasant enough, but where he lived they didn't seem all that interested in university boys with their half-pint rounds and their cold walks home. He opted for the gentle let-down: 'Look,' he ventured, 'I *would* like to come out with you tonight, but I can't.'

'Why not?'

'I've got to do some work.'

'You can't work tonight, it'll be too dark.'

'No, that's what I mean.' He took a deep breath and then dropped the bombshell: 'I'm not actually a pitcher, you know.'

'*Oh yeah?*' she replied, eyeing him suspiciously, 'then what are you?'

'Well, I'm a research fellow at university.'

'A *what?*'

'A research fellow. It's more or less the same thing as being a student but you use bigger words and you get paid a little bit more. Well, I used to get paid a little more. I'm only working here because I need the money and we're writing a book on the art of pitching.'

Unfortunately, she didn't buy that one. Shaking her head in disbelief and summoning up all the disgust she could muster, she delivered her body blow: 'You bloody spielers, you're all the same – *gobshites!*' and stormed off, pushing her pram at a life-threatening pace, never to be seen again.'

Standing dejected in the rain listening to the sound of Gary's laughter ringing in his ears, Clark consoled himself with the thought that for the first time since he started pitching some-body had obviously mistaken him for what he had been trying so hard for the last few months to become.

When he eventually returned to work at the university, Clark found that he didn't really need this type of proof to convince himself that he had gone native. The effects of having done so were still all too apparent. His voice was continuing to sound as if he'd gone down with a severe bout of laryngitis. Moreover, his head was still swimming with thoughts of doing deals and all the other sometimes grim realities of the cash nexus which impinge on the working life of a salesperson. (The very 'skills' he'd just left behind were soon going to be regarded as an absolute asset in the world of British higher education.) In fact, it took him at least another two months before he could open his briefcase at the start of a class without thinking about what he would have done if, instead of packing it with notes for his lecture, he'd stacked it full of fold-up sunglasses and multi-coloured costume jewellery.

CHAPTER 7

Dodgy Working – Fly Pitchers

You can fall for chains of silver.
You can fall for chains of gold.
You can fall for pretty strangers.
And the promises they hold.

Mark Knopfler, Dire Straits

'Freddy the Fly' told us that a good salesman could talk the knickers off a nun. We got the feeling that he was fantasizing about his own persuasive abilities until, one day, we witnessed him accomplish something very similar and equally unbelievable.

We were travelling home by Intercity train after watching some fly pitchers – those unlicensed traders who make their living by selling goods on the streets – at work. Asleep opposite us was Freddy, no less. He had his suitcase with him, but he wasn't going on holiday. Only a few hours earlier it had been jam packed with hundreds of 'Ferarri' folding sunglasses. At the next station an attractive girl got on the train and sat in the vacant seat beside him. Within a second or so Freddy was wide awake, ready to put in some serious overtime. He started talking:

'That's a nice ring you've got. It's a bit like mine, isn't it?'
'Yes, it was my grandmother's.'
'Was she as pretty as you?'
Before the train had even left the station they were talking

170

like old friends. His patter was so smooth we expected him to slide off his seat any second. He was shameless too. He started telling the girl he'd bought his wife some kinky underwear and he couldn't wait to see her wearing it. Out it came from his case and they began comparing notes on the colours, materials, styles and merits of other types of lingerie. We didn't dare look at each other in case one of us made the other laugh at the preposterousness of it all. Freddy began to tell the girl how he was uncertain as to whether the underwear was suitable for his wife. Ten minutes later he'd convinced her to model the underwear for him in the train toilet.

Freddy seemed to personify the cash-on-the-hip, live-by-your-wits, keep-both-eyes-open-for-the-main-chance lifestyle of the fly pitcher. During the time that we knew him he told us all about the exceptional difficulties that fly pitchers face when trying to sell, and the dodgy and sometimes illegal tactics to which they sometimes resort.

Fly pitchers like to view themselves as being a breed apart from market pitchers. This feeling seems to be mutual. Although straight workers and fly pitchers both use an elaborate sales spiel to attract and sell to a crowd of people, *en masse*, the similarity effectively ends there.

Fly pitchers do not have a legitimate market pitch; nor do they have a licence to trade anywhere else. Consequently, they have to choose the place where they work very carefully. They have to be ready at less than a moment's notice to move on, and many of them employ look-outs to warn them in advance of any approaching police about to descend upon them. Fly pitchers are also called street hawkers, a term that aptly captures the way these traders hunt for buyers. Like a bird of prey, they travel, seek out, then pounce (in this case verbally) upon their custom.

The type of stock that fly pitchers sell under these circumstances is obviously limited to items that are easily transportable and small enough to be carried in something like a briefcase ('peter'). Typically, they sell jewellery ('tom'), perfumes ('fun-kum'), watches ('kettles'), cassette tapes, and socks. An up-turned milk crate usually suffices for a stall, and their executive briefcase doubles up as a counter upon which to display the goods. Freddy reckoned:

'When you're fly pitching you cannot build up a big flash, you cannot flash all your gear out and get a big display. That's a problem because people like to see a lot of stock, especially when you tell them it's bankrupt stock [laughs].'

FLY PITCHING VENUES

The best places for fly pitchers to set up 'shop' are usually on main shopping streets where there is plenty of passing trade, enough room for a crowd to gather without obstructing the pavement, and a number of possible escape routes. They can also be found working, though not usually for long, in some of the walkways between the regular stalls in both open and covered street markets.

As Freddy told us:

'You look for a place that, number one: it's got to be busy. There's got to be people. And most towns have shopping precincts now. You look for a position in a precinct where – there should be two of you, there's usually two of you. If there's only one of you, er, you just have to keep your eyes open. But you look for a position where you can see and where people can see you, right? Where you can put down – where you're not obstructing anybody's doorways, anybody's shops. If you're selling something that's on sale in a shop nearby you're not gonna reign for long. You'd be lucky to get two minutes before he rings the police. Why should he stand for you outside his shop? The most important thing is to find somewhere that's busy. And then, obviously, somewhere where you can see if there's any policemen approaching. Not that *that's* a big worry.

I don't think – um – ninety-nine per cent of policemen just aren't bothered. But you do get one or two young coppers, they know they can get you for obstructing the highways. Some policemen are not bothered. They don't *all* nick you. You just say: "I'm trying to get a living. Leave me alone, will you? I'm not doing anybody any harm."'

The fly pitchers in Freddy's home town formed a loose-knit 'community'. They would often meet after a day's work to compare sales figures, swap tall stories and talk up any incidents that had occurred during the day's trading. But their favoured places of working always seemed to remain a closely guarded secret. Freddy:

'Well, you know that, don't you? Nobody will tell you the best venues to work. *Me*? I'm not bothered. They'll all tell you where it's bent though; everybody will tell you where you cannot work. There's a café nearby where all the fly pitchers go to on a morning. "I'm going to X." "Oh, don't go there, it's double bent." They'll tell you where it's bent, they'll *not* tell you where it's any good.'

Given the restricted range of stock a fly pitcher usually carries, and the limited amount of time they are typically able to 'reign' or 'dwell' at any one location, not being able to evoke an interest in the goods can have a disastrous effect. Freddy again:

'Many of the straight workers pull out a toy, say, at fifteen pounds and drop it to a fiver. He might get a dozen out in one pitch. Then he drops it and goes on to something else. We don't work like that. When we pick something up we have to make them want it. We can't just put it down and go on to another line because we haven't got one.'

This problem is exacerbated for the fly pitcher because their potential clientele perceive them as having far less credibility than traders who sell from high-street retail stores or from a legitimate market stall.

Because of their 'here today, gone today' character, fly pitch-ers do not have to worry about selling to more or less the same pool of customers or passers-by week in, week out. Consequently, the fly pitcher's world is one with fewer constraints, and this certainly manifests itself in the special techniques they use to persuade people to buy.

They rarely have enough time to sell in the way straight workers do, by elaborately creating bargains or using the people who initially gather to build an execution pitch. They employ far fewer, if any, audience management and commitment-inducing tactics, and only rarely do they conduct an extended build-up and then a slow run-down to the final selling price. Perhaps the most noticeable difference between fly pitching and straight-working market pitchers is the use of confederates ('ricks') in the audience who pose as customers. This difference can be seen from the very beginning of a sale.

Pulling a pitch with 'the hook'

Fly pitchers face the same problems as straight workers in getting people to stop and listen to their sales spiel. Because the task of attracting people to a briefcase, even an executive briefcase, is, however, harder than that of attracting them to a bona fide market stall, a fly pitcher is likely to resort to a variant of this ploy called 'the hook' (see Chapter 1). Here, a series of very low and decreasing prices is announced and passers-by are encouraged to stop on the assumption that the goods will eventually be sold for an even lower price. This strategy is evident during the following two sales of sets of jewellery:

P   *Right, then*, it's the *very last* of these look, an' I'm gonna *clear* them out of the way now, at prices, look, you will not believe POSSIBLE. Now watch. An' *never mind*, look, FORTY pence or thirty pence. Watch this. Never mind twenty pence. Look. For the purposes of the advertisement I'm gonna make them the *cheapest* you've *ever* seen them. If I say cheap I mean *exactly* what I say, and I say *exactly* what I mean.

P   You can buy them in the 'News of the World'. There's
      only one difference, they charge you POUNDS, I'm
      gonna do it for PENNIES. And *NEVER MIND
      FIFTY PENCE, AND NEVER EVEN MIND
      FORTY PENCE*. 'Cos if I attempt to charge you *forty
      pence* each for them, all I say to you is this: *WALK
      AWAY!*

The lowest of these prices bears little, if any, relation to the
actual selling price of the goods. In the two sales above, the sets
of jewellery were sold for £3 and £2 respectively. Freddy:
      'We always start off with "Never mind ten pence, nine pence
or eight pence." All we've said is "Never mind . . . ", and they
think then, the greedy bastards think they're gonna get something cheap. But once you've got a few people stood round you
by doing that, then you can go to work.'
      It is obvious that some of the people who do stop after
hearing this type of spiel genuinely believe that these extremely
low prices are what the actual selling price will be. We have seen
people gathering round a fly pitcher with the small amounts of
money mentioned in 'the hook' already in their hands. By the
time the actual and higher price is announced, many of these
people will have been convinced by other strategies that the
goods are worth buying and will in any case pay the final price
demanded.
      By offering the goods for sale in collections, the fly pitcher
who employs 'the hook' is provided with a convenient way of
dealing with the obvious discrepancy between the low prices
mentioned at the start of the sale and the higher selling price. If
anyone complains about this price difference, the fly pitcher will
invariably reply that the prices initially announced referred to
only one of the items for sale, not the collection as a whole. The
fly pitcher's next response is likely to be something along the
lines of: 'Sorry, I'm not allowed to sell them on their own.'

DESCRIBING AND SELLING THE GOODS

Having attracted people to a sale, fly pitchers then go on to describe and sell their goods in a way that is quite similar to that of straight workers; but only up to a point. For instance, both types of sellers 'fanny' the goods. Freddy:

'All right, so if we're describing the jewellery. You pick up a rope chain, it's *just* a rope chain, and then it becomes a *"fabulous* eighteen-inch rope necklace. Look, it's plated with a precious nine-carat gold. Er, it will add grace and elegance to any lady's neck." Right? It becomes a – *everything* is *"fabulous"*, and "Here's the one that *everybody* likes" – [starts laughing] you usually use that for the one that *no one* wants. That's the way you do it. Most of the time though you just have to bollock 'em.'

When they have plenty of time to sell, fly pitchers also use price contrasts and lists of declining prices in order to enhance the worth and the bargain status of their goods. This happens in the following sale:

SETS OF JEWELLERY
P   The one, the two, the three, the four. With *either* the lady's
     or the gent's. *Forget* about costin' you well over thirty
     quid. Ah'm 'ere to give you a bargain. Times are hard, an'
     ah'm gonna go a lot, lot cheaper. *Not* thirty, *not*
     twenty-five, *not* twenty, not even fifteen, *not even* twelve,
     [CLAP] an' ah don' even want a *tenner*, an' at a tenner for
     that set there, for the *five* pieces includin' a ring, it's
     absolutely for nothing. But times are hard like ah've just said
     so ah'm gonna go a lot, lot cheaper. That suits everybody's
     pockets. Ah'm not even gonna charge *you eight* pound,
     ah'm not even gonna *charge you seven* pound, an ah'm not
     even gonna charge you *six* pound. *Where do I get them
     from? Mind your own bloody business*! But ah'm not even
     gonna charge you *a fiver* 'ere today. If *you wanna* bargain,

the one, the two, the three, the four, either the lady's or the gent's, *all* brand new an' *perfect*, which weigh between four an' five grammes the rings, ah'm gonna take *silly* an' level money. The *first* ten of you to say yes, 'cos I 'aven't got many chains left, an' ah'll take a silly price, *not even* four quid. The *first ten* of you to say yes 'ere today before that bobby comes up the road. *What* you see is *what* you take away [CLAP] for *three quid* for the whole set here today.

Those fly pitchers who are particularly pressed for time are likely to conduct a series of rapid-fire single sales. In such cases they are able to exploit to the full the benefits that can be obtained by 'twirling the edge' to attract more passers-by and generate additional custom. This happens in the following sale. We note that the fly pitcher is using a compressed version of a hard-sell spiel. This is referred to as 'working strong', and the type of pitch he is making (notably his claim that he is selling solid gold jewellery) is called 'blagging the punters' or 'getting moody'. The fly pitcher heightens the assembly-line atmosphere of the sale by stressing the last word of every phrase he announces. This gives his spiel a hypnotic, 'said it (and sold it) all a million times before' quality:

SETS OF JEWELLERY

P   There's been a *robbery*. Of twenty-six *million pounds' worth*. Over three tons were *stolen*. It's *never* been seen *since. One*, there it *is*! A nine-carat gold *rope*. It costs thirty *pound*. A twenty-four-carat gold *belcher*, thirty-*two*. An eighteen-carat gold *cobra*, and a *Gucci bracelet*. Forget about ninety *pound*, give me two pound for the *lot*. [Hands jewellery over to a buyer] Put it away, *it's stolen*. [To everyone] When you buy stolen property you don't get a *receipt*. A nine-carat gold *rope*, a twenty-four-carat gold *belcher*, an eighteen-carat solid gold *cobra*, a hallmarked bracelet is *forty pounds*. Give me *two pounds* for the *lot*. [Hands jewellery over to a buyer] Put it away, *it's stolen property*. I can't give you the money to buy it *with*. The gold *rope*, the gold *belcher*, the eighteen-carat gold *cobra*, the *Gucci bracelet*, gimme two pound for the *lot*. [Hands jewellery over to a buyer]

Selling by suggestion and misrepresentation

Although we can see from the examples above that on some occasions fly pitchers attempt to sell their goods by misrepresenting what they actually are – for example, that their gold-plated or gold-coloured jewellery is solid gold – on other occasions they only hint at these possibilities, albeit in the strongest possible terms. Mention may be made of jewellery being 'stamped':

P   They're *all stamped*! If they're not *stamped*, with pleasure go an' get that policeman down there with the beard. He'll be more than pleased to nick me.

. . . but while it is likely that there will be an inscription printed on the jewellery, it almost certainly won't be a genuine gold hallmark. Another strategy used in jewellery sales is to invoke the kind of precise density and weight measurements that are characteristic of the assessment of precious metals, gold in particular:

P   It's a twenty-two-inch, *solid* Italian rope necklace and weighs *exactly* one and a quarter ounces.

P   [They] weigh between four an' five grammes the rings.

Freddy elaborated on this principle of selling by suggestion:

'Look at that bottle of Gavroche [perfume]. Gavroche? *Rive Gauche*! Everything's suggestive. I mean, I've found it hard the last few weeks 'cos I haven't had the Gavroche, I've had to work one called "Outrage". I mean, it *is* an outrage, but we've had to name it "Oh-trahge". And you *have* to use a rick because you've got to say, er: "Who's ever bought 'Oh-trahge"? "Ah've bought some." "Did you buy it duty free?" "Aye, the wife bought it on the plane, five ninety-five." "Well, there you are," you say, "they sell at a tenner, you buy them duty free they're five ninety-five. If you want them from me, *watch*."'

Well-known brand names may be brought in to play to provide a form of suggestive selling *par excellence*. We saw at least five fly pitching squads grafting 'Ferarri' folding sunglasses. Although in each case not as much was made of the famous name as one would expect, it was plastered in large enough lettering on the left lens of each pair of sunglasses, as well as on the leather(ette) pouches, for everyone to see. Only those eagle-eyed people who had an intimate knowledge of spelling or an avid interest in performance cars would realize that the legend 'Ferarri' emblazoned on the sunglasses was not the same as that belonging to the Italian car manufacturer Ferrari.

With perfume, where the odour of the scent can apparently be a significant clue as to the quality of the merchandise, the tactic of selling by suggestion can be taken to the extreme. Freddy:

'What we have done in the past — where you could get into illegalities, I suppose — is to spray the entire gaffe with a bottle of Anais Anais perfume. We spent a tenner on a bottle — wholesale, mind you — and sprayed the whole place with it. All day long people kept stopping and saying, "Ooooh, that's nice, isn't it?" We didn't tell them that it was the perfume we were selling. They just thought it was.'

The sale of counterfeit goods is not unheard of either. We observed one squad of fly pitchers selling phoney 'Opium' perfumes in a city high street. The gang, which seemed to consist entirely of youths playing truant from school, used crude sales techniques, and their ricks were blatantly obvious to all but the exceptionally gullible.

Selling stolen goods

Customers buying from fly pitchers are usually suspicious as to whether their goods are stolen. Most of the time they will be encouraged to think this by the fly pitchers themselves. Practically every fly pitcher we studied played upon the widely held belief that they were selling goods whose origin was, to say the least, extremely dubious:

SETS OF JEWELLERY
P   The *first ten* of you to say yes 'ere today before that bobby comes up the road.

SETS OF JEWELLERY
P   *Are they stolen?* That's what's going through your mind. *Are they stolen? Mind your own bloody business.* I don't worry where you people get your money from. Don't you worry where these rings and these chains come from.

This does not of course mean that the goods actually are stolen. In fact, they rarely are. But mentioning that the goods have been obtained in a less than legitimate way provides an aura of criminality that seems to attract rather than repel custom. Such information provides a rationale that accounts for how allegedly expensive goods can be sold at such cheap prices. It also taps into and feeds off people's greed. Freddy summed it up like this: 'People like to think that they're buying stolen goods and all they're getting is something that has been bought cheap in a warehouse.'

Indeed, it can pay handsome dividends for a fly pitcher to look and act like the classic English spiv. All they need is an oversized camel-coloured overcoat with a black moleskin-type collar and pocket flaps (creating the impression that there is probably some expensive, illegally obtained stock sewn into the lining), a pair of shifty eyes forever on the look-out for the law, a nervous tic borne out of the years of stress selling 'stolen' goods in a public place, and their business image is almost complete.

One ex-fly pitcher claimed that all the regular fly pitchers in one big city had an informal and more or less equitable 'arrangement' worked out with the local police whereby every so often, and in a very public way, a fly pitcher would be arrested and frog-marched off to the police station. Each trader would take it his turn at the dubious 'honour' of being made an example of. They would be charged with the usual offence of trading without a licence or obstructing the public highway, released almost immediately, and eventually had to pay only a nominal fine. This arrangement, though distinctly favouring the police, seemed to suit everyone. Other fly pitchers would refer to these incidents in their spiel, pointing out the fate of their unfortunate associates, if one of them was being arrested in the vicinity, as evidence that their own goods were stolen and should therefore be purchased immediately. Local shopkeepers would feel happier that the police were taking some action against unlicensed street vendors obstructing their doorways and window displays. The police, in turn, were able to chalk up another arrest and took far less flak from shoppers and shopkeepers as they were being seen to uphold the law.

Ricking

The difficulties fly pitchers face in obtaining custom can be solved even more effectively by employing a 'rick' who will be planted in the audience to pose surreptitiously as an ordinary customer. Practically every fly pitcher made use of at least one. Freddy told us: 'Your rick is indispensable. You need a rick. You need a front.'

'Do most fly pitchers use them?' we asked.

'Most people do, yeah. Anybody who's taking it serious. You only know how bad it is without one, you know, when you don't use one. When I can't get a "front" to work for me, to stand at the front and rick for me, I'm stuck. My takings go down ninety per cent.'

'Really?'

'Yeah, *really*. Yeah.'

'*Is it* as bad as that?'

'It's as *bad* as that.'

The first task for a rick is to attract people to the sale. By standing facing the fly pitcher, the rick makes it easier for others to stop. People's reservations about being the first person at the sale tend to vanish if they can see that someone else is already present (see Chapter 1). Freddy:

'People walk past and they think, "Oh, hello, what's going on here? Here's a crowd." That's why you always put somebody at the front first. If you put somebody at the front and they are stood watching you then other people don't feel so embarrassed about standing to watch as well. Otherwise, if you're working on your own it's hard to get people to stop. They think: "Well, there's no way that *I'm* gonna be the first person to stop."'

Indeed, the fact that it is an unusual occurrence for a crowd to gather in the street can work to a fly pitcher's advantage and act as a lure to attract even more people. Because the fly pitcher is usually squatting over something like a milk crate, from a distance passers-by will only be able to see a group of people standing around as if in a huddle; they will not be able to see the fly pitcher. A small crowd such as this is likely to provoke other passers-by to stop and see what unusual event has taken place – has someone, for instance, had a heart attack?

As well as helping to attract passers-by, the other main task of the rick is, of course, to stimulate audience responsiveness and buying activity. If the rick is the first to express an interest in the goods, it reassures other people present that at least one person other than the fly pitcher thinks the goods are worth buying. Freddy:

'That's why the front shoots his hand up first — "I'll have some." And they think, "Well, he's got some, they must be okay." When you say: "Who can use them if I make them cheaper than one pound fifty?" He's there with his hand up, or she's there with her hand up. *"You can. You can."* And other people, as soon as that hand goes up, *they'll* put one up. Sometimes you don't do it like that, you come straight to the price. The rick leaps forward with the pound or whatever: *"Ah'll have some."* And everybody else thinks: "Oh God, ah'd better have some as well", because they're so scared that they might miss something. *Bollocks to 'em.* They'd feel a bit silly if they put their hand up and they were the only person and everybody turned round and said, "Ha ha ha, you're getting nobbled", so they like to see somebody else do it first.'

The main reason for using a rick is to exploit the imitative basis of opinion formation and, if at all possible, to whip the crowd into such a frenzy that they lose their faculties of economic reasoning and buy before they have time to think about what they have let themselves in for. Freddy:

'You wait for the hand to go up — be it the hand of the rick or be it the hand of the punter. A hand *must* go up. And if it doesn't go up you say [pointing to non-existent people in an imaginary crowd], "You'll have some there, lady there, you want some as well." Then they all go: *"Oooh, ah'm confused, ah'd better buy something."* And before you know it they've pulled their purse out, given you the money and they're walking away thinking to themselves, "Why have I bought this crap?"'

To be an effective rick is in itself an art (see Chapter 6). For one thing, most people appear to be particularly alert to the likely presence of confederates in these types of sales. In particular, they are suspicious of anyone who looks like an exceptionally enthusiastic buyer. One way round this is for a fly pitcher not to employ the obvious type — the callow youth or some other 'ne'er do well'-looking adult male. Instead, wives and girlfriends, looking suitably prosperous in fur coats and the like, and even innocent-looking senior citizens, may be employed.

Another strategy (already mentioned in Chapter 6) is to conceal the rick's attempts to influence others at the sale. Mack the potato-peeler demonstrator recalls that, when he used to rick, his behaviour had to be far less obvious than most people expected:

'I'm in the audience. I stand there and I don't move. No movement whatsoever! As though I'm dead. And when he comes to the bat I don't do anything dramatic. I just simply change my stance. And as soon as I move they think it's time to pull up and they punt.' Just thrusting up a hand at the appropriate point can give the game away. A rick has to behave exactly like an ordinary member of the public, perhaps more so; he or she has to have all the stock of reticent responses that genuine shoppers use. Head-nods will have to replace verbal responses; the rick will avoid the pitcher's eyes, stand away from the seller and look elsewhere occasionally, as if distracted and not initially interested in buying. When asked to confirm factors such as the higher selling prices of stock in magazines, they must also make it obvious that they don't already know what that price is.

There is another potential problem with the rick. Even if other shoppers do not immediately realize that there is a confederate in their midst, the rick dramatically thrusting a hand up in the air or lurching forward cash in hand to be the first to buy the goods can still disrupt a sale. If this apparently bona fide member of the public is *not* served first people may begin to wonder why not, and may then assume that he or she is a confederate. Yet if the rick *is* served first the fly pitcher wastes a few important seconds which could be better employed taking genuine money.

Some of the less skilled workers we saw wasted selling time in this way by going through the motions of conducting a sham sale where they took money from, handed the goods over to, and sometimes even gave change back to a rick. Mack's strategy of employing only the slightest of movements at the appropriate points in a sale can be enough to convince other people to buy, particularly in a tightly packed edge. It also has the advantage of being less likely to make the audience cotton on to what is happening. In this way the first buyer with a hand up waiting to be served is a genuine customer (at this point the rick can often be found fumbling in his or her pockets as if looking for the correct change). Other experienced fly pitchers will provide a plausible reason for either not serving the rick first, such as 'I'll serve you in a minute, who's got the correct change?', or not serving him or her at all. In the following example, which occurs after a selling price has been announced, the rick (who is the fly pitcher's wife) is prevented from buying the goods:

PERFUMES
P   [To R] I'm sorry, you've had two sets, love. [To AS]
       She's had two sets off me, she's come back for *more*.
R   [Looks suitably sheepish]
AS   [Smirks and laughs]
P   [Motioning R away from the sale] Come on, give other
       people a chance.
R   [Stays at the sale]
P   [Pushing R away from the sale]. *Come on*!
R   [Stays at the sale]
P   If there's any left ah'll serve you. They're here to be *sold*.

Such theatricals also help to remind the audience just what a bargain they are getting. To build upon the extra sales that can accrue by using these types of staged encounters, ricks sometimes pretend that they are legitimate market stall-holders or shopkeepers who have come to buy the goods from the fly pitcher because they are so cheap:

SETS OF JEWELLERY

R   Ah want a *hundred* sets.

P   AH'M *NOT* SERVIN' YOU. YOU CAN TAKE YOUR MONEY AWAY.

R   Ah want a *hundred* sets.

P   I've been told to sell these to the general public, not just to other traders.

R   I'll buy *all the lot*.

P   They're going to the general public. *Ah'm sorry*.

R   I can't sell them in my shop because you're selling them too cheap. Ah'll buy the lot.

P   If I *want* to sell them cheap *I'll sell 'em cheap*.

R   AH'LL BUY *THE LOT*.

P   Ah'm not servin' you. You're takin' them off me an' sellin' them for profit an' gain.

R   *GIMME IT ALL*. AH'LL BUY IT *ALL*.

P   [Ignores rick and continues to serve customers]

R   [Walks off in disgust]

The judicious use of ricks certainly seems to speed up the process of hand-raising and buying responsiveness. The people standing round a fly pitcher will often shoot their hands up much more quickly than they would at a straight worker's stall, and there are not as many responsiveness 'blind spots' (see Chapter 5) immediately after the announcement of the selling price as there are in straight routines. This further emphasizes the skill of the straight worker who overcomes such difficulties without having to resort to a rick.

ENDORSEMENTS AND TESTIMONIALS

Those fly pitchers who are able to work in one location for longer than usual will often extend their sales patter with things like external endorsements of their wares to enhance the status of their goods as well as of themselves. Often, as with regular pitching, shoppers will be asked to handle the goods and inspect them closely in order to convince others that they are, in fact, what the fly pitcher has claimed them to be. For instance, when selling pieces of jewellery, a shrewd fly pitcher will select the heaviest item in the set as the one to be passed out for examination to a member of the audience. This item will then be dropped into the endorser's open hand, from a good height, in order to accentuate its weight:

P   *Come on, the last few before it rains.* AH'M *NOT*
     TAKIN' THEM HOME WITH ME. Look at
     these. *Oooh*, look at this one. *'Ere*, just feel the weight
     of this one. [Drops chain in someone's hand] 'ERE,
     FEEL T'WEIGHT OF THEM IN YOUR
     'AND 'ERE.
P C [Reacting to the girl feeling the weight of the item of
     jewellery] *Oh yeah! Heavy.* It is, isn't it? It's heavy.
P   TEN PENCE. Look at these. [To another A who
     is also feeling the weight of the jewellery] Nice is
     that, isn't it?
A   [Nods]
P   That weighs an *ounce* and a *quarter*. An' that's how
     you know – that's how you know it's worth money.
     Watch. Before it rains, watch.

When external endorsements are brought into play the sources are designed to be impeccably credible and objective. Showing advertisements of identical (or at least very similar) products in newspapers and magazines is an especially favoured ploy:

SETS OF JEWELLERY
P   If you think ah'm *joking*, when I tell you the price in
     a minute you'll feel like *choking*. [Holds newspaper
     advertisement in the air] Because it *does state, quite*

clearly, in black and white in the 'Daily Mirror', it does state there, in black and white, it does say there: 'Pound crisis forces the sale of a *large quantity* of HEAVY, eighteen-carat gold-plated chain and bracelet sets.' So, in other words, if they're not *heavy*, they're not the *same* ones.

SETS OF JEWELLERY

P   [Holding up advertisement] *There's* the rope set from the 'Daily Mirror'. [Pointing at ad] *There's* the price it sells. It's ten pound ninety-five. Plus a pound post an' packing, the cheeky buggers. Ah'll make that set number *one* for *nothing*. It sells in the 'Daily Mirror' at ten ninety-five. There's a beautiful twenty-two-inch Prince of Wales chain. It's beautifully diamond cut an' finished. They sell at four ninety-five.

Individuals and organizations of high repute will also be used to endorse a product. One trader we saw selling sunglasses had what he called a 'test bench', allegedly on loan from a 'major scientific laboratory', yet to us it looked like it had been knocked together from two-by-two timber out of an odd-bin from the local hardware store. A pair of these sunglasses – 'The latest in designer summer eyewear' – was placed on this bench and one of the lenses was then bashed with a penny coin, 'just to prove that they won't shatter and so all of you cyclists don't have to worry about grit thrown from the wheels of the car in front of you.' In case this wasn't enough to convince people to buy, the trader then stood erect, paused momentarily to muster some authoritative terminology, and then continued with: 'These glasses have been subject to the most stringent possible tests – in the laboratory in Scunthorpe – and, ladies and gentlemen, I've got all the certificates to prove that they passed every test.' The most successful sale of perfumes we ever encountered involved Freddy showing people a copy of *The Royal Love Story* magazine featuring the then-not-separated Prince Charles and Lady Diana. Inside this magazine were a number of illustrated advertisements featuring the perfumes he was offering for sale. On the back was a full-page advertisement of Freddy's own jewel in the crown – Gavroche. To build the worth of his collection into an exceptional bargain he would ask various individuals in the audience to verify that he was selling the same perfumes at a much lower price than that advertised in this magazine:

P   You *don't* have to buy them from me here today, *go to any newsagent the length and breadth of this country*, go to W. H. Smith's or Menzies, and then buy it, and I know a lot of you ladies have bought it already . . .

A   What?

P   [Holds the magazine up in the air] *Buy a copy*, look, of the 'Royal Love Story' magazine, it's on sale in the newsagents at ninety-five p. [Flicks through the pages of the magazine so that people can see the pictures of Charles and Diana and the other adverts] It's all about, look, Charles and *Diana*. Look, on the back page, of every one of them, is a full-page advertisement for Gavroche perfumes, now am I right?

A   [Nods]

P   [Shows magazine to rick] And can you tell me, sir, what's the price of the perfume there? A bottle?

R   Ten pound.

P   *Ten pound.* [Shows magazine to second A] Am I right, love?

A   [Nods]

P   [Shows magazine to third A] 'Cos they do say that what doesn't speak doesn't lie, am I right?

A   [Nods]

P   *Thank you*, that's number one and I'll give you that one for *nothing*.

This strategy is based on the advertisement itself being beyond dispute. It has been published in a magazine about royalty – something certainly independent of the pitcher – and, as such, the implication is that the perfume itself has received the royal seal of approval. Also, by getting a series of people in the audience to verify the price directly from the magazine, the pitcher enhances the credibility of this external warrant. This was more than enough evidence to convince most shoppers that he hadn't simply made up the price and that he was offering them a real bargain.

We had our own suspicions that these advertisements were not genuine. Yet when we looked at the magazine closely we found that exactly the same perfume was being advertised and, moreover, the recommended prices in these ads were exactly as Freddy had claimed. This was a puzzler. Perhaps the perfume he was offering was counterfeit? When we asked him for an explanation it was pretty obvious from the way he skirted around our question that something was amiss:

'Tell us about this funkum you were doing last year. Tell us about that, about the magazine and all that.'

'Well, that was very, very clever because the people who supplied – who supply the funkum are based in [city]. Now a shop in [city street], the bottles – there's about ten different bottles to choose from. All the perfume that we sell, um – we have – with – with each order we get a brochure, a fabulous colour brochure. And in that brochure, bottles of perfume are priced higher than what we sell it for. And it says "Suggested retail price" in small print. They're priced from between – between five to ten pounds. But they *are* on sale at those prices, in one shop in [city street]. That makes it legal. Now the company that sells funkum – it's been about a long, long time has funkum, it's been about years. *We* considered it *dead* two years ago, *wouldn't touch it*; we thought it was a joke, the funkum. What they've done is packaged it *well*. It looks lovely. It's in a package, it looks *fantastic*. They're not bothered what it smells like. And also they've given us with it a fabulous colour brochure. With the advertisements showing the prices. People can't argue with it.'

And, indeed, they didn't. But when we asked him to tell us more about the magazine and, specifically, where the whole-salers from whom he bought the perfume acquired it themselves, he went silent. When we pressed him again he claimed not to know. We found out later that the perfume wasn't counterfeit. Rather, the magazine itself and the advertisements within it were an elaborate sham, manufactured to be sold as a job-lot fly pitching kit.

NAUSES

Fly pitchers inevitably attract a fair share of complaints. Freddy was not an exception:

'I can stand there, an' if I've got gold-plated jewellery, and I sell a chain at forty pence – a nice-looking chain – how many people do you think ask me, during the course of the day, "Is it gold?"'

We shrugged our shoulders and shook our heads in puzzlement.

'That's just how stup— "Is it gold?" "Are they gold?"'

'Do they *actually* ask that?'

'Yeah, an' they *believe* it too. They think it is.'

'So what do you say to them when they ask you that?'

'"Are they gold?" [Laughs] "If you want gold I can get you a shovel and you can dig for some." "Well, if *you* can't tell the difference, love, *nobody else can.*" It's as simple as that, isn't it?'

We heard many a tale showing just how quick-witted and skilful a fly pitcher can be in dealing with even the most recalcitrant of complainers – for example, the occasion when one of Freddy's customers developed an allergic reaction to the perfume he was trying to sell:

'She said, "Well, I will have to try it before I buy," so I sprayed some on her. She said: "Well, I'm going to have a little walk around to see how it wears." I wasn't bothered because I knew she would come back. She came back ten minutes later. With a rash on her arm.'

'*You're joking*?'

'*Straight up*! "Look what your perfume's done." I said: "Now *excuse me, dear*, I rather think that is a flea bite." She said: "What? *What*?" I said: "*It's a flea bite*. I've been bitten myself; look at the back of my leg." She stood for it! [laughs]'

Such repartee generally seems implausible and unconvincing. Fly pitchers often seem forced into substituting one piece of implausible 'fanny' for something equally suspect and unconvincing. This happens clearly in the following sale:

SETS OF JEWELLERY

P   Like a lady said, you'd have to be daft or drunk to walk away from them at this price, wouldn't you? Well, just watch.

N   All the gold washes off of them.

P   [To AS] *'Ave you heard that*? 'All the gold washes off them.' She can't afford gold. THEY'RE *NOT* GOLD. I didn't say they *were* gold. But all I say to you is this: this is the nearest they come. They might even be worth *more* than gold. *Watch*!

It's almost as if the old adage 'the bigger the lie, the more chance there is of getting away with it' works for the fly pitchers. Such 'lies' seem incredible in the cold light of day, but at the time they are spoken they do seem to work remarkably effectively.

Although fly pitchers undoubtedly trawl for custom along the thin line that separates overstated exaggeration from outright deception, Freddy still believed that in terms of giving people a bargain it was traders like himself – with his low overheads –

who held the moral high ground in comparison with the high-street shops:

'You go into some of these stores and all they've got going for them is fancy lighting, fancy displays, fancy salesgirls all tarted up saying "Sir this" and "Sir that". And what do you pay for all that? Fancy prices! We give people bargains, a "Thank you" and a piece of tissue paper to wrap their gear in. (. . .) I never give anybody nothing but value for money. Everything we've had — and you've seen the lot of the stock we've had — it's been value for money. There's nothing wrong with it. It's just that we've described it — legally — as a little bit more expensive, and made it sound cheap.'

He even showed us some proof to back up his conviction:

'You can work a sixty-inch pearl-type bead. It can be bought in a warehouse for fifty pence and sold on a street corner for a quid. From the same manufacturer in London, that same bead is on sale in a major high-street store at five pound ninety-nine. Who's the villain? *Who's the villain now?*'

As further support, Freddy also told us this story about a trading standards officer:

'We had an argument with a trading standards officer while we were grafting. An' he came down an' bought— we'd been selling five chains for two pound. And one of the people who'd bought this set, after a few days it'd like changed colour. The gold wears off. When you put gold plate in contact with skin it comes off. And it comes off quicker on some people. [Laughs] Sometimes it leaves a black mark round their necks!'

'The ones that don't get washed?'

'Yeah. Well they wear them in the bath and everything. They're proper nutters! So he's come down — this guy — and he says: "It's about this jewellery." And he's made his presence known. It's like, you know, I said: *"Not me!"* [Laughs] Anyway, I said to him: "What's the problem?" He says: "Well, look, somebody's bought some jewellery from you, they've taken it away, worn it, and this is what's happened, it's changed colour." So we looked at it, and it *did*, it looked schmatty. Anyway, he had a little go at us, like he does: "Where did you get it from?" And we had a receipt for it, of course. And, um, then he said: "How much did you charge?" I said: "What? *For the lot? The five pieces?* Two pound." And the TSO said: "Do you mean to tell me that I'm down here because somebody spent forty pence on a chain? That's why I've wasted a whole morning?" And he said himself: "What's up with them? *What's up with them?*"'

Of course, fly pitchers are not the only traders who use unscrupulous techniques to sell. Regular market pitchers, too, have been known to resort to such dodgy tactics, especially when trade is slow or people display more than their usual reticence to buy. But the difference between these two groups of traders is more than the result of the different type of selling conditions they face, or the lack of credibility that fly pitchers tend to suffer, or the relative propensity of fly pitchers to resort to the more dodgy techniques in order to increase sales. It is also a difference in attitude. Fly pitchers, as we have seen, tend to view their customers with utter disdain. They are not seen as people who need to be coaxed and convinced into buying goods, but as gullible, weak-willed 'sucker punters' ready for the taking, whose sole purpose in life is to provide the fly pitcher with a steady source of ready cash. Freddy:

'You say you want to know why people buy things?'

We nodded our heads.

'It's because they're *stupid. Greedy* and *stupid.*'

'And you exploit that, do you? Is that your game?'

'Yeah. *Absolutely.* Now without conscience any more. I *used* to have a conscience. Now I haven't got a conscience because for the first year or so I used to feel sorry for people.'

'Yeah?'

'And then I realized, well, if *I* don't take their money off them somebody else will. I've had people come up to me and say: "Well, lad, ah've bought them before. They're no good. But ah'll have some more." They're gonna have another go with them, like. Am I supposed to feel sorry for a person like that? For anybody in their right mind to seriously believe that they're going to get thirty pounds' worth of goods for three pounds and that the salesman is gonna— is gonna make his profit as well, there's something wrong with them. You've got to accept the fact that if they're stood in front of you there's something wrong with them in the first place. I mean, you know and I know that if it's thirty pound and the man offers it you for three pound you've saved twenty-seven pound.'

'Yeah.'

'But *they don't*, you see? 'Cos they don't think like that. Most people don't think logically. 'Cos most of them are [shakes his head in despair] — I would say ninety per cent of the people in this country you can sell them anything. *Anything*.'

This somewhat cynical view of his potential customer is equalled only by the low opinion the fly pitcher holds about the goods he sells to these people. Freddy:

'Normally we give five pieces of gold-plated jewellery, right, for three pound. Or it might be for two pound. It depends on the quality of the piece. But at the end of the day, right, the gear is *shit*. *They know* it's shit when they buy it. I mean, what do you expect when you pay forty pence for a gold-plated chain?'

'So what makes them buy it, then? Is it the spiel or what?'

'Because they can't afford gold. The spiel's part of it, but it's also because they look nice and they are nice. An' if you wear them once for going out and they're okay, what do you want for forty pence?'

Fly pitching is not the only way in which people attempt to sell goods using unscrupulous techniques. There is another, far more lucrative, complex and fraudulent way of selling to a crowd of people with a sales spiel. This routine is not so much the close cousin of fly pitching as the black sheep of the straight workers' family, and has the honour of having a special Act of Parliament passed in order to ban it. This is the 'mock auction', which we now turn to examine.

CHAPTER 8

'Going, Going . . . Con!':
the Mock Auction Sales Fraud

We were standing outside a squat shop in the north of England listening to Bald Bill the Mock Auctioneer avoiding telling us how this lucrative sales con worked.

'Nobody's ever sussed it out.'

'Ever?' we asked.

'*Never.*'

'Well,' we replied, trying to sound confident, 'we— we're going to have a try.'

Bill, of course, looked totally unimpressed with our plans. He even started to voice his scepticism:

'It's no use it being half-truths, you know. You've got to tell it right so that all the auction boys will say: "*Yes!* They're *fucking right*, what they've said." It's no use it being half-truths, d'you know what I mean?'

We certainly did. We'd already started analysing five recordings of this sales fraud and we still didn't really have the foggiest idea how the con worked. So far, we hadn't even come up with a half-truth. What made matters worse was that nobody else would or could tell us how it worked.

Most of the straight-working market pitchers we spoke to claimed to know as little as we did. All they appeared to be concerned about was making sure we didn't confuse their way of selling with the mock auction. Daft Dicky, for instance, had nothing but disdain for mock auctioneers: 'I'm totally against

196

them,' he told us, 'and I think any decent pitcher would be totally against them. They're giving us a *bad name*.'

The mock auctioneers themselves didn't mind talking to us, but they would never reveal anything of real significance. Bald Bill, at first, would only go so far as to say that 'It's high-pressure selling – with my team we psychologically pressurize them.' When we egged him on to tell us just a little more, he started making ominous noises. They were from the soundtrack of *Jaws* and signalled the presence of a shark, as well as the certain doom of at least one more unfortunate swimmer: '"Da-dum. Daaaaaa-*dum*." It's like *Jaws*,' he recalled enthu-siastically, 'it heats up as it goes along. You tickle them, *then you nab 'em*! It's a *Jaws* pitching run. *Up* the hill, then take all their *dough*. You take them on and *win. Every time*!' He thought about it all for a few moments, gave us another small clue – 'Motorized money!' – then he clammed up again.

Ralph, a retired mock auctioneer, was even more cryptic: 'The mock auction is a battle of wits where the punters are unarmed.' His wife, who used to assist him in the con, assured us that it was 'smarter than the means of a trick'.

What the mock auctioneers never failed to tell us, though, were all their outrageous tales about incidents *indirectly* ass-ociated with the con. Ralph, for instance, claimed that he was the first person in Britain to advertise this type of sale on TV ('though I didn't tell 'em it was a mock auction, of course'). When the look on our faces said we didn't believe a word of it, he produced the receipt from the television company concer-ned. A couple of minutes later he started talking about an incident that occurred during a mock auction sale in a high-street shop. Apparently, the crowd were so hyped up about the bargains he was about to offer that the floor caved in. He proudly showed us a copy of the next day's local newspaper. On the front page was a photograph of one of the injured being carried away on a stretcher at Ralph's 'One Day Sale'.

Carl, another mock auctioneer, couldn't wait to tell us about the time ('The one and only time') it had all gone wrong for him when a woman had started complaining about having been deceived:

'A right posh nause she was too. I said to her: "Madam," I said, "have you ever been unfaithful to your husband?" And she come back with: "I most certainly have not!" "*Yes you have!*" I said. "I've just fucked you in front of two hundred people.""

Bald Bill was also pretty vocal when it came to talking about his own ability as a mock auctioneer. And judging by what he told us, there was also no doubting his commitment as a salesman:

'Last summer I was working for Harry on a percentage of the bunce. I'd been out the night before, and was feeling really rough. *Rough as fuck*, y'know what I mean? I'd had an Indian and a bad pint on top. And— and— *get this*: just as I was coming to the bat – I'd nailed about twenty-five punters, and a few others were eager to punt – just as I was coming to the bat, I touched cotton.'

'*Touched what?*' we asked

'*Cotton. I shit myself*! *Followed right through*! I had no control over me arse *whatsoever*! I thought, "Sod this," so I continued with the pitch as if nothing had happened. The punters couldn't see 'cos there was a stall in front of me, but the crew copped a whiff and were spraying all over the back of my kegs with fly-killer – it was the only thing they could get hold of to deaden the stench. Anyway, I ended up having to get a taxi home. *Mind you*, I was back grafting *within the hour*!'

All these stories were very insightful, to be sure, but they told us absolutely nothing about the secrets of the con itself. We ended up having to talk to 'outsiders' to try to get the information we required – trading standards officers, journalists, and the victims themselves. We even watched all the annual exposés of these sales by the various consumer rights programmes on TV. Each of these accounts provided something that helped us in our quest to understand this type of selling, but rarely did they provide us with anything decisive. But by taking on board these different perspectives, and by comparing and contrasting them with our own analysis of the tapes we'd collected, we gradually began to fit the various pieces of this incredibly complex jigsaw puzzle together. Indeed, the more we learned about this con, and the more we showed what we had learned to the practitioners themselves, the more, in return, they ended up revealing to us. Eventually, we obtained what we believe is the first full account of how the mock auction sales fraud really works.

THE ANATOMY OF THE MOCK AUCTION

In the mock auction a salesman lulls a crowd of shoppers into buying goods at prices that are much higher than what they had been led to expect. The con, which lasts between one and two hours, consists of a preliminary phase and a main sale. In the preliminary phase, a variety of items are given away or sold at exceptionally low prices. Some of these items are offered only to those members of the auction audience who show a willingness to pay the stipulated 'bid price', yet these bidders usually do not have full knowledge of what the goods they are bidding for actually are or precisely how much they will cost. Successful bidders are allowed to participate in the main sale and are rewarded with 'treats' – substantial price reductions or extra goods provided free of charge. As the auction progresses and more expensive goods are offered, the requisite bid price rises and greater discounts are given. In the final and most expensive sale, however, the bidders, who have pre-paid for their goods in the expectation of receiving even greater 'cash and kind' re-munerations, are given no cash discounts and obtain treats that, invariably, turn out to be only cheap goods.

Successful mock auctioneers can take pretty serious money. In the UK it is usually the case that around ten to fifty people each part with between £10 and £50, sometimes more, in a single mock auction sale, and at least five auctions can be conducted daily at some sales sites. Some individual victims may also part with up to £100 in one of the special sales that are conducted at the end of these events. In the last mock auction we visited, forty people parted with £20 each, a further eight with £200, and two individuals with £1000 each.

In Britain, mock auctions were originally worked at fairs, street markets, galas and other places where crowds were to be found (such as horseracing meetings and outside factory gates). Nowadays, largely owing to the effect of the Mock Auction Act 1961 (which has the honour of making this type of sale a criminal offence without recognizing the central deceptions that take place), it is to be found in less high-profile environments such as at coastal resorts during the summer holiday season, and in one-day sales in church and village halls. Nevertheless, it is still not uncommon for mock auctions to be conducted in vacant high-street stores ('squat shops'), at racecourses, and even on street markets on a one-off ('here today, gone tomorrow') basis. In America we recorded a mock auction taking place in a 'sales theater' in the downtown area of a major city. In France, during a special one-day city market, where all the main shopping streets were closed to road traffic so that shopkeepers and market traders could sell their wares out in the open, we witnessed a version of the mock auction being conducted in a marquee about five metres away from the door to Clark's apartment.

The sale is usually conducted from a raised platform behind a long and high sales counter. A variety of goods are displayed on this counter and around the walls of the sales site to create an atmosphere closely resembling a run-down retail store that is clearing out its liquidation stock. The sale is staffed by a crew consisting of i) the mock auctioneer (the 'Top Man'), who conducts the sales; ii) someone whose task it is to attract an audience (or 'edge') at the start of the routine (an 'edge puller');

and iii) a number of assistants ('floor workers'), who are usually to be found between the sales counter and the front of the audience, moving in and out of the crowd at various points in the sale collecting money and distributing goods.

The Top Man is invariably male. Typically he appears to be both a 'regular bloke' and also someone who could turn nasty, if necessary. The edge puller is often an apprentice Top Man. Ideally, floor workers should be short in stature so that when they mingle with the audience – who remain standing for the duration of the sale – their precise location is more difficult to determine.

Insiders call the mock auction the 'Run Out' or the 'Run'. In America, it is called the 'Royal Run', a name that hints at its British origins. The term 'Run Out' does not stem, as many people believe, from the occasional need for the mock auctioneer and his crew to beat a hasty retreat from hostile victims at the end of the sale; they are more likely, in fact, to start the next sale with another group of prospective victims. Rather, it symbolizes the dramatic power and typical success of the selling techniques employed. It is a con that is often so successful that it only ends when the victims have 'run out' of money.

And this point was what had always puzzled us. In the mock auction, as with many other confidence tricks, the swindle or 'sting' is perpetrated by means of confidence-building, false representation, an appeal to greed, and a betrayal of trust. But this sales strategy differs from other cons in three important ways. First, the deception is undertaken on a group of prospective victims, *en masse*, not on isolated individuals. Second, its success doesn't seem to rely on the deceiver hiding the fact that conning may be the name of the game. Victims of traditional cons usually only realize that they have been deceived when the swindle is over and the perpetrators are well out of harm's way. Throughout the mock auction, though, the Top Man will often hint at (and sometimes even flaunt) the possibility that wrongdoing and deception may be on the agenda. Third, and perhaps most surprisingly given our previous points, this type of sale is usually conducted in an orderly and non-hostile manner; few of the victims complain directly to the auctioneer, seek immediate redress for having been deceived, or have to be 'sweetened up' or 'cooled out' after the sale has finished.

The typical routine has five basic stages:

1. 'PULLING A PITCH' (Attracting a crowd to the sale)
2. 'STEAMING UP THE EDGE' (Getting the crowd excited and in the frame of mind to take buying risks)
3. 'THE NAILER' (The first mass sale)
4. 'THE RAM' (The main sale)
5. 'END GAMES' (Where bonus sales are made)

1: PULLING A PITCH

Before the mock auction begins, an attempt is made to attract the largest possible crowd to the sales site. As with regular pitching, this is not simply because the larger the audience the greater the likelihood that mass sales will be obtained – the mock auction relies heavily on getting the audience to sell to each other, and this is made easier with a large and compacted crowd.

In 'one-off' sales – say for a single evening in a village hall – local householders will be leafleted in advance with handbills publicizing the sale. Promises are made that goods will be sold at around one-tenth to one-twentieth of their normal retail sales price. The scale of these reductions contrasts sharply with those usually found in regular high-street sales. The handbill advertises video recorders for sale at £25, and unused colour TVs (albeit 'slightly soiled') for £10. At fixed sales sites (e.g. at coastal resorts) the edge puller will attract passers-by into the shop. The methods used are again similar to regular pitching (see Chapter 1) but, in this type of sales setting, the edge puller faces even greater difficulties because people are often reluctant to make the ill-fated move from the pavement into the shop. Passers-by are invariably suspicious of such unusual sales tactics and remain 'on their guard'. Consequently, more flamboyant means usually have to be employed. In the American sale we recorded, the edge puller spread a number of dollar bills on a paste table in front of him in the doorway to the shop. As he announced the bargain offers he slowly moved the table into the store, taking his newly acquired audience with him. Sometimes women are employed as edge pullers on the grounds that passers-by are less wary of a female.

As with any pitching routine, the edge puller will explain why the goods are being sold so cheaply. Items are often described as 'bankrupt stock' or 'fire salvage'. To offset further the reservations of those who have stopped, a number of guarantees about the authenticity of the sales offers and how fairly the sale is to be conducted will also be mentioned:

EP   There's *no* point in me standing up 'ere this evening, telling you good people that *that's* a fiver [i.e. the price of a 'ghetto blaster'] – just a minute – that *that's* a fiver, if ah'm gonna charge you *twenty* pounds for it. Obviously, you'll just turn round an' say, 'Well, you told me it was a fiver', and you wouldn't buy it, and you'd be quite right in order not to do so. *Nobody* will force *anybody* to buy *anything* they *don't want*. What I'm trying to say to you is this, ladies an' gentlemen. It's as simple as this: you're under *no obligation whatsoever* in this shop. When I start this sale in a moment's time, if all you wish to purchase is an electric toaster at a pound, then you wish to go on your way, then you're quite welcome to do so. *Nobody* will force *anybody* to buy *anything* they *don't want*.

The reason the goods can be offered so cheaply, and that such guarantees can be expressed, is quite simple: these sale items are, as we shall see, never actually sold and the guarantees do not, therefore, have to be met.

2: STEAMING UP THE EDGE

When a large enough crowd has been gathered the edge puller will hand over the running of the sale to the Top Man, who then attempts to foster a sales atmosphere suggesting unparalleled generosity on the part of the organizers. This is achieved by conducting a series of mini-sales where goods are either given away free or are sold at cheap or token prices.

Plundering the edge

The Top Man begins by distributing items such as pencils, combs and packs of playing cards ('plunder') to the audience, often free of charge and, ostensibly, to break down the audience's reluctance to respond ('To wake you all up a little bit'):

TM *Right*, to make a start. 'Ere, *these're nice*. They came out of Woolworth's last night. *At half past twelve*.
AS [Small laughs]
TM *Nobody* knows they've gone *missing* yet!
AS [Small laughs]
TM What they are, they're odd packs of playing cards. There's fifty-two in a pack, an' two jokers, rather like me an' him down there [i.e. FW]. *My price*, I think you'll like. FORGET about *forty* [pence], *thirty* or *twenty*, the *first* half-dozen of you, with your arms up in the air, *anywhere* in the shop, *very quickly*, [BANG] ah'll take FIFTEEN, *who wants a pack?*
AS [Practically everyone in the crowd raises a hand]
TM *Quickly. You* do, *you* do, *you* do, *you* do, *you* do, *you* do. *Who*

else wants one? *They're nothing*! *Quickly*. Gentleman there, one over there. Can you *close in off my doorway*? Either *close in*, or *carry on walking*. DON'T BLOCK UP MY BACK PASSAGE!

The plunder is thrown fiercely into the crowd, loosely in the direction of those people who have raised their hands. These goods are often aimed at the heads of the audience – especially at those standing near the front of the sales counter. To protect themselves, many of the audience raise their arms and attempt to dodge these missiles before scrambling for the goods on the ground. By throwing the goods towards the front of the crowd, the Top Man is able to entice the audience nearer to him. If he is working from an open-fronted shop the noise and commotion this generates will, invariably, attract additional people to the sale.

The hintern and smother

This commotion is accentuated by offering to sell larger and vastly more expensive collections of goods ('lumps' or 'combos') at extremely low prices. Before doing this, the Top Man makes it clear that he is going to offer these goods only to those people who respond first. The goods are typically the stock the edge puller talked about earlier to attract passers-by to the sale, or stock that was advertised as special sale lots in the handbills:

TM With *that* clock radio, *on the top*, you get a two-band radio. With *that* lot there, you've got a personal hi-fi stereo. And to make it into a *nice line*, *there's* a pocket calculator. [BANG] Ah'll *take a* POUND, who wants *that* lot?

AS [Many hands are raised and shouts of 'Here' and 'Me' etc. to attract the Top Man's attention]

TM [To FW] Ah think they're waking up a bit now. Ah think it was a *toss-up*, between *that* gentleman there and *that* lady there. Who was first?

A   It was *me* first. [A is the 'lady', referred to above]

TM [To the 'gentleman' referred to above] You like winning,
    don't you? All right, wrap 'em up an' charge a pound. [To
    A, the 'lady'] Ah'll find you a lot. [To FW] While you're
    wrapping *those* up, 'ere, wrap *these* up. There's *two of 'em*.
    [To AS] Who smokes cigarettes in 'ere? *Who smokes?*

AS [Many hands are raised]

TM One or two of us. There's two glass ashtrays, *sets* there,
    first two of you [BANG] NOTHING. *Who wants a set?*

AS [Many hands are raised]

TM [Pointing to individuals in the audience but talking to
    FW] Give him a set. Charge 'im *nothing*. Give that
    gentleman one, charge 'im *nothing*. Wrap those up. While
    you're wrapping those up, ah'll tell you what. [To AS]
    Who, in the audience, who *didn't* get a pack of cards for
    nothing? Who *didn't* get one?

AS [Many hands are raised]

TM [Throwing packs of playing cards into the audience] *You*
    didn't, *you* didn't, over there, over there, *over* there . . .

Only some of these goods are actually sold. The hintern is so
called because the sale essentially is fictitious – it is only 'hinted'
at. The individual the Top Man appears to address and sell the
goods to, for instance, the 'gentleman' in the sequence above,
does not exist. In this sale only the cheap items – the ashtrays
and playing cards – were handed out; the most expensive items
were returned surreptitiously by the floor workers and hidden
behind the counter ('scheisted'). The audience usually remain
oblivious to what is happening and all this is down, in large
part, to the skill of the floor workers:

'When you're a floorman you haven't got to watch the
punters, you've got to watch the Man,' Johnny the Floor
Worker told us. 'When he ricks a combo [i.e. pretends to sell a
hintern lot], he'll say "slap it into the pitch", right? You then
have to try and dodge the punters – when they come one way

you go the other. But you've got to make it look as if *somebody's* getting the gear. If you're getting in difficulties he might call you back and tell you to pack it up properly. That lets you off. Then you just walk round the back with the gear – you pretend to be wrapping it up, and instead you just hide it under the counter.'

In fact, the items that are sold (goods known as 'ream') are handed over to the audience solely for the purpose of deflecting attention away from (i.e. smothering) a hintern lot as it is being replaced under the counter by a floor worker.

For the hintern to work successfully, the 'smother' lots have to provide a sufficient distraction for the audience. It helps if these goods look expensive, but they never are. They are more likely to be gaudy schlock such as glass or even plastic vases which are cut to give the appearance of being high-quality crystal. These are offered for markedly contrasting cheaper prices than the goods that have been hinted (e.g. 'nothing' versus 'a pound' in the above example).

A rapid-fire series of hintern and smother sales is usually carried out. Johnny the Floor Worker:

'You've got to do a few hinterns, of course. You've got to get moody with them. Just to get them together; to get them worked up, like. When you're winding them up you're scheisting the gear – like you've just seen us doing – and all the punters are thinking: "Oh, we're gonna get something in a moment for nowt."'

The audience jostle and compete with each other for the opportunity to purchase the goods that are apparently being sold. June, a mock auction victim, recalled that:

'At first me and my mother were both stood there, and she kept saying to me, "Get your hand up. *Go on*, get your hand up." And I was embarrassed, because what I was feeling was that everybody was gonna think: "Look at her, putting her hand up for everything", you know? *"She's bloody greedy."* But *everyone* was doing it. And in the end I moved further to the front, away from my mother. I moved to the side, and sort of, like, squeezed in between people. I was thinking that if I was closer he might notice me a little bit more. I was stood on my tip-toes – I mean, I'm tall anyway – I was stood nearer shorter people so that I could stand on my tip-toes and he could notice me more.'

The excitement and commotion which occur at this point in the sale prevent the audience from recognizing that many of the goods are not being handed over. Few would-be buyers dare look away from the Top Man to see who has been lucky enough to receive the (hinted) goods for fear of not catching his eye and thereby missing their own opportunity to receive the next (fictitious) line that will be offered.

Because the hinted goods are never going to be handed over to the audience, the Top Man can fulfil the edge puller's promise to sell the previously announced range of goods very cheaply. As such, the Top Man can indiscriminately choose any item of stock – the more expensive they look the better – and seemingly sell those goods at a ridiculously low price to hype up further the frenzy of buying excitement which occurs. The audience now typically come to believe that the sale is being conducted by someone who appears to have taken leave of both his senses and his wallet. At this point in the sale it is not by any means unheard of for fights to break out between members of the audience seeking to attract the attention of the Top Man.

Taking the gamble

The final part of this stage of the sale consists of the Top Man engineering bids for goods at a particular price, and then rewarding the first person to make a bid for reacting quickly and taking a gamble. This 'lucky' member of the audience not only wins the auction and thereby receives the goods, he or she also receives a massive reduction in cash or kind. Typically, the goods are, again, not handed over as this bidder is also fictitious. The floormen again collude in the conspiracy, but now they do so by nodding and pointing to where the non-existent bidder chosen by the Top Man would be standing. To enhance the plausibility of this deception, the Top Man may have a make-believe conversation with the chosen bidder. The audience 'hear' the non-existent bidder's responses by virtue of the Top Man talking as if he were responding to all the positive things the fictitious individual in the audience actually had said about the goods (e.g. 'What's that you said? . . . You like that? . . . Fantastic . . . That's what I like to hear').

By this stage some important principles have already been instilled into the audience. They have learned that the sale is unorthodox; that it is a series of mini-sales of unparalleled generosity; and that only a few fortunate, quick-responding individuals will be lucky enough to receive the goods being auctioned. They have also been shown that this is a sale where risk-taking pays off for the fortunate (though, so far, usually fictitious) individuals who have had the courage to take a gamble and have responded quickly to the sales offers.

3: THE NAILER

This stage – the first mass sale – prefaces the upcoming main ('ram') sale. A 'nailer' is an item of stock, such as a necklace in a box, which is offered to the audience 'blind'. The audience are asked to, and usually do, purchase these unseen goods and part with their cash (most often £1 to £10, sometimes £20) before having full knowledge of what, if anything, the boxes contain. The main incentive for participating in such a sale is that the opportunity to receive the even bigger bargains forthcoming in the main sale is made conditional on them buying one of these nailer lots.

The nailers serve a number of purposes: they help to locate

suitable individuals for the main sale (the 'ram'); they help the Top Man to separate these individuals from non-buyers and sceptics who may have a disruptive effect when the mock auction reaches its climax; they ensure that these prospective victims do not leave prior to the main sale; and, furthermore, they reaffirm the unorthodox, risk-taking, bargain-receiving nature of this type of sale.

Instead of attempting immediately to get mass sales of unseen and unspecified goods – a difficult task for anyone to accomplish – the process of nailing is managed step by step. First of all, one individual is tempted to buy the nailer. The Top Man does not reveal what is inside the box and will often state that it may, in fact, be empty. Once this person has confirmed his or her 'bid' for the possibly empty box, the box is opened, the item revealed and the bidder offered these goods at a vast reduction in price for having 'taken a gamble':

[The Top Man has secured one bid for the box]

TM [Talking to the bidder] What I'm gonna do with you, on *this* occasion, [gets a small china figurine out of the box and shows it to A and the audience] do you like that? It's a *proper* china one.

A [Nods]

TM *Is* it worth two pounds?

A [Nods]

TM *It's worth a lot more*. But because you said yes an' raised your hand (. . .) [Talks about going away on holiday and, apart from making 'a little bit of holiday spending money', not caring about making any profit] But what I'm gonna do, *there's* your figure, *there's* your two pound. On *this* occasion, *because* you're a gambling sport, I want you to pay level cash. [BANG] *Twenty pence. How's that? All right?*

A [Nods enthusiastically]

AS [Sounds of approval]

The bidder then hands over money and receives the goods. The audience have now seen someone take a gamble that has paid off in the form of the bidder receiving a very large price reduction.

Another member of the audience is next asked to bid for unseen goods, sometimes in a different and larger box. Now, however, the risk is much greater in two ways. First, the bid price is higher. Second, the bidder is asked to hand over his or her cash before receiving (and seeing) the goods to demonstrate that the bid is genuine. The Top Man holds on to the goods and the bidder's cash is returned. The price of the unseen goods is then reduced, and the same treat is offered to the rest of the audience at the same reduced price:

TM Somebody take *that* one, [another item in a box] *fourteen* [pounds], *thirteen, twelve, ten*, cost *over* fourteen quid's worth, I want *one* price for this one. *Whoever* says yes, I'll make that buyer say *bloody thank you. One* caller, [BANG] FOUR QUID.

AS [Many hands raised]

TM Lady there. *Pass* up your four quid. *Pass* up your four quid.

A [Passes up a £5 note]

TM Lady there. [TM pretends to blow his nose disdainfully on the £5 note – as if the money was of absolutely no interest to him. To A] Now, *madam, you bid* four quid on the *one.* Instead of me treating you as *one*, could I treat you all? (. . .) What I'm gonna do, I 'ave got now *twelve lots.* Instead of me charging you four quid, *like the lady's bid*, could I 'ave twelve lots out on this occasion? (. . .) So what I'm gonna do on this occasion, [hands £5 note back to A] instead of me charging *you* four quid, could I treat *twelve* buyers, [to A] and you're number one. [To AS] Could I treat *twelve buyers* to *bid* me, *not* four quid, 'ere, [stops and thinks for a moment] *bugger it, half price*, (. . .) [BANG] TWO POUND.

AS   [Hands raised]

TM   [Counts each hand individually] (. . .) Twelve buyers bid me two quid each. *Did you mean it*, yes or no?

AS   [Yesses]

TM   [To A] That didn't sound like twelve, love, *did it*?

A   [Shakes head]

TM   [To AS] DID YOU MEAN IT, *YES OR NO*?

AS   [Yesses (now more emphatic)]

TM   *Right*. Pass up your two pounds and show that the bid is genuine.

AS   [The hand-raisers pass up their £2.]

TM   [To an Asian male in the crowd who hadn't expressed an interest in the goods] *Black arse*, pass up your two quid!

By selling, at first, to only one or two willing buyers, sceptical members of the audience are provided with a more credible reference point – one from within their own ranks – as to both the desirability of making a purchase, and the trustworthiness of the seller. In addition, with these preliminary sales, the Top Man accentuates his seemingly flagrant disregard for sensible sales practice: he has now sold goods at prices lower than he could have obtained, and he has returned money to people in the audience which he could have kept.

The discrepancy

After the money for the nailer has been collected, the Top Man will mention a discrepancy that has arisen between the greater number of bidders' hands raised and the actual amount of money received. The Top Man speaks of there being people who have attempted to outwit him and obtain the goods for free ('cheating buggers'). This discrepancy is fictitious. The objective of this ploy is to instil consternation and competitiveness in the audience. The possibility that genuine bidders are being outdone by others of a more deviant inclination also puts additional pressure on would-be buyers to respond early and more emphatically. The discrepancy, as we shall see, serves an important purpose later in the nailer routine, as well as in the main ram phase of the sale.

Separating the buyers from the spyers

The final stage of nailing takes place when the Top Man separates those members of the audience who have purchased a nailer (and their friends and family) from those who have not.

Precisely how this separation is carried out depends on whether the sale is being conducted in an open or closed setting. Open sales sites, where passers-by cannot easily be prevented from joining or leaving the audience, make this type of separation difficult. At these types of venues the Top Man will send non-buyers to the back of the store and will turn off his microphone or speak less loudly so that only those people who have purchased a nailer will be able fully to hear what he is saying. If the routine is being conducted in a lock-up shop then the non-buyers ('spyers' or 'monkeys') will be told to leave, the doors or shutters being closed behind them. The Top Man will justify needing to undertake this somewhat ominous course of action by claiming that he is only trying to prevent the non-buyers from jumping onto the bargain bandwagon:

TM   Ah want my customers round me! *Come forward* if you
        spent a pound [i.e. purchased a nailer] or you're *with*
        someone that spent a pound. [The nailer buyers move
        forward] *Right*, ah'll tell you what. There's, er, twenty-
        four of you that spent a pound. Ah'll tell you what, sir, [to
        an individual who purchased a nailer] have you ever been
        to a zoo?
A   (Response audible)
TM   *Yeah?* Just turn round and have a look at the monkeys out
        there.

AS [Laughter]

TM *Ah'll tell you what, those* people are *dying* to know what you
lot've got for your pound. *In fact*, they're *more* worried
about *your* pound than *you bloody are. Ah mean it.*

AS [Laughs]

TM They're *too tight*, an' *too bloody mean*, to part with a pound.

AS [Titters]

TM But they'd *love* to know what's in that box. But ah tell you
what ah'm goin' to do to those miserable buggers. If you
haven't spent a pound, the next free show will be up the
[local tourist spot] at half past ten tonight. *Until then,
thanks* for callin' by, *call by again. Clear the back of the shop
out.* Thanks very much indeed. [The floor workers usher
the non-buyers out of the shop and pull down the shut-
ters] *Right*, ah'll tell you *why* I kicked those miserable
buggers out. For a very simple reason [turns microphone
off]. The other night I had a sale in 'ere. There were
twenty-five people who had spent a pound. (. . .) At the
back of the shop was a much bigger crowd that hadn't
spent a shilling. When I started picking up my cheap lots,
the people at the back charged forward, started grabbing
at stuff, and somebody actually finished up getting hurt.
To me one customer is better than having twenty-five
Nosey Parkers stood outside. I can now serve you people
with a *bargain*.

The individuals who are asked to leave usually do so. It is also
very rare to see any nailer purchasers leaving at this stage of the
sale or, indeed, expressing any sympathy for those individuals
who have been asked to leave.

The people who remain have the common experience of
having purchased something at this sale (or are with purchasers). As such, the potential number of non-buyers, sceptics
or onlookers who could disrupt or openly revel in the downfall
of others during the upcoming sale is significantly reduced.

The nailers are not immediately handed over to individuals who have paid for them. The Top Man gives a reason for this by referring back to the previous discrepancy and to the possibility that there are still one or two cheats in the audience.

We can now begin to see the real role of the nailer as a precursor to the main sale. The price of this item of stock is designed to be low enough to create a large response to an unusual and risky sales offer, but it is also priced high enough to 'nail' the feet of the buyers to the sales site until they do receive the goods. Johnny the Floor Worker put it this way: 'You cop their harvey and keep the nailer so they can't schmitze. They've gotta stay now, haven't they? That's how you get more poke out of them later on.' In essence, the nailer stage ensures that a large number of people who all share the same 'sucker-punting' history both remain and are primed for the main sale.

4: THE RAM

The ram is the main and most profitable part of the mock auction. Everything the Top Man has done before this point is designed to come to fruition here.

Taking a bigger risk

As in the nailer phase, and for exactly the same reasons, the Top Man starts another sale by working on specific individuals in the audience. Now, both the risks as well as the potential rewards the bidders may receive are far greater. For example, instead of asking for a bid of, say, £1 to £10, the Top Man will usually ask for £15 to £50 (sometimes £100). These individuals may, again, be asked to bid on unseen goods, or something even more vague such as 'What's on my mind', or 'What's in my other hand' (that is, the hand the Top Man has placed well inside the front pocket of his trousers):

[The top man is offering a collection of goods]
TM   Who'll bid me *fifteen* on that lot?
AS   [Many hands are raised]
TM   [To FW] Who was *first*, Walter?
FW   [Points to an individual in the audience]
TM   That lady there. Who was *second*?
AS   [Hands raised]
TM   *Right*. [Points to another individual] Ah think that gentle-
     man there. Right, if *she* can't pay, you've got it, Stripes.
AS   [Small laughter regarding A, the gentleman with a striped
     sweater, being referred to as 'Stripes']
TM   [Pointing to other hand-raisers] If *he* can't pay ah saw *your*
     arm, *your* arm, *your* arm an' *your* arm. Sir, [i.e. to 'Stripes']
     you were second, ah'd like you to go away with some-
     thing. Are you a gambler?
A   Yeah.
TM   Yeah? Ah'll tell you what. Will you bid me fifteen pounds
     for what's on my mind an' leave the rest to me?
A   Yes.
TM   Is that a *genuine* bid? *Can you pay?*
A   Yes.
TM   Right, if *he* can't, *who would*?
AS   [Small number of audience members (approx. 5–7) put
     hands in the air]
TM   *Right*. [Points to another hand-raiser] If *he* can't, *you've*
     got it, sir. *Okay*? But ah think he can, though. [To FW]
     Walter, we've had *two* bids now at *fifteen*. Ah want you to
     go round, to those two customers, an' ask them, if their
     bids are genuine bids, to tend me up the cash. [A floor
     worker collects the money]

This higher risk at a higher price is used to preface the higher
risk and the higher price that will be required from those
audience members who bid for the items in the imminent ram
sale. It is also used to get the audience to display the more

substantial sum of money needed (i.e. around £15 to £50) – a procedure that is a small but significant step along the road to getting them actually to part with it.

This type of sale is not resolved immediately. Before taking any money from these individuals, the Top Man moves on to describe the goods that will be offered in the main sale. At this point all the audience have at stake is the money most of them have given for the nailer (which has not yet been handed over), although a couple of individuals have given up substantially larger sums of money for items in the above sale.

Describing the goods

A selection of goods is offered for sale (such as watches, jewellery, car stereos, clock radios, rings, china, crystal glassware, cutlery, carving sets, compact disk players, videos and computer game consoles). Offering a choice enhances the possibility that more people will bid for, and be seen by others in the audience to bid for, at least one of those goods in the collection. The Top Man builds these goods into bargains largely by using the same techniques as straight-working market pitchers use – contrasts, three-part lists, etc. (see Chapter 2). Only after having done this are the previous bidders dealt with.

Resolving the risk

The money obtained from the previous bidders is now returned. However, these bidders receive plunder items and, given that they are handed over free or for a nominal charge, these are accepted with exceptional enthusiasm. Along with the rest of the audience, these bidders seem willing to overlook the fact that their bids were originally for other items of stock:

TM Sir, you sent me up fifteen pounds for what's on my mind. Where're you from, sir?

A Nottingham.

TM [Lines omitted regarding the alleged sexual proclivities of women in Nottingham] Firstly, Mr Nottingham, if my mind is empty, who does your money belong to?

A Me.

TM *NO.* It belongs to *me*, don't it? If my mind's empty *it belongs to me*, an' ah *can't think of a bloody thing.* [Laughs]

AS [Nervous laughter]

TM Give 'im a fiver change. [FW moves in the direction of A]

TM He's nearly fainted there. *I'm only joking* (. . .) Take your cash back, *take it back.* [Hands back £15 to A] You can 'ave as many lots as you like this after— this evening 'cos you're a sport an' ah like that. What's on my mind are two articles, there's something for yourself an' something for your home, but they're *not* on my mind at *fifteen pounds*, they're on my mind at *fifteen pence*. Will you pay me fifteen pence?

A Yeah. [TM hands over two plunder items]

The delay in dealing with these bidders is meant to play upon any remaining fears the audience may have about the trust-worthiness of the seller. By now the audience should be think-ing along the lines of 'Is this higher risk not going to pay off as the previous risks taken did?' (i.e. in the hintern and smother phase). By not immediately handing back the risk-takers' money, these suspicions are enhanced, a procedure that makes their eventual subversion seem even more dramatic. The audi-ence have now been given more proof to convince them that they can trust the Top Man after all. This makes it somewhat easier for the Top Man to obtain mass purchases, because other people in the audience are now much more likely to take such a gamble themselves. Yet the gamble they are about to take will not pay off in the way they are likely to have anticipated.

Working on the first ram bidder

The Top Man now returns to describing the selection of goods on offer, and asks for bids on these goods. But instead of asking these bidders to pay for the goods immediately, the Top Man again addresses only one of the bidders (another presumed 'divvy'). He asks, first of all, if the bid was 'genuine'; secondly, if the bidder 'can pay'; and finally, what item the bidder has 'chosen'. The item of stock selected is then placed on the sales counter. The Top Man goes on to state that this bidder will be treated further. But one important caveat is added: he asks the bidder to state whether or not they would be happy if they handed over their cash for the goods and there was no additional discount given. In all the mock auctions we observed, the bidders stated at this point that they would be happy. This is an important admission because it paves the way for the main con – it implies that the bidders have nobody to blame but themselves if the gamble does not pay off.

The Top Man then states that *he* would *not* be happy if there was no additional discount given; rather, he promises to 'treat' the bidder 'further'. The cash the bidder has handed over to demonstrate that the bid is genuine is now returned. The phrase to 'treat further' and the handing back of the bidder's cash are designed to suggest strongly that the bid price, or at least a substantial portion of it, will be returned to the bidders for having taken the gamble. Given the previous sales that have occurred, as the risk has now been increased (price-wise) the rewards may also be anticipated to be greater.

Obtaining mass bids

The other members of the audience who have expressed an interest in the goods and have made a bid by raising their hands are now individually asked the same three questions. No mention is made of having to pay for these goods. In each case the Top Man states that he will 'treat' the bidder 'further'.

The miscount

As a pretext for getting those people in the audience who have expressed an interest in the goods to *display their bid money*, another discrepancy is raised, now between the number of goods set aside and the larger number of people who have bid for these goods. This discrepancy is effected by the Top Man either counting some hands twice or inventing fictitious hands. The bidders are asked to get out their cash and hold it up in the air to prove that they are genuine and, as such, can pay for the goods.

To get these bidders to *part with their cash* the Top Man announces that his sales staff have become confused. Although the goods apparently are ready to be handed over to the bidders, a floor worker will state that he has not been paying attention and does not know which particular individuals are supposed to receive which particular goods. The fact that a variety of different goods have been offered for sale gives credence to this confusion. In response, the Top Man requests the bidders, again, to show their money to indicate that they are genuine bidders. While each bidder is being addressed individually (with 'If I treat you further, will you say thank you?'), the floor worker goes round collecting their money.

The ram

In comparison with the elaborate build-up, the ram itself is a model of simplicity. The goods are handed over and little else happens apart from the Top Man reaffirming that 'if he has promised nothing then he owes nothing'.

Only after the ram goods have been passed out are the nailer items finally handed over. If a very proficient Top Man is working, he will hand over the nailers in such a way as to create suspicion among the audience that these items may, in fact, be the only treat they will receive:

220

TM I've now been round to *each one* of my customers, I've
    told you the price on the goods, I've said that there's
    nothing with them, *no* discount, you're happy, you've *told*
    me you're happy, the money's in the till. By the laws of the
    land, if I've promised you nothing, [BANG] *what* do I
    owe you?

AS [Shouts of 'Nothing']

TM I do owe you something, I'm very sorry, I forgot all about
    it. (. . .) I owe you what's inside this box, *don't I*? Your
    pound box [i.e. the nailer]. Ah'd better do that next. Ah'll
    tell you what, though, *what* did I say was inside 'ere for
    your pound?

AS [Responses of 'nothing']

TM *Nothing.* Ah said it was *empty*, didn't ah? An' if I said it was
    empty, what are you all legally entitled to?

AS [Responses of 'nothing']

TM *Nothing.* An' if you *got* nothing, what would you say?

AS [Responses of 'nothing']

TM *Ah bet you bloody would!*

AS [Laughs]

TM [Looks inside box] (. . .) *No.* What's inside actually —
    shushhh – comes out of a jeweller's shop, it came out at half
    past twelve last night. *I* threw the brick an' *Walter* [i.e. a
    FW] ran like bloody 'ell.

AS [Laughs]

TM An' when you get these, *don't* tell people where you got
    them from, *otherwise* you'll do the days an' I'll do the
    bloody nights.

Delivering the treat or 'topments'

The nailer isn't the only treat the ram purchasers receive. What
they also get, though, is not the massive reduction in price they
expect but, rather, extra goods free of charge on top of what
has already been bought ('topments'). Like the nailers, the

topments are wrapped up in order to conceal their identity and, in particular, their cheapness. As a means of claiming that the goods are high-value, the Top Man will allude to the possibility that they have been obtained illegally (e.g. 'Put it in your pocket, don't show anyone what it is. If a man in a blue uniform [i.e. a policeman] asks you where you've got that, you've found it, you didn't get it off me.').

5: END GAMES

An optional part of the mock auction, used after the ram sale has successfully been conducted and when some of the victims have remained at the sales site to see if any further bargains will be offered, is for the Top Man to sell more goods to members of the audience on a one-to-one basis. Here, individual victims can be 'bled dry' – that is, taken for all the money they have got or, if they have credit cards in their possession, are willing to part with. One such sale is the 'MOT' ('Money on Top'), where the victims buy goods and also receive their bid money back from the Top Man, although they still make a loss on the sale. Ralph recalled what he used to say during the 1960s when he had got somebody to bid £10 for a canteen of cutlery:

"'You've bid me ten pounds. I'll tell you what I'll do, love, gimme your ten-pound note." You take her ten-pound note, you open the canteen, you put the ten pound in and shut the lid with the ten pound hanging out. You say: "Madam, your ten pound in cash, and the canteen at twenty-seven pound is worth— how much is that?" She says: "Thirty-seven pounds." You say: "Right, you've got thirty-seven pounds of commercial value there, including the money, bid me twenty pound for the lot, money as well." She says: "Ah'll have it." You're selling her her own tenner back, but you're copping twenty quid.'"

The victims of the MOT effectively buy their own money back. The success of this con rests on the confusion-inducing speed at which the sale is conducted and the buyers not realizing (at least until well after the goods have been purchased) that they have helped create the exceptional bargain offered by contributing their own money.

Today, it is not unusual for Top Men to take between £50 and £1000 from individual customers at this stage in the sale. This can be quite a profitable activity.

This type of 'end game' selling calls for even more finesse and courage than usual. We heard many tales of the exceptional skill needed to get people to part with their cash under these difficult circumstances. So entranced will these people be by the prospect of receiving even more 'bargains' that, sometimes, it can pay the Top Man to foster the impression that the one or two individuals who are participating in an end game are part of a much larger crowd of willing buyers. Gentleman John, the straight worker, told us about the occasion when he witnessed one such individual being worked on by a mock auctioneer:

'I have seen one of the most incredible – one of the best, if not *the* best run-out worker – a kid named Richie Barnes. I watched him once at this fair in the south of England. He was stood three stalls away from me, pitching a bit of a run-out pitch. And the only guy— there was only one man in front of the stall other than the four of us [i.e. other pitchers]. Richie Barnes had this bloke hypnotized. He kept saying: "No. Not you, sir." And I watched him take fifty-odd quid off this bloke, right? This was years ago, remember. If this bloke had ever turned round and realized he was on his own I don't know *what* would have happened! But he was so spellbound this guy. Richie was going: "No! Not you, sir, the gentleman here was first", and all this. And the guy kept popping up his money. I don't know how we kept a straight face, but Richie was like that. He was a marvellous run-out worker but he worked off imaginary people.'

DECEPTION AND THE MOCK AUCTION

One way of trying to understand why the mock auction is so successful would be to study the victims and search for reasons to explain why they take part in this type of sale and also why they tend not to complain when deceived. We might find that such people have an abnormal penchant for taking risks; that they possess more money than they have sense; that they have an abnormally greedy or an unusually gullible disposition; or that their lack of confidence or puny physical stature renders them incapable of pursuing redress over the economic injustices perpetrated against them. But explanations like this tell us nothing about the amount of effort and the special techniques that the Top Men and their associates employ to manage a successful deception, regardless of who gathers at the sale or actually becomes a victim of this con.

In some ways the success of the mock auction stems from the Top Men deploying the same selling techniques as are used in more legitimate sales situations. Their special methods for attracting people to the sales site, price contrasts to generate apparent bargains, supportive explanations to account for the lower-than-normal prices of the goods, capitalizing on the imitative basis of buyers' actions to obtain additional sales, obtaining preliminary commitments to buy from prospective customers, using individual opinion-formers at strategic moments during the sale – all are techniques we have documented already (see Chapters 1 to 5).

But the mock auction is also a highly unusual shopping scenario, and many of the techniques that the Top Men bring into play contrast sharply with those deployed by pitchers and other types of salespeople. For instance, most shoppers are not in the habit of receiving free goods and additional treats, bidding for unseen items, handing over money without knowing precisely what they are buying and what (if anything) will be the required payment. Nor are they likely to have had much experience of being physically separated from non-buyers and locked in a store until they have made their purchases.

On the one hand, this unorthodox character of the mock auction is perhaps the main reason why at the beginning of the sale most of the audience, who are likely to be encountering this form of selling for the first (and, one presumes, the last) time, act as if they are particularly wary about being deceived and pressurized to buy. But, on the other hand, it is the sale's very unusual nature which also enables the Top Men both to convince them to participate in such a sale and not to complain.

Much of the success of the mock auction rests on the fact that the audience is unfamiliar with, and certainly not immediately able to see through, elements in the routine that are designed deliberately to mislead, such as the hintern and smother, addressing non-existent members of the audience, creating a false discrepancy between bidders and buyers, and getting individuals to purchase their own money.

The length of time it takes to conduct a mock auction also makes it difficult for the audience to comprehend exactly what is going on. A single sale often lasts for between one and two hours, and the many twists and turns that a typical routine takes are an essential part of the deception. There are over fifteen key activities that must be employed for the deception to stand a good chance of being successful and for the sale to be orderly. But these stages do not follow each other in a way that would enable the audience easily to figure out the underlying pattern or the 'hidden agenda' of the routine. The key activities are hidden within other types of dialogue, such as establishing rapport, telling jokes, expressing philosophies of life, etc. These seemingly off-the-point ramblings make the mock auction difficult to understand without some form of insider knowledge; this perhaps explains why many of the accounts of the mock auction by journalists and TV consumer rights programmes are ill-informed and inaccurate. To the uninitiated the selling process has the appearance of being haphazard and chaotic when, in fact, it is exactly the opposite. All this confusion and chaos is more than likely to have been planned well in advance. As Ralph told us:

'If you don't know how the run's done you can't work it out, no matter how long you stand in the audience writing the spiel down. That's why the law can't do 'em. To prosecute you they've got to know where the conspiracy occurs, *but they don't!*'

Indeed, rogue workers who have learned the mock auction by covertly recording the routine (rather than serving an 'apprenticeship' with actual crews) are able to obtain only an onlooker's view of what is going on. In failing to appreciate crucial features, their profits suffer and the prospect of receiving complaints and physical violence from those they have deceived is dramatically enhanced. When we asked Bald Bill if it ever goes wrong, he said:

'Of course it does! By bad workers. Not by professionals. *By bad workers only.* Not by people like us. If you're like me, and have a sense of moral and intrinsic value, you try to give them the best value that you think is possible. But if people – *mugs* – come into it thinking it's an easy game, an' take the piss out of every punter, then— [gesticulates a castration] We don't want them in the game.'

The relatively rigid nature of the seller's patter also makes the routines conducted by different sellers all sound the same:

'Well, every run-out worker has their own sense of style, y'know,' Ralph told us. 'The run is a piece of poetry, right? You've got to remember it like you would a poem, see. But each grafter that works it has his own interpretation of it. But the *method*, it's the same from A to Z – it's the same right through.'

This sense of sameness can also create particular confusions for outsiders. For instance, one trading standards officer we interviewed thought (incorrectly) that a 'Mr Big' had written the script for this con and was controlling all the mock auction operations in the UK. One of the victims we interviewed listened to one of the routines we had recorded (not the one she had heard, nor one worked by the same sales crew); she was convinced that the person she was listening to was the one who had conned her.

Moreover, the unusual nature of the mock auction is what enables the Top Men actually to bring into play these deceptions and other activities that are central to the success of the con. The Top Men create a particular (and no doubt peculiar) sales world, complete with its own unorthodox rules and standards of conduct, propriety and morality. Because most of the audience are unfamiliar with this type of scenario, the Top Man has, fortuitously, to act as a guide and advise his 'pupils' of the appropriate behaviour at each point where the audience encounter an unfamiliar situation. In this way the victims effectively learn to be deceived.

For instance, from the very beginning of the sale the audience's understanding of what is likely to happen next is drawn mainly from observing or taking part in all the unusual preliminary sales that take place and observing their outcomes on others. The various repetitive elements of the routine – the variety of treat-receiving, price-reducing preliminary sales which are conducted, and the discrepancies between the number of bidders compared to 'genuine' buyers – provide precedents for understanding what occurs and for the audience to predict what is likely to happen in the main sale.

Of course, to add credibility to the con, the Top Men and their aides also work as a team. Throughout the routine, and particularly at those points where the veneer that protects the Top Man's portrayal of the sale as a legitimate one becomes very thin and fragile (such as during the hintern and smother phase), the auction crew collude to project a shared, and thus more persuasive, definition of the sale as being a bona fide one.

As we have seen, the 'treat' in the ram phase is the principal deception of the mock auction. Its success, however, relies upon a variety of earlier deceptions (e.g. misrepresentation, misrecognition, sleight of hand, duplicity, and illusion). All of these play a crucial role in paving the way for the central deception – the ram sale. In the ram an ambiguity is generated. The actual treat in store for buyers is never fully specified. It is only suggested. More accurately, the audience, armed with the precedents created by the prior deceptions and the preliminary sales, wrongly put 'two and two together to make five' by thinking they will receive a substantial treat in either cash or kind. But the Top Men cleverly avoid making an explicit link between the treats given in the early sales and the treat promised in the main sale. This makes it more difficult for them to be held accountable for having deceived anyone. The deception is accomplished by the Top Men creating confusion over who is responsible for this ambiguity that has arisen. The victims are caught in an interpretive 'twilight zone', and most often act as if it is their own fault for misreading the ambiguity that emerges.

When a mock auction is coming to its end, some of the people who have bought the goods do seem to recognize that they have, in some sense, been deceived. June told us:

'When they were bringing things out at the time [i.e. the ram sale items], my mother said to me – she started laughing – she said, "Well, I think we've been done, you know?" And I said, "Yeah." But we were laughing, because we were getting just what we paid for. We were under the impression that he was going to put other things with each lot, like he had with the television [part of a hintern lot].'

Although some of these victims do seek redress – though most often at some later date, and with outside authority figures such as the police and trading standards officers – the deception is managed recurrently in an orderly and non-violent fashion. The fact that the revenue obtained by this con derives from the sellers taking a relatively small amount of money from many victims rather than a large amount from a few plays some part in keeping the audience quiet. In this way the Top Men make it far easier for the victims to rationalize their loss by convincing themselves that it was not significant after all.

Nevertheless, the Top Men and their crews conduct the sale in such a way as to minimize the likelihood of receiving customer complaints and physical hostility. These particular strategies are designed to ensure that the victims' losses are reviewed in private contemplation, rather than by recourse to either public or official complaint. For example, the Top Men define the sale as a kind of entertainment among thieves, with the implication that by the end of the con, and by purchasing the goods, their audience have become criminally complicit.

Throughout the mock auction, as we have seen, the Top Men also imply that they are dodgy characters who often engage in wrongdoing such as receiving stolen goods. Factors such as the audience's apparent greed and their eagerness to take advantage of a salesman who appears to have lost all his faculties of economic reasoning seem to divest the audience of the moral authority needed to complain. In this respect the victims become accomplices in their own deception and ultimate quietude.

Furthermore, by obtaining affirmations from each buyer that they are satisfied with the terms and conditions of the main sale, the Top Men make it harder for the victims to complain when the (unspecified) treat does not live up to their expectations. These affirmations serve to 'cool out' the audience before the con is finally hammered home. It primes them and then obliges them to treat the final sale as a gamble that did not pay off rather than as a deception.

The Top Men also take great pains to ensure that the various groups of people that comprise an audience (individuals, friends, families, etc.) remain isolated and estranged from one another in order to minimize the chances of them ganging up on him with their grievances. The principal means by which the Top Man achieves this is by separating the nailer buyers from the non-buying 'sceptics' just before the start of the main sale. But, as we have seen, the Top Men also foster competitiveness between members of the audience throughout these sales. This makes it more difficult for individuals suddenly to become allies and to develop any fellow feelings for each other at the point where their complaints would be most appropriate.

Most victims of cons do not wish to acknowledge publicly that they have been deceived. They are generally treated unsympathetically by their peers, and their misfortune is often quietly held by others to be indicative of embarrassing personal deficiencies such as greediness and gullibility. For instance, one victim who had bought a faulty watch at a mock auction was continually asked for the correct time by friends and colleagues at work who had learned of her misfortune. These victims tend, therefore, to rationalize their predicament and, in an attempt to maintain or restore their self-esteem, will privatize the event, treating it as something that, although unfortunate, can nevertheless be shrugged off and 'put down to experience'.

CHAPTER 9

Street Entertainers and Urban Hustlers

The noise that woke us would be immediately familiar to any British football fan – the repeated honking of an ear-piercing klaxon horn. But it sounded totally out of place here on the hot sands of Venice Beach, Los Angeles. This was *Baywatch* country, famous for its film stars, muscle-heads, 'beautiful people', and the hordes of odd-ball characters who had already provided us with plenty of fun for free.

The noise – and by now it was incessant – was coming from along the boardwalk behind us. Yet from where we were lounging there wasn't a single football fan in sight. We looked again. The owner of the airhorn was a smaller and more manic version of Eddie Murphy wearing a stetson hat. He was zig-zagging across the boardwalk, airhorn high above his head, behaving like a real nutcase.

To add to his din he started shouting to anyone and everyone in earshot willing to listen: *'Folks, ah've got jokes. Come an' get 'em!* Don't wait to see me on Johnny Carson, *COME ON DOWN AND SEE ME LIVE!'*

We were wide awake by now and set off to catch a piece of the action. As we got nearer we noticed a young girl brazenly walking right past him, avoiding his eyes as if he weren't there. But he *was* there. *'OH SURE*, I know what *she's* saying,' he shouted, trying to make sure that such an event didn't happen again. *'"HEY, let's ignore the comedian. MAYBE HE'LL GO AWAY."* Never happens. *Never happens.'*

He started pointing at two women walking right in front of us. 'Come right down to the front,' he shouted, frantically waving his finger at the ground ahead of him. 'You see this lump down here?'

The two women nodded.

'This is front-row seats, no waiting.' He stepped back a pace or two to make it easier for them to move closer. 'You see,' he added, 'I work from back here.'

The women took their places on their imaginary seats. We sidled in behind them. This scenario was already looking very familiar to us – the 'comedian' was building an edge, exactly as we had seen the market pitchers do. The video camera we'd brought along from the university was put to work.

'Come on, come on, *come on, come on.*' He was pointing out every passer-by to get them to stop and watch his show. *'Miss!* Come on, come on, *come on, come on.* Okay, come on, sir, put that bike down.' He sounded his horn again. *'Y'all better come on.* We've started.'

As a result of all this effort he'd gathered about twenty-five people around him. One man, hugging the shadows behind us, was obviously standing too far away. The comedian waved him closer:

'Sir, come on.'

The man didn't move so the comedian tried again: *'Come on.* I'm not gonna stab you. *Come on.* What's your name?'

It was Tony but his response was almost inaudible.

'Are you nervous?' the comedian asked.

'No,' he answered, but he was.

'Sure?'

'Yeah.'

'You're standing way back. It's like: *"Black comedian, maybe he'll stab him!"* AAAAAAARGH,' he screamed, *'AAAA AAARGH!',* and he ran off along the boardwalk doing his madman impression again. When he'd composed himself he returned to apologize to what, by now, was beginning to look like a proper crowd: 'Sorry. Excuse me. I went off to Mars there for a moment.' He took off his stetson, wiped his forehead, and finally introduced his show:

'Now, folks, I don't know whether you're anything like me. You've probably got *places to go* an' *people to do*. So I'm not going to hold you long, okay? *Five minutes* of comedy then I'll send you on your merry way. Now watch how we start this thing out. The first joke's gonna be very cutesy-cutesy, then they'll slowly get *more* and *more risqué*. BUT I *SWEAR*, they'll never get dirty – trust me, ma'am, I've got a PhD in comedy. I know what I'm talking about, *okay?*'

His choice of the word 'slowly' to describe the development of the jokes was an accurate one – we were still standing there, with the rest of the crowd, over twenty minutes later. His claim that he had a PhD in comedy, however, was not strictly accurate. This Eddie Murphy look-alike certainly told jokes. And there was also no doubting his ability to get the crowd to laugh; some of them laughed so much they looked like a game-show audience. But the truth is he was not really a comedian and the fun he'd provided was not for free. In fact, he was selling his jokes and what we had seen was a sophisticated sales routine. When we recorded his second performance, from another camera position, what he said was almost a word-for-word repetition of his first show. In this second show, which lasted for twenty-four minutes, there were seven jokes. These jokes took only six and a half minutes to tell and, as such, they accounted for less than a quarter of his show. Almost all the rest of the time was spent building and maintaining a crowd and then obliging people to make a contribution for having watched his performance. This 'comedian' was not so much a street entertainer as a patter merchant using humour as a means of persuading people to part with their money. What is more, he was employing almost the exact same rhetorical and inter-actional skills as market pitchers use to sell their goods. If he had a doctorate in anything, it must have been in sales rhetoric and crowd management. After all, he even managed to get ten bucks out of us.

STREET ENTERTAINERS AND MARKET LURKERS

Most street entertainers behave totally differently to the comedian we recorded on Venice Beach. The vast majority are similar to market lurkers in that they do not rely upon an elaborate verbal sales patter to persuade passers-by to stop, watch their performance and then make a contribution at the end of the show. Of course, some of these entertainers – like the Charlie Chaplin impersonator we saw outside the Forum des Halles in Paris, the mime troupe in London, the robotic duet in Brighton, and the human statue in Brittany – are prevented from saying anything by virtue of the type of (silent) entertainment they provide. Many others, such as buskers, jugglers, fire-eaters and the like, however, rarely make eye contact with, let alone talk to, passers-by. Only a few design their entertainment around a structured verbal routine that involves explicitly selling their performance to bystanders. Without this routine, the performance alone is what is being relied upon to attract the interest of and contributions from passers-by. In effect, an upturned hat, sitting apologetically on the ground in front of them, is left to say it all.

By working from the assumption that their 'goods' will sell themselves, street entertainers of this type rely inordinately on finding a venue where there is plenty of pedestrian traffic. There is often so much competition for the most popular pitches that at some prime sites time-slots are allocated between performers. At the Piazza complex in Covent Garden, London, auditions are even held before permission is given to perform.

Lurking a performance rarely seems to be as economically successful as pitching a performance. We have seen street entertainers accomplishing the most spectacular feats of juggling, break-dancing, fire-eating and musicianship in front of small, disorganized and soft-edged crowds. On other occasions we have seen street entertainers performing in front of massive crowds but, because they rely on their performance alone to do their persuading for them, the proportion of people who end up making a contribution was, almost invariably, a small one.

This is not to say that these entertainers do not ever utilize sales ploys to increase their earning power. One tactic is to provide people with the type of entertainment appropriate to the venue. The string quartet we saw playing outside the Royal Festival Hall in London, for example, had obviously chosen their location carefully and targeted their music to suit the likely preferences of passers-by on their way to a classical concert at the nearby South Bank centre.

A hat with a little money already in it – showing that other people have previously deemed the performance as worthy of a contribution – is widely recognized as being more likely to attract additional money than when the performance is conducted from behind an empty hat. A cute puppy (and, on one occasion, a rabbit) asleep next to the hat usually obtains a higher proportion of extra contributions from adults who have children with them. A shrewd street entertainer will also ensure that most of the coinage in the hat is silver rather than copper, thus hinting at the level of appreciation felt by others and, more importantly, at the appropriate size of future contributions. Placing an already part-filled hat some distance from where the performance is being conducted ('Though not *too far* away. It might get nicked') makes it easier to obtain contributions, because people can maintain a safe distance between themselves and the entertainer. They also do not have to intrude into the performance area.

Revenue can also be increased by employing an assistant to go round the audience with the hat rather than leaving it on the ground. One member of a violin-cello duet we talked to, who worked in London, claimed that she collected four times as much money when someone solicited contributions in this way. The importance of this strategy was highlighted by the fact that the assistant received an equal share of the takings. This assistant told us that she went round the crowd surreptitiously and, whenever possible, she would try to sneak up on people on their 'blind side'. Because of their surprise and embarrassment at being caught out watching for free, such people were less able to refuse a contribution.

Some entertainers who recognize the difficulties involved in attracting the attention of and obtaining money from passers-by may seek to work in locations where they can guarantee having, quite literally, a captive audience. This was the case for the buskers we saw performing next to London theatre queues, and the groups of musicians working the tube trains on the London Underground and the Métro trains on the Chatillon–St Denis line in Paris. In the latter cases the musicians had an audience who were, in effect, trapped in the carriage between stations. As such, the passengers were obliged to remain for the full (albeit brief) show – even if they occasionally tried to make it obvious that they were not listening to the music by, for example, burying their heads in a book, or falling asleep. The chances of such performers obtaining a contribution is enhanced, not only because there are likely to be more people listening to the performance than they could have attracted elsewhere, but also because the onus is now on the passengers to refuse to make a contribution when the hat is thrust under their noses. The Parisian Métro buskers – an accordion troupe – would assist the hat-holder at this point by playing the popular but ominous theme tune from *The Godfather* film.

All these strategies, even when they work well, are a world away from the level of success obtained and the techniques employed by street entertainers who use a more elaborate sales spiel to persuade people to buy their performance.

PITCHING STREET ENTERTAINERS

Most of the street entertainers who made a special verbal effort to sell their performance employed the same kinds of rhetorical skills as market pitchers. The similarities between these two types of enterprise were most apparent in the process of attracting and building an audience.

Building an edge

The first step in persuading passers-by to stop is almost always a version of the 'pull-up' (see Chapter 1). The entertainer makes a noise to announce his or her presence (such as sounding a klaxon horn). Then, while briefly announcing what the performance will consist of (e.g. 'Folks, ah've got jokes'), the entertainer will attempt to persuade a succession of individuals to stop and watch. The Venice Beach comedian gave those people who did stop two incentives to stay. First of all, he stated that his show was only going to be a short one ('Five minutes of comedy then I'll send you on your merry way') and, secondly, he implied that his show would get better the longer people stayed ('The first joke's gonna be very cutesy-cutesy, then they'll slowly get more and more risqué').

A pair of skateboarders, working further along the Venice Beach boardwalk, attracted people by performing a particularly impressive acrobatic feat. Standing on their skateboards, they would casually flip them over with their toes and, in the same movement, end up balancing precariously on the board's edge. This feat alone was enough to differentiate them from other skateboarders nearby who were using their boards only for their own enjoyment or as a means of transport rather than as a vehicle for making money. To stimulate people's curiosity, the skateboarders would occasionally (and deliberately) fail to pull off this trick, thereby making it seem even harder to accomplish and, hence, all the more impressive when they actually succeeded. After a few attempts, one or two people would gather to watch and, soon, a crowd would start to form. A ghetto blaster was then turned on to signal the start of their full dancing show.

The next step is often to use those people who have stopped to attract a bigger crowd to their show. Unlike market pitchers, who attempt to do this by getting people to laugh and raise their hands in unison, these street entertainers usually aim to get a more appropriate form of collective response – applause. The Venice Beach comedian used a 'cute/cheap trick' to do this:

SE Now we're gonna start off by doing a cute trick, okay? (. . .) [Brief chat with T. Pinch – the camera operator – about whether he is ever going to put a contribution into the comedian's bowl] (. . .) Okay, when I get to 'three', I would like *everybody* in my audience to *APPLAUD, SHOUT*, and *CHEER*, as *loud as you possibly can*. Like I said, ma'am, it's a *cheap trick*, but it *always works*. People come from everywhere, they say: '*What the hell is going on over here?*' You know what I'm saying?

AS [Laughs]

SE Now remember, folks, there's only two rules to this. Number one, I don't want to hear none of this 'Yeaaaaaaah' [i.e. half-hearted clapping and responsiveness] *shit*!

AS [Laughs]

SE No, no, I want you to be *enthusiastic*, to *come from your heart*, and make me *proud of you*. And *secondly*, if I see anybody in my audience that's *not* participating, I will come into the crowd and *stab your ass*!

AS [Laughs]

SE *Okay*? All right? Here we go, on 'three', *everybody* a loud shout, a cheer, a joyous roar and watch folks come running from miles around. This shit'll work. Are you going to help me, sir?

A   *Yes, sir*.

SE You really like that stuff, huh? [i.e. apparently feeling himself in his trouser pocket].

A   [Smiles]

AS [Laughs]

SE Okay. Okay. Here we go. On three. *One, two* – don't let me down. Make me proud of you – *THREE!*

AS [Loud applause, cheers and other noises of approval]

Cheap or not, the trick worked. The comedian soon had about sixty people around him, most of whom seemed to have joined the crowd solely to find out what all the noise was about.

A particularly enterprising juggler (studied by the sociologists Mike Mulkay and Gerard Howe), performing in the heart of an English mediaeval city centre, used exactly the same ploy:

SE [Talking to the people who have already gathered around him] We are going to do these people [i.e. passers-by] a favour. We're going to bring them down here by using a tiny show business trick, which is *me* bending down low so the people behind cannot see what is happening. I count to three. On the count of three everybody standing here *bursts* into spontaneous applause . . .

AS [Laughter]

SE . . . for absolutely no reason at all. Not only that, the men shout 'more, more' . . .

AS [Laughter]

SE . . . women throw their children into the air . . .

AS [Laughter]

SE . . . everybody gets absolutely crazy. And you watch, it's really funny, you watch 'em come running down the high street and running up the back here. So here we go.

AS [Start applauding]

It may not be a coincidence that both the comedian and the juggler made it difficult for passers-by to see why people were applauding. Both crouched down on the ground while they were being applauded. Mulkay and Howe mention that the juggler even joined the audience while they were still applauding him and started clapping himself. This accentuated the curiosity of passers-by to find out what was happening. As we have seen, fly pitchers, who often work from a seated position, are able to attract interest for the very same reason (see Chapter 7).

During the crowd-building process a street entertainer may also set about organizing those people who have stopped in such a way that they form a tightly packed crowd. A fire-eating escapologist working the plaza at the side of the Pompidou Centre in Paris first attracted people's attention by emitting an ear-piercing whistle. He then proceeded to move the people who had stopped closer together into a tighter circle:

SE [Whistles four times] Move forward [whistles]. [Talking to one of his assistants] Oh, they're hard-faced, heh? [To AS] Move forward. [Pointing to an imaginary line on the ground] No, no. Up to there. Please close the door [i.e. bunch up closer together]. Look, there's airstreams . . . [whistles] Ladies and gentlemen, move forward. *Move forward*. Don't be afraid. Do it like you did at school. Move the ranks closer, please.

By closing up any gaps between the people who have stopped, the street entertainer enhances his or her chances of attracting more people to the performance. Any passers-by will now find it more difficult to ascertain what the crowd is looking at and are more likely to join the crowd to find out.

Another reason for closing the ranks in this fashion is that it can prevent passers-by from straying into the performance area and disrupting the crowd's attention. When this happened during one of the Venice Beach comedian's routines, the comedian didn't let the intruder pass without comment:

A [Walking between the front of the crowd and the comedian] Excuse me, please. *Excuse me*. I'm going past here.

SE [To AS] All that fucking space out there. He can't get no attention at home so he cuts through my fucking show.

AS [Laughs]

SE [To AS] Okay. All right. [To A] Hey, *wasn't that fun?*

A [Laughs]

SE *Oh, oh*. Come on, come on, go through again. Come on, we've got an audience here, man.

A I can't do it no more.

SE *No*. Come on. Do it one more time. It's fun. [To AS] Applaud for him.

AS [Applause]

SE Okay. *You lose?*

A Yeah.

SE *Are you through?*

A *Yeah*.

SE Can I get on with my show? Are you through?

A YEAH! I wanna see your show. That's what I've come here for.

SE [Mimicking A's voice] That's what you've come here for?

A *Yeah*.

SE *For?* Okay. All right.

By getting the crowd to applaud the intruder and thus 'show him up', the comedian manages to persuade this passer-by to stay and watch the show. The intruder's claim that to watch the show 'is what he came here for' appears to be a rationalization to cover up his having been put on the spot.

Attracting and building a crowd is no less difficult for street entertainers than it is for market pitchers. Many people recognize that stopping to watch a performance, never mind moving

nearer to the performer, involves a heightened sense of obligation to make a contribution. One way in which this can be seen
is from the closed and protective body postures of individuals at
street entertainers' shows. The body positions taken up are
identical to those that tend to be adopted by people standing at
the front of market pitching stalls (see Chapter 1).

Certainly, the Venice Beach comedian had one or two minor
problems moving his crowd closer to him:

SE   Now wait a minute. [Pointing to a cluster of white people
      standing to his left] *All*— you're all cool over here.
      [Talking to a cluster of predominantly black people stand-
      ing some distance away in front of him] *You folks* are too
      scattered. Can y'all *come forward*?
A   No! [Turns and walks away]
SE   [To A] All right, then you *take a hike, pal*!
AS   [Laughs]
SE   [Still talking to the same group of people] Folks, can y'all
      walk forward?
AS   [Laughs. Some people slowly move closer]
SE   [Talking to people standing some distance away behind
      him] Come on down. What do you think these people [i.e.
      the white people in his audience] are gonna say? '*Hell*,
      black folks won't get close, you know *we won't*!'
AS   [Laughter]

To help offset the reservations about standing close to a street
entertainer, confederates may be placed surreptitiously in the
crowd to initiate and encourage the forward movement. At the
L.A. skateboarding show, when one of the skateboarders asked
people to move nearer, a 'rick' was the first person to do so, his
arms outstretched in a beckoning manner to lead the way.

Having gathered an audience, pitching street entertainers
begin the performance proper. More importantly, they also begin
the process of obliging the crowd to pay for the performance.

THE DIFFERENCES BETWEEN STREET ENTERTAINMENT AND MARKET PITCHING

It is after people have been attracted to a performance that it becomes most apparent that street entertainers face different kinds of problems to those confronting market pitchers. Consequently, they cannot rely on the same strategies as market pitchers to achieve economic success.

For a start, although both build crowds comprised of casual passers-by who have no particular interest in buying goods or paying to be entertained, street entertainers have nothing physical to sell. As such, there are no appropriate goods (or bags or wrappers and the like) with which to solicit displays of interest and an obligation from people in the crowd (see Chapter 4).

Moreover, pitching is conducted in surroundings where the activity of buying and selling is both expected and appropriate. Street entertainment is often provided in an environment where the people are present for reasons other than being entertained.

Pitchers sell goods while street entertainers provide a service and, as Mulkay and Howe have pointed out, this service is 'consumed' before it is paid for. In the case of musicians in particular, the service cannot be restricted to those people who have stopped to listen and watch the performance. Furthermore, in having nothing physical to sell, these entertainers cannot, by right, claim any remuneration for the service they provide.

Nevertheless, there are a variety of ways in which street entertainers are able to persuade people to proffer a contribution for watching their performance. One of these is by means of heightened individual audience contact.

Audience contact

Getting an audience to respond collectively to the performance with laughter and applause is one way in which street entertainers evoke a feeling of obligation. These kinds of responses indicate a sense of appreciation of, and, therefore, a willingness to 'buy', the performance. Yet because these responses are overwhelmingly collective, the obligation that people feel is a relatively vague one. In market pitching this type of responsiveness is built on by soliciting actions such as hand-raising to indicate an 'interest' in the goods on offer, and sometimes handing out carrier bags or even the goods themselves before these goods have been paid for. These responses separate and distinguish one group of people in the audience from another and, therefore, render the obligation that the responding individuals show a more explicit and ineluctable one.

Street entertainers can do much the same thing by means of establishing contact with and involving individuals in their crowds. One of the most obvious ways this is done is by getting individuals to volunteer to be assistants in the performance. The heightened sense of obligation that volunteers feel is one reason why people in a street entertainer's crowd try to avoid being chosen as the volunteer. The Parisian escapologist-cum-fire-eater we saw working beside the Pompidou Centre had difficulty persuading people to tie him up in chains:

SE Are there volunteers among you who'll put me in chains, with sixteen metres of chain?
AS [No response]
SE *No?*
AS [Silence]
SE Nobody? Well, then, I'm just going to have to choose somebody at random. [Moves forward to a likely person] Ah, sir.
A   [Starts walking away]
SE *Where are you going?*
A   [No response]
SE [To AS] You don't have to take any risks. It's *me* who risks everything.

The English juggler studied by Mulkay and Howe used a particularly effective technique for getting round the difficult task of obtaining a volunteer. He picked someone standing next to the person who everyone thought he was going to select as his next volunteer. This strategy took into account and subverted people's reluctance to participate:

SE   [Talking to a prospective male volunteer in the crowd]
      Excuse me, sir. When you woke up today, did you know it
      was going to be a special day for you?
A   No.
SE   [To AS] He didn't know that *he* would be the *one* man in
      my audience, the *one* man standing right there [pause]
      right behind the one person to help me in this next trick.
AS   [Laughter]
SE   [Guides young woman from the front of the audience into
      the ring]

In general, the more people actively and publicly participate in a show, the more they feel a sense of obligation to pay for it. Street entertainers don't employ volunteers simply to save on the wage costs of an assistant. Volunteers are often those individuals who are most likely to make a contribution after a show. Crowds are liable to be much more sympathetic to and ready to applaud volunteers – if only out of a sense of relief that the person press-ganged into volunteering is someone other than themselves.

But measures such as this can heighten the sense of obligation felt by, at most, only a few individuals in the crowd. One solution is for entertainers to establish contact with and involve other individuals in the crowd. The Venice Beach comedian was obviously aware of the economic importance of doing this. In the second performance we recorded – the performance we recorded in full – he made explicit verbal contact with twenty-three people in his crowd.

This contact took a variety of forms. At the start of the show, for instance, he shook a number of people by their hands to thank them for stopping to watch. He made brief contact *en passant* with other people, by saying things like 'That's right, dear' and 'You know what I'm talking about here, sir?' He also pointed people out and made them the butt of his humour, as in this example where he sees a man with his hands stuck nonchalantly in his pockets:

SE   Sir. Please take your hands out of your pockets. Do you know you can go blind like that?
AS   [Laughter]

But he also used far more explicit strategies. For example, he would get more intimate with people by asking them to tell him their names:

SE   First of all, what's your name?
A   Joe.
SE   What do you do for a living, Joe?
A   *Everything*.
SE   *Oh shit*, you unemployed too, huh?
AS   [Laughs]

These names would often be repeated later on in the show and served as a reminder both to the person who was being named as well as to the crowd in general that the entertainer was marking people's (obligation) cards during the performance.

Given the obligating nature of a response such as laughter, it was not surprising that the comedian also made it clear that he was aware of anyone distinguishing themselves from the rest of the crowd by laughing louder than normal. To one loud laugher he remarked: 'Oh, you got that shit, huh?' With another, who was laughing with exceptional gusto, he had the following exchange:

SE Now, I wanna thank you, hon', what's your name?
A Me?
SE Yeah.
A Donna.
SE You are so lovely. *What's your name?*
A Donna.
SE Donna? [Shakes A's hand and looks her up and down]
Damn, you're beautiful. And most importantly you're a
good laugher. And *I appreciate that*.
A [Laughs]
AS [Laughs]
SE *NO NO NO!* I appreciate that 'cos it's really *weird* for me
to see a woman *laugh* when I'm *NOT making love to her*.
AS [Laughs]

He would also run up to and stand very close to people as he
was telling jokes. This seemed to break all the rules as regards
the normally accepted personal space to be maintained between
strangers in a public place. On one occasion he stood so close to
someone in the crowd that their noses were almost touching.
The comedian then flashed his eyebrows at this individual and
said: 'See how that shit works?'

Each individual contacted and put on the spot in this way has
a heightened sense of obligation to contribute at the end of the
show. From our videos it certainly appeared to be the case that
the people with whom he made such contact, however fleeting,
were far more likely to pay at the end of the performance.

To avoid the obligation that such responsiveness entails,
some people in the crowd resisted any form of contact with the
comedian. This usually took the form of not responding to the
comedian's questions:

SE What's your name, buddy? You are laughing your ass off.
What's your name?
AS [Laughs]

A   Mine?

SE   Yeah.

A   [Name inaudible]

SE   What do *you* do for a living?

A   [No answer]

SE   Far too long, buddy! You on the blood, huh? [i.e. selling his blood for money]

AS   [Laughs]

SE   Are you? *What do you do?*

A   [Silence]

AS   [Laughs]

SE   Nothing? WHAT DO YOU DO?

A   [No response]

AS   [Laughter]

SE   We can just wait 'cos we don't have *any fucking* place to be, *okay?*

AS   [Laughs]

SE   Wha— wha— what do you do for a living?

A   What do I do for a living?

SE   Yeah. Why d'you have to think about the shit so long, man?

AS   [Laughs]

SE   Do you feel like you're on the spot?

A   No, I—

SE   *Then answer the fucking question!*

PUTTING PAYMENT ON THE AGENDA

That the audience's involvement and the sense of obligation it instils will eventually have to be transformed into economic reward for the entertainer is, of course, implicitly recognized by the audience. Indeed, throughout a performance, and especially as a performance is coming to its close, an entertainer may have prepared for this point by mentioning money in casual and often humorous asides. For example, some of the instances of contact established between the comedian and individuals in his audience revealed the former's interest in the latter's economic circumstances:

SE What's your name, hon'?
A   Michelle.
SE *Michelle?* [Looking at A closely] *Damn!* You're almost a Michael [i.e. Jackson], huh?
AS [Laughs]
SE *Shit!* That's okay. Now you got on those dark glasses, what do you do for a living, Michelle?
A   Well, I'm kind of a legal aid.
SE *A legal aid?*
A   [Nods]
SE Okay. All right. So you've got big bucks on you.
AS [Laughs]
SE Okay, we'll talk about that later, okay?
AS [Laughs].

. . . or implied that there was a price attached to standing and watching the show:

SE [Pointing to a man in the crowd] What's your name, sir, with the hat and the sunglasses?
A   Steve.
SE Steve. What do you do for a living, buddy?
A   I am a stuntman.
SE *A stuntman? NO SHIT? How about that?* [Deep and ominous voice]. 'Cos it's gonna take a hell of a trick for you to get your ass outta *this* audience.
AS [Laughs]

One musical ensemble we observed at the Street Entertainer of the Year competition at Covent Garden in London closed their show with a song called 'We Want Your Money', written expressly for this purpose. The song was accompanied by a variety of elaborate gestures involving the musicians delving into the pockets of their Bermuda shorts, pulling out money (usually in note form), and placing it in their hat.

BUILDING ON THE OBLIGATION

Many of these street entertainers leave the best part of their show until the end in order to hold their audience to the point where making a contribution is most appropriate. The problem with this strategy is that it can help people to predict the end of the show and, thus, the best time to leave if they want to avoid making a payment. The Venice Beach comedian was wise to this. He carefully avoided saying exactly how many jokes he was going to tell during his show. Just before he announced that he was about to tell his last joke, it also became clear that those people in his crowd who had expected the fun for free had, in fact, stayed too long. Suddenly and unexpectedly their obligation to pay was made even more explicit:

SE   All right, *now* before I tell this last joke, you might notice folks like Joe, they start tippy-toeing outta here, when they hear me saying 'last joke', *see*?

AS   [Laughs]

SE   They say: 'Last— *last joke*? *Oh shit*! He'll probably wanna *pass the hat soon.*'

AS   [Silence]

SE   [Smiling] Well, yeah, *that's true.*

AS   [Laughs]

SE   *But— but* you don't have to *worry about it*, because you *don't have TO PAY, TO STAY*! You see, police say I've gotta tell you this: there is *NO* – I'll say it one more time – *there is NO obligation* to *pay* the *street performers*. However, folks, let's keep one thing in *mind*. I could be in your homes, *right now* [holds up a large photo of himself], *taking* [i.e. stealing] *the stereo equipment*, but *no*—

AS   [Laughs]

SE   *No*, I'm out here trying to make it legitimate, *let's keep that shit in mind! Okay?*

AS   [Laughs]

SE   Now I know what you're saying: 'No—' I know what you're saying. You're saying: 'No, he couldn't be in *my house*, because he *don't know* where I *live*.'

AS   [Silence]

SE   *You are wrong!*

AS   [Laughs]

SE   Yeah, I *bumped* into some of you, I've *got* your wallets, *I KNOW WHERE YOU LIVE!*

AS   [Laughs]

SE   Now the police *stopped* me from doing what I used to do, I used to tell the jokes, and *pass my hat*. The police said: 'No! Can't pass no hats out here. That is called solicitation.' So I said: 'Right. *Cool*.' I went and got a *bowl*. [Reveals a large plastic collection bowl]

AS   [Laughs]

SE   They said: '*No*. You can't pass that shit *either*. You can *sit on the GROUND*, but you cannot *pass it*.' Now they didn't say shit about *kicking it!* [Kicks bowl closer to the crowd]

AS   [Laughs]

SE   *Now*, didn't I *already* say there was no obligation to pay? *Didn't I make that clear?* Still, you're gonna see folks *watching me*, just *waiting* till I'm not looking in their direction, and then you're gonna see them doing all this shit. [Mimics people sloping out of his crowd]

AS   [Laughs]

SE   [Pointing a warning forefinger at the crowd] Now if I *happens* to look up, and catch your *cheap, scheming, conniving ass tippy-toeing outta here*, not only will I *point* you out to the public, but I am liable to say some *NASTY SHIT ABOUT YOU!*

AS   [Laughs]

SE   'Cos it's just a matter of *respect*. *Hell*, I've just stood and made you laugh all this time, all of a sudden my stuff ain't funny *NO MORE?*

AS   [Laughs]

SE   I don't buy that. (. . .) Now all I ask you to do is to (pay). You know, you can't go *NOWHERE*, and have this much *fun*, for FREE. OH SURE, you can walk down the street and pay a dollar twenty-five for a slice of that greasy-assed pizza that's gonna make you *SHIT* in five minutes!

AS   [Laughs]

SE   But *no*, you wanna come to *my show*, and watch for fifteen minutes for free.

To further enhance the obligation, a street entertainer may also attempt to evoke guilt or pity, as did the Venice Beach comedian:

SE   But *most* importantly, folks, remember, I could have been *your son*.

AS   [Laughs]

SE   *THAT'S RIGHT*! So *bring your donations*, at the end of this show, *throw them in the bowl*.

Guilt and pity were also targeted by Mulkay and Howe's English juggler:

SE   I would like to take this opportunity to point out that this is how I make my living, this is how I pay my bills, these *are* all my children [points to a line of children in the audience]

AS   [Laughs]

SE   So if you have enjoyed the show today traditionally *this* is the moment when I hold out my hat [lots of people pay] . . . So I'll say no more except one last thing – please, if you cannot afford the time, the energy or the money to walk the ten yards from where you are to me, then please, whatever you do, don't throw money because there are lots of very small children here with tiny little eyes [pause] and they rip me off.

AS   [Laughs]

SE   So if you *have* enjoyed the show, just form up into four orderly queues.

AS   [Laughs]

SE   Thank you.

AS   [Applause]

SE   People back there leaving now without paying, just remember guilt is a terrible thing to live with. Thank you. Remember it is fun to give. The more you give, the more fun I have.

SPECIFYING THE APPROPRIATE LEVEL OF PAYMENT

The actual size of payment a street entertainer deems to be appropriate is often not left unsaid:

SE   [Talking to a little girl standing with her mother] What's your name? Come here a minute. *What's your name?*

A   Sherry.

SE   *Sherry?* Will you do me a favour? You go tell your mommy that if she doesn't give you at least A *DOLLAR* –

AS   [Laughs]

SE   – to give to the comedian, *she DOES NOT LOVE YOU!*

AS   [Laughs]

SE   *Now*, wait, wait, I don't— I don't expect a dollar for free. I have a special joke for your little girl. [To A2, mother of A] How old is she?

A2   Four.

SE   Four? Can I tell her a cute little joke? *May I? Can I?* She doesn't have to come forward. I can tell her from there. What's her name?

A2   Lisa.

SE   Lisa? Can I tell her a joke? Do you mind?

A2   Sure.

SE   Okay, Lisa, these two lesbians were walking across the park.

AS   [Laughs]

SE   [Pointing to Lisa] *OH LOOK, she already knows it, LOOK!*

AS   [Laughs. Lisa smiles in a shy, self-conscious way.]

SE   *DAMN! I hate it when they know the material, you know what I mean?*

AS   [Laughs]

SE   [A roller skater who is passing by drops some money in the collection bowl] Thank you, brother; appreciate it. That's right, folks, we're not allergic to folded money, you know.

AS   [Laughs]

SE   Now, let me explain something to you folks. I'm not here to put you on the spot. But see, what I want you all to understand is, *I'm a professional.* I don't come out here just to *beg for your change.* No, I take dollars too.

AS   [Laughs]

SE   Folks ask me every show, they say, 'Michael, do you accept *food stamps?'*

AS   [Laughs]

SE   *Yeaaaah!*

AS   [Laughs]

SE *Yeah*. I take *food stamps, green stamps, Canadian money*, I'll
    even take a damn transfer [i.e. a bus transfer ticket] if
    you've got some time left!
AS [Laughs]
SE Now when this last joke is over, if you've appreciated
    what you've seen, I— [Another person puts some money
    in his bowl] – Thank you sir – I wanna see you folks come
    RUNNING DOWN to the bowl, throwing
    CHANGE, and *DOLLARS*, and *WATCHES*, and
    JEWELLERY and shit.
AS [Laughs]
SE *Yeah*, I want you to have a *good time with it*.

The English juggler studied by Mulkay and Howe raised the
issue of payment humorously just before his final and most
spectacular feat:

SE Before I do light these [three juggling torches], I must just
    point out that I am not being paid to perform here today
    so, at the end of the show, if you have enjoyed it, if I've
    made you laugh, then please, very simply take your hand –
AS [Laughs]
SE – put it in your pocket –
AS [Laughs]
SE – take out a contribution. Fold it up –
AS [Laughs]
SE Well, why not? And rush forward and place it into the hat,
    but no one will come to you.

All these tactics worked. Virtually everyone in the comedian's
crowd stayed for the last joke. More importantly, they also
placed a contribution in his bowl. This comedian had, in effect,
achieved mass sales of his jokes.

HAMMERING HOME THE OBLIGATION
TO CONTRIBUTE

As further confirmation of people's obligation to pay, individuals who do actually leave during a show without making a contribution are liable to be pointed out and ridiculed by an entertainer. The Venice Beach comedian did this with a degree of humour – humour that is, given the circumstances, decidedly double-edged:

SE   [To people walking away from his show] Where're you all going?

A   [No answer]

SE   Where're you all going?

A   [No answer]

SE   Where're you all going?

AS   [Laughs]

SE   Yeah. A good time to leave, huh?

AS   [Laughs]

SE   Donation time, huh?

AS   [Laughs]

SE   [Interrupting himself to point out someone who is moving away] Look at this guy. *Look*. Oh-oh, [in mock broken English] *no-speak-English*? No— *no-speak-English*?

AS   [Laughs]

SE   [To AS] *No speak Engli–* ? His ass has stood here an' laughed the last fifteen minutes. Now he *don't speak English*! *Where're you going, man*? *Where're you going*?

A   My wife has to get some jewellery.

SE   Bring your wife back here 'cos this is a *lot cheaper* than jewellery.

AS   [Laughs]

The English juggler did exactly the same:

SE   Now, ladies and gentlemen, before you leave, like that guy
     with the grey hair there.
AS   [Laughs]
SE   *Tight bastard.*
AS   [Laughs]

By pointing out such individuals, pressure is put on other
people not only to stay until the end of the show, but also to
provide remuneration for the entertainer's efforts.

DEALING WITH EXECUTION PITCHES

Outside the Pompidou Centre in Paris the number of people
who gather to watch the performances of the various entertainers is sometimes so large as to be almost unmanageable.

In this situation some of the entertainers we recorded did not
even bother to make contact with individuals during the show.
Many simply sent a number of assistants round with a hat,
seemingly working from the premise that even if only a small
minority of the crowd made a contribution, then the takings
would still be substantial. (In these situations it is not unheard
of for impostors to go around the crowd collecting money for
themselves during the show.) The fire-eating escapologist
working on this site had developed an unusual and much more
explicit method of extracting payment. After eventually getting
two members of his audience to chain him up with sixteen
metres of chain and four padlocks, he then announced the
various astonishing feats he was about to perform. (These
included not only escaping from the chains, but also placing his
bare chest on broken glass and then having heavy volunteers
stand on his back.) Although he had yet to perform these feats
and was still at the start of his show, he nevertheless demanded
(and received) a payment from some of the people who had
already gathered:

SE But, well, y'know, something weird is happening and I'd
better explain it to you now because after the show it'll be
too late. *We are artists*. If we work on the streets it's so we
can be with the people. Consequently this means that
when we're among the people we have no more Social
Security and, believe me, that big refinery behind us [i.e.
the Pompidou Centre] doesn't subsidize us either. Consequently, as we work with a lot of physical effort and use
our body for your greatest pleasure, there's a need for
some kind of guarantee. You know, it's quite simple.
[Looks around at the crowd] There's about three hundred
people around me. Three hundred people. I'm going to
ask twenty persons. Twenty persons to recognize that the
show is for your greatest pleasure. We need a small
guarantee because if I cut myself I'd have to go to the
hospital and they'll ask me for money. So to those twenty
people, I'm going to ask you to put down right there [i.e.
on the carpet with the broken glass on it] a ten-franc coin.
The coins will stay on the carpet until the end of the show.
If you're disappointed, or if I haven't done my job, I'll be
like Darty [a well-known French retail chain]. I've got my
own after-sales service and I pay back too. So, twenty
people. *By the way*, this *isn't* the price of the show. That's
only the *guarantee*. Usually, when the first coin's on the
ground, on the carpet, the others don't have difficulty in
following. So who's going to set an example and who'll
come and put the first coin down? *Come on*! It shouldn't
take as much time as this. [A throws down a coin] There's
one . . . [Proceeds to collect and count out a number of
ten-franc coins]

By the time this entertainer asked for the 'guarantee', the crowd
had already invested a considerable amount of their time waiting for the show to start and they thus had some incentive for
paying up to see the main event.

Similarly, an Indian 'levitator' working at the base of one of the high walls of the Old Red Fort in Delhi would agree to begin his levitation performance only after money had been thrown down to him from those people who had congregated at the top of the wall. In this case, there was no chance of the audience being able to retrieve their money, even if they wished to do so – the levitator was about fifty feet below the audience and there was no easy route down the wall. The other possible option – of the levitator floating upwards and collecting the contributions himself – was never raised.

URBAN HUSTLES

Street entertainers are just one of the many different sorts of traders who have an interest in lightening the pockets of people on the streets. There are fly pitchers (see Chapter 7), windscreen washers and card sharps, to name just a few. The techniques of these hustlers bear some resemblance to those employed by both street entertainers and market pitchers. In particular, to effect their trade most of these traders rely upon the same processes of obligation as we have described in this and earlier chapters.

For example, the street vendors we encountered in India had a habit of handing over their goods before telling you how much they cost. Flowers would be pressed into your hands, flags would be pinned to your clothes, and newspapers thrust into your auto-rickshaw at traffic intersections at a speed that could be registered only by the sharpest of eyes. This reversal of the normal rules of retail exchange, where the buyer initiates the sales transaction, was rather effective. In the UK also this tactic is used by many street sellers. Followers of Hare Krishna, for example, seem to have been trained to catch you off guard when they thrust their texts of enlightenment into your hands as if they are simply returning something unknowingly dropped on the ground.

Squeegees

Squeegees are those people who hang around busy traffic intersections with buckets of soapy water and chamois leathers to clean the windscreens of car drivers who are stuck temporarily in traffic. Typically, this service is provided without asking the driver's permission. Consequently, like the street vendors we have just mentioned, squeegees exploit the principle of possession (of a cleaner windscreen) being nine-tenths of a purchase. What helps reinforce this type of obligation and places additional pressure on drivers to pay up is that, in this situation, the service cannot be returned. Furthermore, because the squeegees have invariably cleaned the windscreen really quickly, there is often little opportunity for the driver to refuse the service. Rather than cause a scene (and make things even worse by holding up impatient drivers in the traffic behind), the easiest option is to pay up and take a minor road next time.

Personal friends

In India, tourists are often befriended by locals eager to act as unpaid guides. This usually happens on a train close to a final tourist destination or when out sightseeing. At some point during the ensuing assisted tour it transpires that this new-found friend can offer unique access to some special warehouse or emporium nearby which 'most other tourists don't ever get to see'. To whet the tourist's appetite, the guide will mention, for example, that the emporium stocks the work of genuine craftspeople, not the tawdry souvenirs that most tourists purchase for shockingly inflated prices. Turning down an opportunity to visit the emporium is difficult because it infringes on the newly formed obligation that is felt by the tourist to the guide. After all, this person, even though he or she is a stranger, has made a big sacrifice of his time and it seems churlish at least not to have a look at what is on offer. Of course, the reality is that these tour guides are working in tandem with the proprietors of these emporiums. This is their profession. The stores they take their victims to are rarely frequented by people other than escorted foreigners. If the visitor does buy the goods on offer, the friendly local receives a pre-arranged commission at some future date.

The Indian urchin hustle

In Delhi we came upon a gang of street urchins working a scam that relied, again, on obligation for its success. (This was a strategy almost identical to the ploy used by the 'Flit Gun Crew' in Cecil Day-Lewis's novel of schoolboy enterprise, *The Otterbury Incident*.) The urchins would stop someone on the street and point out that one of their shoes was covered in dog shit. (A confederate is deployed surreptitiously ten yards up the pavement to foul this person's footwear deliberately.) The target, although obviously embarrassed, is also very grateful at having this unfortunate matter pointed out to him or her. But what is the next step? Dog shit is, as most of us appreciate, exceptionally tricky to clean off footwear without either first removing the shoe (and therefore getting painfully intimate with the offending substance) or going through a conspicuous foot-shuffling routine to transfer it onto nearby grass. This latter course of action is less smelly but equally painful. It is almost always a sign to onlookers (and there are invariably onlookers) that one is in possession of a shit-soiled shoe. It does not therefore take much effort for these urchins to persuade their victims to take off the offending footwear so that they can clean it.

One of the urchins then enthusiastically starts to restore the shoe to its original condition. In so doing a minor fault is discovered – some loose stitching, say – which is in need of immediate repair. (If no fault exists, then no problem – the shoe will be worked on with a stealth and finesse worthy of a cricket-ball tamperer until one is created.) As the shoe is already in the cleaner's hand, and he seems to have come across the fault by chance, the unwary tourist may be tempted to think that it would be sensible to act on the urchins' suggestion that now is the best time to get this problem seen to as well. When the tourist does consent, the shoe is whisked away down a nearby alleyway to a cobbler's where the repair is soon effected. Before the shoe reappears, however, the tourist is informed of the cost of the cleaning and repair job. The price is usually set very high. Victims have, however, little choice but to pay up, unless they want to continue sightseeing in one shoe. Thus, during the course of a series of shrewd moves, the tourist is obliged to pay for a service that he or she originally did not need.

Three-card Monte

The 'Three-card Monte' or 'Find the Lady' is one of the standard street cons. We saw it in operation in London, Paris and at two of the English Classic horseracing meetings. The card-dealer in this con never has trouble attracting the beginnings of a crowd to his stall because he invariably works with five or more confederates who pose as bona fide gamblers.

Three playing cards are spread face down in a line on a makeshift table that is often no more than a piece of board on top of an upended cardboard box. The dealer reveals that one of these cards is a queen. The cards are then shuffled on the table and individuals are asked to place a bet on where the queen is. (Typically the queen is 'palmed' – that is, hidden in one of the dealer's hands or switched before shuffling the cards on the table, so that the audience follows not the Queen but one of the other two cards.) On the four occasions on which we witnessed this routine, the dealer faced major difficulties in getting someone in the audience to place a bet. One way round this problem was for him to try slowly but progressively to oblige someone to place a bet. This happens in the following sequence. The dealer's confederates all behave in a way designed further to encourage the person being obliged to make a wager:

CD [To A – a genuine member of the crowd] Any one you like, sir. Pick any one.

A [Remains motionless]

CD [To A] Just do us a favour. Turn it over. Turn it over.

A [Remains motionless]

CD *Turn it over for free, sir. For nothing*! For free.

R 1 For free?

CD [Nods]

A [Remains motionless]

CD [To A but indirectly responding to R 1's question] It won't cost you anything. [One or two of the ricks are discussing which of the three cards is the queen. One of them – R 2 – eventually points out the likely card.]

A [Points to the same card as R 2 has selected. The dealer turns over the card selected to show that it is the queen.]

CD [To A] 'Ere, it's fifty [i.e. a £50 bet] for you now. Show me fifty.

A [Shakes his head]

CD Go on, ah'm not taking any money.

A [Shakes his head]

CD Go on, honesty's the best policy. Go on, show me fifty.

A [Shakes his head]

CD [To another rick] I'll lend you fifty for nothing. I'll lend you fifty for nothing and I'll do it again. [Hands £50 over to R 2, shuffles the three cards on the table and talks to the audience at large.] The choice is your own, ladies and gentlemen. Any one you want. Look [holds the cards face up]. Two blanks, one prize. [Turns the cards face down and shuffles them on the table] Pick the card for one, twenty, fifty or a hundred [pounds]. Put your money down. On any one you like.

R 3 [Pointing out the card to R 4] There.

R 4   [Replying to R 3 in an audible stage whisper] Nice one.

CD   I can only bring the horse to water. I can't make him drink. Is anyone in? Is anyone in before I stop? For one, twenty, fifty or a hundred. [To A] Turn it over, please.

A   [Remains motionless]

CD   Turn it over. [Just as A points to the middle card another rick tries to bet £20 on the same card.

R 1   Ah'll put it on the middle one.

CD   [Turns the middle card over to reveal the queen. He now talks to R 1] Twenty pound, Johnny? Too late. (. . .) [Turns the cards over again and shuffles them on the table] Like I said before, there's two cards and one prize. Which card?

R 3   [Talking to R 5] *Go on, Pete, put some money on it.*

R 5   [Slowly reaches into his pocket for money]

CD   Will anyone have me for twenty now? [To another A] Go on, put some money down. Put it on, anywhere you like. Just put it on.

A   It's too dear.

CD   [Goes through his spiel again.]

R 2   [Points out a card]

CD   There you are, look. Turn it over.

R 2   [Turns over the card. It is the wrong card. All the ricks express astonishment and disappointment. The dealer leaves this card face up and the other two cards face down]

CD   [Throwing one of three cards away] Now, *now* will anybody have fifty pounds on a two-horse race?

A   A fiver?

CD   [To A] No, fifty's my bet. I can only cover the bets. Is there anyone in for fifty before I stop? For one fifty in a two-card race? Is anyone in? *Anyone?* [Picks up board he has used as a card table and starts to walk away in disgust] *I can make more money selling pork pies!*

Although this dealer was unsuccessful in obtaining a genuine bet, we can still see the process of obligation at work. For example, he asks the first individual he talks to only to pick a card. Then he asks him to turn the card he thinks is the queen face up. Then he asks him to show some money. All these requests, which would betray an interest in placing a bet, are designed to place this person progressively under an ineluctable obligation to place a bet. This is probably why the individual resists doing so. We can also see that whenever this individual does respond, the dealer attempts to transform the response into an obligation to stake a wager.

SIMILARITIES BETWEEN STREET ENTERTAINERS AND MARKET PITCHING

Although there are obvious differences between street entertaining, urban hustling and market pitching, these differences are generally outweighed by the similarities. Whether it is telling jokes in Los Angeles, juggling firesticks in an English mediaeval city centre, getting people to stand on your back while your chest is resting on broken glass in Paris, or working a shit-on-the-shoe scam in India, the same fundamental processes of persuasion and people management seem to apply. Two similarities typify these encounters. First of all, pitchers, street entertainers and urban hustlers tend to rely on obligation, in some form or another, to persuade people to part with money. This obligation is built up, progressively, during the course of a show, sales routine or hustle. The second similarity is the employment of humour to manage problematical tasks. As we have seen, street entertainers and market pitchers use humour as a central feature of their routines to deal with the problems of people standing too far away, people not responding in a sufficiently enthusiastic fashion, and the like. Such humour is used most noticeably, however, by street entertainers.

For example, in the second of the Venice Beach comedian's shows – which lasted twenty-four minutes – the comedian managed to get the audience to laugh on 104 occasions, or about once every fourteen seconds. Yet only twenty-six of these instances of laughter took place during, or were the result of, the seven jokes he told. These figures are almost exactly the same as those found by Mulkay and Howe in their study of the English juggler. Only eight minutes of the juggler's twenty-eight-minute performance were devoted to juggling. And although he told no jokes during this performance, he nevertheless managed to get the audience to laugh on 116 occasions – that is, about once every fifteen seconds. In both cases, and as with market pitchers (see Chapter 5), this constant stream of humour also helped to maintain the audience's attention and stimulate other passers-by to stop.

CHAPTER 10

Tele-Shopping

Our discovery that the methods of persuasion employed by market pitchers were almost identical to those employed by the more vocal and enterprising street entertainers and urban hustlers was very satisfying. It suggested that there was a group of common communicative procedures and principles of persuasion which had to be adhered to by these traders in order to 'sell' successfully. The fact that we had witnessed these strategies in countries (and cultures) as diverse as Britain, France, India and America only served to strengthen the significance of this discovery.

When we encountered an American demonstrator pitching kitchen knives from behind a wooden butcher's counter, however, our belief in the significance of what we had discovered was redoubled.

This man, who was saying and doing exactly the same things as practically all the pitchers and demonstrators we'd seen hitherto, was selling the 'Miracle Blade'. Just after he started his pitch, he encouraged people to move closer to his stall: 'Now come round the side. In fact, you can lean on the counter if you want to, just as so we don't block up the aisle.'

Like many of the goods sold on street markets, this knife, as its name suggested, was unique: 'A very special knife; a knife so special it comes with a lifetime guarantee.' The demonstrator was also using the classical rhetorical device of three-part lists to describe the various components of the knife: 'That handle's [1] made of Nylac by Tupol, [2] virtually indestructible,

[3] *dishwasher safe!*' and 'That blade is [1] surgical [2] stainless [3] steel' and '[1] hardened, [2] tempered and [3] guaranteed in writing a lifetime'.

To prove just how miraculous the Miracle Blade was, and how confident he felt about offering it with a lifetime guarantee, he started to subject it to the same kind of over-exaggerated and punishing test we'd seen crockery pitchers use. To verify that the handle was virtually indestructible, he gave it a good bashing with a hammer; to certify the sharpness, strength and durability of the blade, he didn't just slice up a tough steak or an over-ripe tomato, he cut through a boot sole, hacked chunks off his hardwood counter, and sawed away at the head of a metal hammer. He then rounded off these startling demonstrations with a contrast: 'I'm giving that knife more abuse [A] in ten seconds than [B] you'd give it in five years of use and abuse in your kitchen.'

Even when he came to the price he stayed true to form. Like many British and European demonstrators, he chose not to build up the value of the bargain by dropping the selling price step by step; instead, he announced the price and added a variety of extra goods on top, free of charge: 'You spend thirty-nine ninety-five with me here today, I'm gonna spend probably *five times* that right back with you. You watch what I do. *You buy the first knife*, now that's *all* you buy, 'cos I'm gonna give you the second knife free.'

Around this point in the sale a number of the people at his stall, already convinced of the bargain, started waving their money in the air trying to catch the demonstrator's attention. Their behaviour was exactly the same as we had seen at the Family Rider sale described at the beginning of this book. But this demonstrator also wasn't interested in making a sale straight away: '*Now hold on to your money*,' he shouted at everyone, holding his hands up in the air. The money-wavers were visibly disappointed, even though he was continuing to build the value of the bargain: 'Now you've got one for your tackle box, your motor home, one that stays in the kitchen – you've already got *two* for the price of one. I'm going to give you one of the paring knives. Look, it's like a little razor blade with the handle on. Thin, sharp, flexible. I'm gonna give you one of those, *that's free*. The little spiral knife . . .'

The money-wavers interrupted him again, all to no avail: 'Now *hang on*,' he pleaded, 'I've got more and more. It gets better and better by the second.'

And, indeed, it did get better. There were also two plastic fruit juicers, and a garnishing kit, complete with instruction book. And there was a utility knife, and a six-inch flay knife and, on top of all this, a set of four steak knives, all for the same original price of $39.95.

To us, the response from the people gathered around his stall was, by now, unsurprising – practically everyone wanted part of the action. What *was* surprising, though, was where this sale was being conducted. We weren't standing on a street market or visiting an indoor trade fair or an 'Ideal Home'-type exhibition; we were sitting at home watching television.

Far from being an archaic and, for some, insignificant form of economic exchange conducted by barrow boys and the like on the margins of the orthodox economy, the techniques of pitching are now being employed in one of the most recent and most successful developments in mass television retailing – tele-shopping. This finding only served to confirm that market pitchers have their fingers firmly on the pulse of a set of fundamental, perhaps universal, principles of persuasion.

INFOMERCIALS

The Miracle Blade demonstration turned out to be only one of a growing breed of 'infomercials' – direct-marketing broadcasts taking the form of an extended twenty-to-thirty-minute televised sales presentation where viewers are invited to call a toll-free telephone number to make a purchase. These goods are typically low price/'low risk' purchases such as exercise equipment, polishes and cleaners, skin-care creams, and kitchen and hobbyist gadgets. Between 1987 and 1992 infomercials generated sales that mushroomed from $750 million to $1.5 billion within the USA alone.

One of the leading companies in this field is the National Media Corporation Inc., based in Philadelphia – nominated as 'one of the hottest stocks of 1992' by one of the *Los Angeles Times*' staff writers. This company, along with its subsidiary, Quantum International, places its infomercials on over 900 cable, terrestrial and satellite stations worldwide. In Europe, Quantum International broadcasts 125 hours of infomercials weekly, via three European satellite stations, and reaches over thirty million homes.

Many of the infomercials the National Media Corporation produces to sell its portfolio of over fifty products use a celebrity or special guest to demonstrate and extol the virtues of their products. Many sales are also conducted within a high-energy game-show-type format, complete with host, demonstrator and a highly vociferous studio audience. Regular breaks are provided within these sales presentations to summarize the sales offer (usually in the form of a more orthodox TV advert) and to invite the viewers to order the product by credit card on a toll-free number. To offset any reservations viewers may have about buying directly from television, all products are backed by a thirty-day return policy.

These infomercials, as we shall now see, are remarkably similar to the sales routines of market pitchers.

Building an edge

Where market pitchers often face the problem of having to attract and hold otherwise uninterested passers-by at their stalls, infomercial producers have to battle with the channel 'surfer' and remote-control 'zapper'. The solution in both cases is much the same – information is provided, usually in the form of an unsolved puzzle, designed to stimulate the curiosity of the viewer:

QUANTUM: FLYING LURE
H   This is the first half-hour programme devoted to a fishing lure. Stick around and you'll see why.

In the Purrfect Punch infomercial, which promotes a gadget enabling people to create embossed wool designs on their own clothing, the host enters the sales arena to unbridled applause and cheers. He then whets the appetite of viewers by contrasting the quality of a sample of the finished embossed wool designs (being modelled by four people sitting at the front of the studio audience) with their low price:

QUANTUM: PURRFECT PUNCH
H   [Having just shown a variety of embossed wool designs on four people's clothes] I MEAN, THESE LOOK LIKE EXPENSIVE DESIGNS, *RIGHT*?
AS [Shouts of 'Yeah', etc.]
H   [Lower, confiding voice] But what if I told you that because of today's Amazing Discovery called 'Purrfect Punch', come here, look again. [Walks over to first person wearing one of the designs] This design only cost about *three* dollars to make.
AS [Cries of 'Ooh', 'Wow', and clapping]
H   [Walks over to the second person wearing one of the designs] And this design, well, Jason's whole design, less than three dollars to make with the materials.
AS [Cries of 'Ooh', 'Wow', and clapping]
H   [Walks over to the third person wearing an embossed fish design] And *Margo*? Well, *all* the fish put *together*, about *three dollars*.

271

AS [More cries of 'Ooh' and 'Wow']

H   [Walks over to a fourth person who is wearing a cat design] Holly's *kitty cat*? With *all* the little fur and fuzz *like that*? *Two dollars*.

AS [More cries of 'Ooh', 'Wow', and clapping]

H   *All* made with Purrfect Punch. Are *you* ready to see how we made *all* these creations, and see what else you can make with Purrfect Punch?

AS [Cries of 'Yeah', whoops and clapping]

H   *ME TOO!* Let's welcome back our queen of crafts – *CAROL SMITH!*

AS [Cheers and applause]

Describing and demonstrating the goods

As in market pitching and the Miracle Blade demonstration, the goods on offer often have unique properties (e.g. 'There's no other lure like it'), and product descriptions are often packaged in three-part lists:

QUANTUM: LEATHER AND VINYL RESTORER

D   On leather goods, [1] it *cleans*, [2] it *shines* and [3] it *waterproofs*.

At the end of one infomercial, Alex Langer, the inventor of the 'Flying Lure' fishing fly, uses two consecutive three-part lists when he exhorts the viewers to:

H   [1.1] Just try it, [1.2] just try it for a day. [1.3] Give it an honest try. [2.1] It has worked for people north, south, east and west. [2.2] It has worked for pros. [2.3] It has worked for people that have never caught a fish before on a lake they've been fishing for years.

Do-it-yourself gadgets and implements for hobby enthusiasts which require a degree of manual dexterity to use are often packaged in three simple steps (using short and simple words) to indicate just how easy these goods are to use. In the Bedazzler Plus sale, all the user has to do is: 'Snap, press and pop'. In the Purrfect Punch sale, all they have to do is: 'Punch, lift and slide'.

These types of description are often supplemented with contrasts:

QUANTUM: VICTORIA PRINCIPAL SKIN CREAM

D   [A] Now if you think quality skin-care means complicated steps and expensive packaging you're in for a big surprise. [B] Because this skin-care is [1] simple, [2] fast and [3] practical. Just three steps in three minutes.

. . . and many of these contrasts are reinforced visually with, for example, 'before' and 'after' shots showing the difference between, say, an ordinary paintbrush (slow and messy) and the Europainter Paintpad (quick and effective).

The kinds of punishing test we saw the Miracle Blade undergo are routinely employed to emphasize the unusual capabilities or durability of these products. In one infomercial, featuring a paint restorer and protector, the demonstrator set light to the bonnet of a car treated with the product to show that the flames would not penetrate the protective coating it provided. To persuade any viewer who was still, by any chance, sceptical of the paint restorer's merits, there was another test still to come:

QUANTUM: COLORCOTE 2000

D   We're gonna put ColorCote 2000 to a very *punishing* test by sandblasting the hood [i.e. the bonnet] of *this seventy-five-thousand-dollar* Porsche 911 turbo.

AS   [Cries of 'Ooh' and other sounds of astonishment]

D   And we're gonna do that with a *force* that is strong enough – are you ready for this? – to *shatter glass*.

Needless to say, after this test the car bonnet remained unmarked and looking as new.

Testimonials and endorsements

During product descriptions and demonstrations, a variety of different types of testimonial and endorsement are provided to validate and enhance the claims being made:

QUANTUM: VICTORIA PRINCIPAL SKIN CREAM
D   After using the products I noticed that people have told me, a lot, that, er, 'Oh gosh! You have lovely skin.' Or 'My goodness! You hardly have any wrinkles.'

Of course, the almost constant whooping, cheering and applause of the studio audience in the game-show-type infomercials serve to provide a very convincing barometer of what 'ordinary people' like the viewers at home should feel about the goods on sale. Members of the studio audience, like people standing at a pitching stall, are invited to assess the product for themselves. This happened in the ColorCote 2000 infomercial. Four volunteers were invited to try out the paint restorer on four differently coloured pre-scratched car bonnets:

QUANTUM: COLORCOTE 2000
H   [Addressing the first volunteer] How does it look?
V1   Oh, this is great. I tell you what, I've gotta brand new car. It's got scratches on it already. I'm getting some for *my* car.
AS   [Applause]
H   *All right. Terrific!* And over here on the gold hood. How're you doing?
V2   This is *awesome, it's really working*!
AS   [Applause and cheers]
H   Okay, *awesome*. I love that word. [Chuckling as if

surprised] *Sure!* [Moving to the next car hood] How do
we look on the red?

V3   It looks *amazing*.

AS   [Applause and cheers]

H   Okay, amazing is a word that *I love too!* [Moving to the
next car hood] And here we are on the silver hood, how
are things going here?

V4   Goes on easy, comes off easy [higher-pitched voice] an'
covers the scratches.

AS   [Applause and cheers]

Over sixteen minutes of the twenty-five-minute Flying Lure
infomercial are dedicated to presenting thirty-two clips of tes-
timonials from ten professional and five amateur anglers (as well
as the inventor himself) who say things like: 'There's no other
lure like it', 'You can catch any type of fish', 'It's so easy, even I
did it.'

One of the most sensational endorsements occurred during
the Bedazzler Plus infomercial. A whole rack of clothing decorated with Bedazzler Plus studs and sequins was placed in a 'very
exclusive' Beverly Hills clothes store ('When you shop there
bring a lot of money'). A hidden camera captured a member of
the public purchasing one of these items for the same price as
professionally produced designer-label clothing. The infomercial then cut back to the sales arena showing the host with a
clipboard and pen in his hands about to report the results of
some calculations he had just made:

H   [Breathlessly excited] Now look at this. Look. For that
black jacket we paid under forty dollars and we just sold it
for 179 dollars.

AS   [Claps, applause, whoops and cries of 'Yeah!']

H   WE'RE MAKING MONEY! THIS THING'S A
MONEY MACHINE!

AS   [Applause, whoops and shouts of 'Yeah!']

More generally, the behaviour of the hosts is another way in which the credibility of a product claim is validated and enhanced. Although their role is officially that of impartial observer, summarizer and master of ceremonies, hosts often act as stooges by, for instance, reinforcing and upgrading the demonstrator's own assessments of the goods:

QUANTUM: PURRFECT PUNCH

D. [Showing the host an embossed Teddy bear created with the Purrfect Punch on a child's sweatshirt] Now this is the little project that we're going to do. Isn't it a cute little bear?

H *Oh, this is adorable!*

QUANTUM: EUROPAINTER

D Save *time*, save *paint*, but most important of all, remember – the price, the price – *save money*.

AS [Cheers and applause]

D Can you afford *not* to paint?

H [Looking impressed] What do you think, audience?

AS [Cheers and applause]

H I think the Europainter has *truly* been an 'Amazing Discovery'.

The hosts also raise objections about the goods – objections that the viewers at home are obviously unable to raise themselves:

QUANTUM: PURRFECT PUNCH

H [Talking to AS about the embossed Teddy bear created with the Purrfect Punch] *Look at the little bear, with the yellow ribbon*, this is beau— [sudden change to a deeply suspicious voice] *Wait a second!* You gotta know something *about sewing* to do this! This— you have to be an *artist* to do a pattern like that! *Come on!*

D No, Mike, all the patterns are already done for you.

QUANTUM: BEDAZZLER PLUS

H   [D is showing a denim jacket decorated with Bedazzler
     Plus studs] *THIS IS BEAUTIFUL! Now* I see how—
     now are these washable? What happens when you *wash*
     them? *They fall out?*

D   Oh no, you just turn the garments inside out and you can
     wash it just the same.

H   NOW I SEE THAT! THIS IS *GREAT*! Look!
     Ir— iron-on transfers. *You would pay hundreds of dollars*
     for this!

QUANTUM: PURRFECT PUNCH

H   *But wait! Carol, Carol* [i.e. D], these stitches, they don't
     look anything like the stitches on the Teddy bear, the
     Teddy bear looks so mu— so much better.

D   [Small pitying laugh] That's the *back* side, Mike.

AS [Laughter and a couple of gasps of surprise]

D   Turn it *over* and *you'll see the loops*!

H   (. . .) *First time, huh*?

AS [Applause and other appreciative noises]

With the host acting as a suspicious buyer, some of the main
reasons why viewers may not want to make a purchase are
undermined. Judging by the studio audience's reaction, in each
case the objections are rapidly and convincingly dealt with by
the demonstrators.

Building the bargain

The high value and low cost of their goods are established
primarily by the street market demonstrator's strategy of announcing the selling price of the basic product on offer and then
adding a number of extra items free of charge, as happened in
the Miracle Blade sale. Each 'extra' is often presented separately
in order progressively to build up the value of the deal. Flying

Lure buyers don't get one but, rather, sixteen lures. They also receive a special tackle box, and the 'Spinner Bait' lure – all free of charge.

As in market pitching, the sales offer may be posited as being of limited duration in order to enhance the prospect of obtaining an immediate response. Some of the free add-ons, such as the Flying Lure 'Spinner Bait' and the matching steak knives in the Miracle Blade sale, are offered only to those viewers who respond quickly:

QUANTUM: MIRACLE BLADE

D   You call me within the next fifteen minutes and I'm going to throw in the matching steak knives.

H   Oh, right.

D   With the *same* blade, the *same* razor-sharp edge and the *same* lifetime guarantee. John [i.e. H], they're free.

H   Great. [Talking to AS] Isn't that *something*, folks, huh? [Starts clapping] How about that?

AS   [Short burst of applause]

In some shows the host made sure that the viewers received the best deal possible from the demonstrator – another means of creating the impression that they are impartial. For example, at the end of the Purrfect Punch sale, when the host and demonstrator are discussing which items will be added to the basic punch machine, the host went uninvited into the demonstrator's handbag and pulled out a number of other sewing implements (and a banana), and then accused the demonstrator of holding back on the viewers. Throughout all this the audience were chanting 'More, More' until, finally, the demonstrator relented.

THE SHOPPING CHANNELS

Another type of tele-shopping is conducted by companies like QVC (Quality, Value, Convenience) – the largest tele-shopping channel in the US – and HSC (Home Shopping Club). Instead of buying airtime from channel-owners, as happens with the National Media Corporation and Quantum International, QVC and HSC broadcast on their own channels. Rather than producing pre-recorded infomercials, the sales presentations conducted by these companies are usually live and are broadcast twenty-four hours a day for 364 days a year. Typically, each day is divided into a variety of different theme shows (such as QVC's 'Doris Pooser's Must Haves') where products such as cosmetics, discount jewellery, 'collectable' glass, china and ceramic trinkets as well as household goods, kitchenware and DIY items are offered for sale.

Each product presentation lasts for about five to ten minutes. The goods on offer may be modelled or demonstrated by a host, sometimes with the help of a celebrity or expert, who will extol the various features and benefits of the product while it is on screen. QVC employs celebrities such as Joan Rivers ('Can we shop?'), Jackie Stallone and Ivana Trump. Viewers are able to order the product, via a toll-free telephone number, only while the product is being displayed. As is the case with infomercials, many of the sales techniques used in this form of tele-shopping are very similar to those employed by market pitchers. Viewers are, for example, continually being asked (and provided with financial inducements in the form of membership-number prize draws, etc.) to continue watching:

CHSC: JEWELLERY

H   I'm very excited about the jewellery hour, hope you're
     gonna stick around. [Referring to a picture of an item of
     jewellery on screen] Look at the high polish on that. *This*

is twenty inches in length and *you will NOT believe the price of it*! So I hope you have to— well I do, you're going to have to stay with me, that's all there is to it.

One also finds hosts employing three-part lists and contrasts when describing the goods:

CHSC: CAPO DIMONTE SWAN AND SIX ROSES
H   [1] I love the colours, [2] I love the style, [3] I love the elegance!

HSC-USA: GOLD HERRINGBONE CHAIN
H   And you have a thirty-day money-back guarantee. *Of course*! *Wear it* for thirty days. You're *not* gonna do any *damage* to it. *You don't wear out gold.* [1] Ten years from now it's around, [2] *twenty* years from now it's around, [3] FIFTY years from now this piece of gold is still around.

Occasionally, the product is extolled in almost the same dramatic and exaggerated way in which some pitchers 'fanny up' their goods. In the following sale the host implies that the karaoke machine on offer has life-transforming properties:

HSC-USA: KARAOKE STEREO SYSTEM
H   Now let me tell·you a story of a— of a young gentleman, who used this one design that— gosh, I think we sold it *two years ago*. Now this man, he was gifted with a voice that, um— *he knew* he was going places, *he knew* that he was going to be a professional *in* the music industry. *Well*, this *one individual* – and we're talking about a man that was really going to have a career in singing – one— *one moment* he went out, and this was a very unfortunate time for him, [solemn voice] he had a car accident where he was

disabled, and he was physically challenged. Well, this obviously did something to *not only* his *career* in singing, but to how he lived his life and how he went about, er— everyday life, and he *literally forgot about his career in music*. Well, the mother called in one day and said: '*Chuck*, I've got a *son* who er – is disabled and is— is—. literally—' – *physically challenged*, let's call it – and she says: 'He has a *voice* that's simply *phenomenal*.' She goes: 'Do you think maybe I should ge— I should get this?' I said: 'Ma'am, *buy it for him*! Because it's going to bring him out of his *shell*, and it is going to do things for him that *not you* or any other *doctor* could ever do.' Guess what? *That man* has professionally recorded. *That man*, THROUGH USING THE KARAOKE MACHINE, has now been able to bring his talent to the *point* where it is *where it was* before the accident. I'm gonna tell you right now, this deal right here *does more* than what a *doctor* could do, it *does more* than what a *psychologist* could do, this deal right here does more than *ANYONE* could ever do. It brings *personality to those who use it*! *And if you* WANNA SOUND *like Madonna, an' if you* WANNA SOUND *like Neil Diamond, if you* WANNA SOUND *like Garth Brookes, if you* WANNA SOUND *like anyone, YOU— YOU COULD BE THAT VERY PERSON*!

The value of the goods is enhanced by price contrasts (see Chapter 2) which are almost always shown on screen and are often also reaffirmed verbally by the hosts:

CHSC: PAIR OF CERAMIC CHRISTMAS GOOSE HOLDERS
H   *Nine* dollars, *ninety-nine* cents. They are all hand-painted. I
would be happy paying nine ninety-nine for *one*, okay?
Not for two. *It's unbelievable*. But this is *Boxing Day*, and
this is where you *get* those unbelievable sales.
[QVC:USA: seven-inch gold rope bracelet]

H   The *seven-inch, polished* velvet in fourteen-carat gold. It
      carries a retail value of *one hundred and fifteen dollars*, QVC
      price, in the *future*, at *fifty*, but today's special value just
      forty-two dollars, but it's on its way towards selling out.

Some of the more elaborate price-discounting strategies are
almost identical to those employed by market pitchers when
'coming to the bat' (see Chapter 3):

HSC-USA: GOLD HERRINGBONE CHAIN

H   [The 'retail value' of $831.66 is displayed on screen] –
      Eight hundred dollars would be a great price. (. . .) *Seven*
      hundred dollars would be better, *six hundred* dollars would
      be I— I— I'm sure in most stores a 'half off' sale. (. . .)
      Take another hundred off the price everybody gets:
      'That's low, it's five hundred dollars'. Take *another* hun-
      dred off the price, *four hundred dollars*. (. . .) *We* do it for
      $369.75 *they're gone*. (. . .) We'll go *lower*. For the next
      couple of minutes – under 350, 340, *330* – that's a
      hundred dollars a month [i.e. if the viewer takes up the
      'Flexpay' credit option] (. . .) not even 320 or 310 (. . .)
      under three hundred dollars. *Rock bottom price on this*: if
      you can dial in right now for the next couple of minutes
      with Flexpay – *294.75*. That's right, two hundred and
      ninety-four dollars, seventy-five cents.

Explanations are also given to support and account for the
discrepancy in price between what the goods are said to be
worth and their lower selling price (see Chapter 3):

HSC-USA: GOLD HERRINGBONE CHAIN

H   Go to *any jewellery store in the country* – if you wanna have
      the authenticity of the jewellery checked out, please do, it's
      stamped fourteen-carat gold – *price it*, see if you can come
      anywhere near eight hundred dollars.

CVN-USA: JEWELLERY

H   I know you're sitting back, you're saying: 'Charlo', *what's going on? What* are you doing and *where* do you get those price tags?' You know where we get those price tags? *We-buy-in-quantity!* Are— we cut out *all* of the middle-men, *we* go directly to the manufacturer, and *we-get-the-gold. We don't want you* to suffer any of these mark-ups. *No!* That's not what we're here for. CVN can give *you the value on gold!* All you have to do is dial.

Although studio audiences are rarely evident in this form of home shopping, viewers are, nevertheless, regularly invited to call in and provide independent and thus more credible testimony as to the merits and value of the goods on offer:

QVC-USA: SILVER CHAIN

A   (...) I have so many things from QVC, you— you know, my son says I'm a QVC *addict.* [Laughs]

H   (...) [Changes topic and talks about the quality of the jewellery]

A   (...) A lot of times the things turn out looking even prettier than they do on the air. Y'know, when you get them in *person?* It looks beautiful on the air, but when you actually see it on your wrist it looks even *nicer.*

CHSC: CRYSTAL UNICORN FIGURINE ON AMETHYST

H   What do you think about our unicorn?

A   Oh, I have him and I couldn't believe the *colours,* that reflect through his body.

H   Is that right?

A   As well as the gold and the amethyst reflects through it— it's just a *beautiful* piece.

H   Isn't it *gorgeous?*

CHSC: VISIBLE CONTROL FIRMING GEL AND POLISH

A – and it has the money-back guarantee, so you have nothing to lose.

H You have the money-back guarantee and we're paying the GST [sales tax] for you.

A That's right.

H That's wonderful, isn't it?

A That's right. It's an excellent value. Like I say, you have nothing to lose but your cellulite. [Laughs]

As with market pitching and infomercials, a number of ploys are used to instil a profound sense of buying urgency into the viewers. The most obvious is a 'Time Left' and sometimes a 'Quantity Ordered' indicator placed in the corner of the television screen. Items are available only until the 'Time Left' clock returns to zero. The hosts rarely display any reluctance to point out the limited amount of time left for the viewers to make their purchase:

CHSC: PAIR OF CERAMIC CHRISTMAS
GOOSE HOLDERS

H [1 minute 30 seconds is the time left showing on screen] Very, very busy on the phone lines *right now*. We *are* predicting a sell-out on *these* characters *today*, so I *urge* you to dial very *quickly*.

CVN-USA: JEWELLERY

H *We are going to give you sixty more seconds to dial in on this one. Tell you what, I* don't even have enough time to put up a clock! I don't even have time to put up a clock at that kind of *price tag*. The gold's sprouting wings. [Short silence] That sounds pretty stupid but, *really*, this stuff is *flying out of our vault*.

This form of tele-shopping is not just sales rhetoric spliced with a few comments from excited viewers. The Home Shopping Club has sales screens that can relay information to hosts about the number of people calling and the number of goods sold. This information can be used to compare viewers' responses with the particular sales pitch and, if necessary, the emphasis of the sale can be changed. Steve Chaney, one of HSC's hosts, is quoted as saying, 'We're race-car drivers. This is our speedometer.'

Home shopping in this format is a $2.5 billion industry in the USA alone. QVC reaches over 47 million cable and satellite homes in the US; Home Shopping Club goes into 27 million homes. In 1991, QVC made over 61,000 sales presentations, received an average of 122,000 calls every day and has 3,100 telephone lines to deal with customer demand. The Home Shopping Club has 2,000 operators and an automated telephone answering system that can deal with over 20,000 calls a minute.

The sales figures are equally staggering. In 1992, QVC's sales totalled over $1 billion. On one day in January 1993, QVC took orders for over $19 million worth of merchandise. In March 1992, a special 'Fashion Day' brought in 239,118 orders for over $7.4 million; a 'Silver Day' produced 358,732 orders for over $9.6 million. Seconds after the 1993 Dallas Cowboy Superbowl victory, QVC started selling Dallas sweatshirts. Less than six minutes later they had sold over 11,000. On 12 December 1992 a special sale of high-tech toys and electronics produced orders of just under $1.5 million, in one hour.

This industry has grown dramatically and is still growing. The annual sales of the Home Shopping Club grew from $160 million in 1986 to over $1 billion in 1991. Between 1991 and 1992, QVC's net income rose from $19.6 million to $55.1 million. Each month it attracts more than 100,000 new customers. Over 60 per cent of all first-time customers turn out to be repeat purchasers. The total US home tele-shopping market is forecast to reach $100 billion by the year 2000. It would seem that every day in the world of tele-shopping is a 'money day'.

CONCLUSION

In this book we have attempted to describe and explain the various ways in which market pitchers manage sales. In so doing, we hope to have shown that selling – particularly this type of selling – is fundamentally a social and interactional accomplishment. More than anything else, the success of this type of marketing rests upon a pitcher utilizing verbal and non-verbal skills and 'selling techniques' to convince people to buy.

These points are not news, of course, to market pitchers themselves. Almost every one of the sequences in this book confirms that pitchers treat their sales talk as being the most important factor in determining the sales outcome. As such, pitchers are the classic 'patter merchants'. For them, as for salespeople more generally, talk is by no means cheap. In this world of the street market, goods will not sell themselves without the assistance of communicative skills.

This is not to say, however, that the communicative skills used by market pitchers are just any old skills. Pitching is not an anarchical contest where the shopper is verbally beaten into buying goods. The techniques used by pitchers are most often deployed within a framework of social and interactional 'rules' which both pitchers and the people who gather at their stalls share and which the latter rely upon in order to make their purchasing decisions.

For example, to build convincing bargains pitchers must trade on how shoppers measure price differences when shopping, and how they evaluate these differences in terms of getting 'value for money'. Gary reckoned:

'By saying something like "They're worth two pound ninety-nine, give us two pound", you're not appealing to people's greedy instinct; you've only knocked ninety-nine pence off the price. We knock twenty quid off. I mean, how can anybody resist anything that cost twenty-three pound fifty if you can get it for two pound?'

But neither is bargain-building simply a question of appealing to or exploiting people's greed. By studying the way pitchers talk up their goods, build their bargains, establish commitments to buy and announce their selling prices, we have begun to understand the often taken-for-granted processes and everyday reasoning that underpin much of what goes on in this particular selling situation.

Even if there were no legal constraints prescribing limits on what pitchers could claim their goods were worth, and thus how large the worth-selling price contrast could be, there are certainly practical, everyday constraints. Just because a selling price is said to be low does not mean that people are automatically going to treat it as being cheap. In fact, on some occasions we even got the impression that pitchers found it a more difficult task to sell goods cheap than it was to sell them at their 'normal' price. There seems to be a limit on the price contrast bargain formulations that pitchers can build. Here, notions of what an audience would treat as warrantable and reasonable appear to play a significant part. For example, if a pitcher claimed that the worth of (say) a Mars Bar was a thousand pounds and then announced a selling price of one pound, he or she would have produced a price contrast. But this pitcher would not have created a bargain likely to be treated as value for money, because most people know that this item of confectionery can be bought at present for about forty pence. It is no accident that the goods pitchers sell are all items about which there is a degree of price uncertainty.

We conducted a study of sixty of these series of selling prices at the start of our research (Pinch and Clark, 1986) and found that pitchers treated certain amounts of price contrast difference as more plausible and persuasive than others. We calculated the ratio difference between the highest and the lowest price in these series of selling prices – that is, the highest account of what the pitchers claimed the goods were worth, and the final selling price of those goods. The average ratio difference between these two prices was nearly 5:1. In other words, pitchers seemed to be aware that an £11/£10 price contrast would not be treated by shoppers as being as convincing as something like a £50/£10 price difference. And they similarly believed that a price contrast of something like £450/£10 would not be treated as convincing either.

This ratio price difference also tended to get bigger as the selling price of the goods decreased. The average selling price of the goods offered for sale in these sixty price contrasts was £4.74. When we separated all the selling prices that were above and below this average into two groups, we found that the average ratio difference of the worth-selling price contrast elements shifted to around 3:1 and 6:1 respectively. The difference between these two price ratios suggests that those pitchers who were offering cheaper than average items believed that they needed to offer a greater contrastive difference before the audience would treat their selling prices as a bargain.

This type of taken-for-granted price knowledge can be found in other retailing situations, most notably in the percentage price reductions used by high-street stores to publicize their sales. Consumer research shows that 5 per cent price reduction from a 'normal' or recommended retail price is not likely to be treated as being as appetizing as something like a 50 per cent reduction. On the other hand, a reduction of 95 per cent will undoubtedly arouse a shopper's curiosity, but it is also more likely to encourage them to think that the offer may not be a genuine one, or that there may be something wrong with the goods offered in the sale.

Pitching, as we hope to have shown, is a particularly

felicitous way of studying real-life selling, marketing and consumer behaviour. This sales context provides an excellent scenario for determining why customers actually make the purchases they do. Because pitchers are engaged in a process of persuasion they have to attend to and make explicit the normally implicit processes of reasoning, perhaps even the reservations, that customers hold and share.

Sales outcomes can be seen to be understandable more in terms of the manner in which pitchers capitalize on culturally held social conventions than in terms of economic theory or of any abstract criterion for the comparison of selling price and economic worth. In other words, the normative principles that underlie and inform the activities and sales outcomes conducted in this sales context seem to be distinct and separable from the factors usually cited by economists and marketing researchers to account for the outcomes that arise.

Perhaps the most obvious example of this is that market pitchers recognize that while shoppers often act in a systematic way, they rarely behave as rational consumers. For instance, when we asked Terry if market shoppers searched for the lowest prices before they bought goods, he replied:

'*That's nonsense*! I've *never* heard so much nonsense! Yesterday I had one particular customer – a married couple – and they're by no means the exception, I'm citing them as the norm. They bought a saucepan set, a set of knives, a set of towels, a set of cut-glass lamps, a Teddy bear and something else – I can't remember what. And, initially, they were walking past me! Now there is not an economist, a psychologist – you or *anybody* – who could convince me that they had passed me with a shopping list in their hand which read: "1: saucepan set; 2: Teddy bear . . ." To cite another example, I get cheques, *obviously*. Now – not more often than not, but it's certainly not unusual – at the end of the day I'll have three or four different cheques from the same person. That indicates very strongly that what they bought were impulse buys.'

Consequently, any attempt to understand how people sell should, we believe, start from an analysis of how sales are an interactional process. Although we have already pointed out that there are some similarities between the communication skills used in pitching and other forms of selling – namely in terms of how a sale is structured and how products tend to be described and explained (see Chapter 4) – many of the pitchers we spoke to viewed their form of selling as being almost the antithesis of the skills that they claimed were often employed in more orthodox sales situations. Many pitchers, in fact, viewed their way of persuading people to buy as being a more collaborative and certainly a less adversarial form of selling.

For instance, Terry, who had once worked as a sales representative, claimed that the selling techniques used in other sales situations would be of no use on a street market:

'The basic difference is that as a sales rep, however much I tried, I was alienated from the people I was dealing with. It's as though you're on a different planet; you're not in tune with them. It's you and them – it's a battle. Look at what companies give to salespeople for training – they give them charades to carry out. They'll throw twelve customer objections at them and they'll train them how to overcome those objections as though selling is some form of obstacle course and, at the end of the day, the goal is for the customer to say "Yes, I'll have it" and the salesman says: *"Whaaa-hey!"* and then he goes back to the sales director and they open a case of champagne together. Now if you take pitching, it's almost as if the pitcher and punter are buying the thing together in as much as you would say: *"Bloody 'ell*, 'ave you seen the prices of these in the high street, sweet? *Robbing buggers!* 'Ave you seen them on the telly?" In other words, you're not fighting with them all the time. There is nothing we can learn from normal sales techniques. *Nothing*. All they serve to do is alienate the seller from the buyer.'

Terry reserved the greater part of his contempt for those salespeople employed in retail stores:

'If you walk into some of these high-street electrical retail stores you are suddenly *attacked* – and that is the only word that I can think of – by a spotty youth in a cheap pinstripe suit. Every single one of them rubs his hands together and they all cock their head to one side when they talk to you. Now that's very polite, and that's how they've probably been trained, but that's *not* how you talk to people. That way you're dealing with customers as if they are some sort of child. How many times have you heard shoppers say: "I'm just looking"? Now if they go to a market and they buy their fruit and vegetables you'll get: "Hello, Doris, how's the kids, all right?" It's as though they are talking to their own kind. I talk to customers the same way that I talk to my next-door neighbour or my friends in the pub. In pitching you talk *with* not *down* to the customers.'

This view of the type of sales skills used in more orthodox selling is not without foundation. For instance, in a study we conducted of a sample of forty-eight telephone sales interactions between people wanting to place an advertisement in the classified ads section of a newspaper, we found that tension and antagonism between the salesperson and the prospect was the rule rather than the exception (Clark, Drew and Pinch, 1994). In thirty-four of these forty-eight calls the prospect initially did not accept the deal proposed by the salesperson. In every case where this happened, the salesperson either ignored any hints prospects made that they did not want to buy or, when prospects markedly objected to or rejected the salesperson's proposal, in every case they still attempted to pursue an acceptance of the sale they had initially proposed.

Although sales eventually occurred in all of these thirty-four cases (which was not surprising given that these prospects had telephoned the newspaper on their own initiative with the express intention of placing an advertisement), the final price was invariably lower than that which the salesperson had first proposed. Indeed, the revenue obtained from these sales was approximately two-thirds lower than that obtained from an 'average' sale, where the prospect immediately accepted the salesperson's proposal.

In many cases it is not the salespeople who are responsible for these selling strategies, it is the people who employ and train them. And the difference between the sales techniques used by market pitchers and salespeople in more orthodox sales situations appears to stem from a difference in the way in which the role and status of selling in the marketing mix is perceived.

Many sales trainers, for example, still tend to work from the assumption that 'selling only begins when the customer says no'. Because of this, selling is viewed as being a form of economic conquest – a means of leading potential customers step by step through a maze, overturning their objections, not attending to customer reservations, not breaking silences until a sale is won. This is a qualitatively different pressure to that employed by market pitchers. As Terry told us:

'As an example, if you get a top "closer" selling double glazing or kitchens he'll create this minefield for himself by getting objections. A pitcher is more subtle and thus more effective. For instance, he recognizes what objections are in a different and more effective way. He recognizes them before they even happen.'

This effectiveness is seen by pitchers as deriving from the close contact they have with their customers. Henry told us that pitchers are: 'on a one-to-one selling basis with the public and provide a very personal service. Our customers know me, I know them. Often, in shops, you don't really see the boss. The boss is sat up in an office somewhere making the "big" decisions. On a market, invariably, whoever you're dealing with is the owner of the stall. And when it's your own business the shopper is always looked after that little bit more carefully. I believe that these days far too many high-street chains lose contact with the general public. I've always said to people that if you wanted to learn anything about selling then don't go into retail stores, spend two or three days on a market stall dealing with Mr and Mrs "Average". You'll learn more in one day about human nature and life than you would in any shop.'

The key to understanding the pitchers' strategy is expressed in the maxim 'the best way to control people is for them to control themselves'. By the use of imitative behaviour, humour, grand gestures and the like, pitchers are able to turn a group of isolated shoppers into a responsive and sympathetic crowd. But they do it, more often than not, without seeming to force people or cajole them into buying. A loud sell is not necessarily a hard sell.

Pitchers, then, as Britain's army of indigenous sellers, perhaps have lessons to teach those engaged in other forms of selling, marketing and persuasion.

Pitching goods is one of the oldest forms of selling. References to this technique, and to street-hawking, can be found in literature written in Medieval times. During the Victorian era most goods on street markets were sold in this manner. One pitcher proudly told us how his grandmother used to sell shoes on a Northern street market, working with essentially the same rhetorical ploys as he used today to sell towels and toys. Pitching on street markets has been in decline since its heyday in Victorian times when markets were much less regulated. Today, local market regulations often prevent more than one pitcher from operating on a market because of concerns that the large crowds which pitchers attract might block up narrow market alleyways. Norwich market, for instance, one of the largest in Britain, now no longer has any pitchers. Pinch, as a boy in the 1950s, can remember being taken to see the 'Pottery King' who ruled Norwich market and provided one of the highlights of a dull Saturday afternoon's shopping expedition. Pitchers feel that these regulations are unfair because often it is the sight of a colourful pitcher at work which gives a market its traditional feel and special character and also serves actually to attract shoppers to the benefit of all market-stall holders.

Looking back through history, the few first-hand accounts of pitching that can be found (e.g. Allingham, 1934) show a remarkable similarity between the methods and language such traders used then and now. Because pitching is a skill which is passed on literally by word of mouth in an oral culture one can speculate that as a method of selling it has changed little over time. We have also been struck by the similarities we have seen in the basic street-selling techniques to be found in different cultures (Chapters 9 and 10). Perhaps the famed patent medicine salesmen of the wild west and today's snake-oil salesmen share a common bond with Britain's best known indigenous sales people.

We end this book by giving the last 'word' to the pitchers as they reflect on their skills.

Terry: 'A few years ago Woolworth's spent – it must have been millions – on a facelift to create the right atmosphere for people to buy. They changed the stores, put in new carpets and different lighting to give them a brighter look: "Have you seen the new Woolies?" But people still have miserable faces as they're walking through Woolies weighed down with their carrier bags. If they stand in front of a pitcher they'll put the bags down and have a laugh. That's the right atmosphere to buy, not fancy lights.'

Terry: 'Pitchers are not only the élite of market trading, which I don't think is in any doubt – it's accepted even within the trade – but I'd even go as far as to say that they are the élite amongst salespeople. First of all, pitching is the oldest form of selling – except for, what is it? Some people say prostitution to that one. We say wholesaling. Well, it's the same thing. [Laughs] Second, it's the most effective form of selling. There is no other sales force in the country that can boast the conversion rate of a pitcher.'

Terry: 'Pitchers are held in reverence by the public, and you musn't doubt that. No matter how much you knock pitchers you've got to understand that people actually love them. If you doubt that look at the success of "Minder" and "Only Fools and Horses" and all those other TV programmes which have those type of characters.'

> It's all about people, right? Making people happy, keeping people happy, giving 'em a lot of nice gear. And at the same time, those people, I hope, don't mind you earning a little bit as you go along, is that right? Not havin' a little bit, earning a little bit. Mind you, I wouldn't mind having a little bit either.

> Daft Dicky, philosophizing while conducting a sale

GLOSSARY

NB: Some of the terms in this glossary have alternative meanings in other, particularly non-British, contexts.

Arnold	Fictitious Christian name given by many mock auctioneers to their assistants. (The name Walter is also very popular.)
Auctioneer	Market pitcher. Auctioneering is the strategy of creating a bargain by announcing a series of progressively lower selling prices.
Back nailing	A method of obtaining more sales of goods already offered for sale. The pitcher states that he or she will sell the goods 'cheaper' than hitherto to purchasers who make a prior commitment. Those who raise their hands are then told the revised price which is, invariably, only a minimal reduction from the original selling price.
Back-to-Back	Pitching one item of stock continuously or working one sales routine straight after another.
Bagging out	Creating a buying obligation by giving carrier bags, wrapping paper, etc. to those people who have expressed an 'interest' in the goods on offer by raising a hand.
Bat	The selling price of goods.
Bent	Illegal; difficult to work.
Blag	Pitching spiel intended to deceive.
Blind start	Attracting people to a pitching stall by extolling the goods on offer while not looking directly at passers-by or individuals already at the stall.

Blow out	A sale where no one buys.
Bobby	Policeman/woman.
Bollock	To criticize, admonish or bully in a heavy-handed way.
Bunce	Profit.
Clock	To look at someone, particularly in the face.
Close	The point at which a sales proposal is made in orthodox selling negotiations.
Cock and hen	Ten, usually abbreviated to 'cocker' or 'cockle'.
Combination (or 'Combo')	A set, collection or mixture of goods offered as a single sale lot.
Cop	To take; get; obtain. Usually in reference to money for goods.
Copper	Police constable/officer.
Crocus worker	Someone who sells 'miracle cures'.
Demicks	Faulty or broken goods that are passed off as perfect or in working order.
Demonstrator	Market pitcher who sells only one item of stock, usually a home-improvement or do-it-yourself implement.
Divvy	Fool; sucker; someone with a suggestible demeanour. A person from whom a dividend or profit can be obtained.
Dough	Money
Drek	Rubbish (when used with reference to goods); shits/complainers/disrupters (when used with reference to people).
Dwell	To stay – for example, at a single location when fly pitching.
Edge	The people who gather at a pitching stall.
Edge puller	The person who attempts to attract a crowd at the start of a mock auction sale.
End games	Sales conducted on a one-to-one basis at the end of a mock auction.
Execution pitch	A crowd of the same magnitude as the number of people who would turn up to watch a public execution.

Fanny	Pitching spiel. Sales talk extolling the virtues of the goods offered for sale in a dramatic and exaggerated way.
Flash	The display of goods on the pitching stall.
Flim	Five pounds.
Floor worker	Pitching assistant.
Fly pitching	Pitching illegally, without a licence. Usually the pitcher sells goods out of a suitcase (see Peter).
Forks	Hands. Forking is a means of creating an obligation to buy through placing the goods in the hands of the audience.
Front	A confederate posing surreptitiously as a bona fide member of the crowd.
Funkum	Perfume.
Gaff	The pitching stall or, more generally, the market itself.
Gee	A plant or confederate of the pitcher who works in the audience (see Rick).
Geeing	Deceiving the audience either by the use of a confederate or by some other form of misrepresentation.
Gelt	Money.
Gobshite	Someone who is talking rubbish or, in a more obvious sense, someone who is 'talking out of their arse'.
Grafter	Market pitcher; more generally anyone who works hard.
Guinea	One pound ten pence.
Harvey	Money.
Hawker	Another name for a fly pitcher or, more generally, a trader who moves about for custom. Like a bird of prey, he or she travels to, seek outs and then pounces on customers.
Hintern	An item of stock used in the mock auction. Hintern goods are not actually sold to the audience. The sale is fictitious – the goods are only hinted at.

Hiring fair	Medieval fair where people went to find work.
Holloway	Women's prison in North London.
Hook	Technique used by fly pitchers to attract custom. A series of very low prices is announced. It transpires that the price refers to only one of the items of stock in the collection on offer.
Jebb out	Renege on a commitment or obligation to buy.
Jeckylls	Broken goods passed off as being in perfect working order (see Schnide — Jekyll and Hyde = schnide).
Joint	Pitching or market stall.
Kegs	Trousers.
Kettle	Watch. (Probably from rhyming slang: kettle and kotch = watch).
Knocking out	Selling oddments of stock very cheaply at the start of a sale in order to attract passers-by and/or to generate responsiveness from those people already at the stall.
Look-outs	People employed by fly pitchers to warn them of approaching police.
Lump	A collection of goods offered as a single sales lot. These goods are usually different from one another.
Lurker	A market trader who does not rely upon an elaborate sales spiel to attract a crowd to the stall and to sell his or her goods but instead waits for individual customers.
Mob handed	Working in a group. (Also 'team handed'.)
Moody	To pretend or misrepresent, tell lies.
Mug	Fool; sucker; gullible or naive person.
Muzzle worker	Someone who sells lucky charms.
Nail	To oblige to buy or otherwise keep people at the stall.
Nailer	An item of stock in the mock auction used to keep the audience at the stall during the remainder of the 'sale'.

Nause	A complainer.
Nick	To steal; to charge with an offence.
Nifty	Fifty pounds.
Nutter	Someone who is crazy or otherwise 'mentally challenged' (from nut = head).
One-up	100 per cent profit.
One up one down	Two-person pitching. One pitches, the other helps. After a couple of sales they switch.
Patter	Sales talk.
Peter	Suitcase, as used in fly pitching.
Pitch crew	Pitching assistants.
Pitcher	Market trader selling goods to a crowd of people at a stall by means of an elaborate sales talk.
Plunder	Items of stock that are sold cheaply, for the purpose of generating responsiveness from the audience usually at start of sale.
Poke	Money; profit.
Pony	Twenty-five pounds.
Proviso	Bargain struck by a pitcher and people at the stall whereby the pitcher agrees to sell the goods below a certain price.
Pull-up	Technique of attracting people to a stall by using the first person who has gathered to help attract others.
Punt	To buy.
Punter	A buyer or prospective buyer.
Quid	Pound.
Ram	The principal deception in the mock auction.
Ramping	Marking stock with prices that are higher than the price at which the goods will be sold.
Ream	Real; genuine. Usually in reference to goods during the hintern and smother phase of a mock auction.
Reign	The amount of time a fly pitcher is able to work before being caught or moved on.
Rick	A confederate of the pitcher used as a plant in the

	audience. Origin is thought to be Yiddish. Rick means 'false'.
Royal run	American name for the mock auction.
Run out	Another name for the mock auction – used by the auctioneers themselves. The term originated not because the mock auction sales crew might have to escape from hostile victims at the end of the routine (as happens so often nowadays with rogue workers), but because during the 1950s and 1960s the deception was allegedly so successful that it would end only when the victims had run out of money.
Running pitch.	Keeping the same core of people at the stall for a number of consecutive sales of different stock. (Also 'rolling pitch'.)
Scheist	To hide.
Schlock	Cheap goods.
Schmatty	Cheap and tawdry.
Schmitze	To hide.
Schmuck	See Divvy
Schnide	False; counterfeit.
Shilling	Five pence.
Skint	Without money.
Smother	An item of stock used to deflect the audience's attention from a hintern lot in the mock auction.
Spiel	Sales talk.
Squat shop	High-street store hired on a short-lease tenancy or used without the owner's permission, often for mock auction sales.
Steaming up	Getting the crowd excited and in the frame of mind for buying.
Straight-working	Working legitimately. Not using any illegal techniques.
Stumm	To silence. Usually applies to someone who is disruptive in a pitcher's audience.
Sweetener	A cheap item of stock given away free to pacify an irate customer.

System, The	A method of working the mock auction.
Tenner	Ten pounds.
Ticket	Price, usually marked on cardboard, used by lurkers.
Tom	Jewellery (rhyming slang = tomfoolery).
Top man	The salesman who conducts the mock auction.
Topment	Cheap item of stock given away as the 'treat' at the end of a mock auction.
Touch cotton	To shit in your pants.
TSO	Trading standards officer.
Twirling the edge	A method of generating additional sales after the selling price has been announced. Instead of immediately serving the customers, the pitcher will try to hold them at the stall in a way that exploits their responsiveness in order to attract additional passers-by, as well as to persuade other people at the stall to make a purchase.
Two bob	Ten pence/two shillings.
Whiff	Smell.
Working strong	Using pitching techniques that are bordering on or transcending the legitimate. (Also 'pitching heavy'.)

BIBLIOGRAPHY

The following bibliography contains books and articles referred to in the text, a selection of keyworks by social scientists who have either studied other types of selling situations and/or communication activities, and some references to previous academic studies we have conducted and published on market pitching and selling.

Allingham, Phillip, *CheapJack*, Heinemann, London, 1934.

Atkinson, J. Maxwell, *Our Masters' Voices: The Language and Body Language of Politics*, Methuen, London, 1984.

Atkinson, J. Maxwell and Heritage, John eds, *Structures of Social Action: Studies in Conversation Analysis*, Cambridge University Press, Cambridge, 1984.

Beattie, Geoffrey, *All Talk: Why it's Important to Watch Your Words and Everything Else You Say*, Weidenfeld and Nicolson, London, 1988.

Belk, Russel W., John F. Sherry, Jnr, and Melanie Wallendorf, 'A Naturalistic Inquiry into Buyer and Seller Behaviour at a Swap Meet', in the *Journal of Consumer Research*, 14, March 1988, pp. 449–70.

Benedetta, M., *The Street Markets of London*, John Miles, London, 1936.

Brigham, Jerry C., and Karlie K. Kenyon, 'Hodacol: The Last Great Medicine Show', in the *Journal of Popular Culture*, Vol. X, No. 3, winter 1976, pp. 520–533.

Burton, Roland W., *Markets and Fairs*, Routledge and Kegan Paul, London, 1973.

Clark, Colin, and Trevor Pinch, 'Micro-Sociology and Micro-Economics: Selling by Social Control', in N. Fielding (ed.), *Structures and Actions*, Sage, London, 1988, pp. 119–41.

—— 'The Anatomy of a Deception: Fraud and Finesse in the

Mock Auction Sales Con', *Qualitative Sociology* 15 (2) 1993, pp. 151–75, 1992.

—— 'The Interactional Study of Exchange Relationships', *History of Political Economy*, special edition on 'Higgling: Transactors and Their Markets in the History of Economics' edited by Neil De Marchi and Mary S. Morgan, pp. 370–400, 1994.

Clark, Colin, Trevor Pinch, and P. Drew, 'Managing Customer Objections in Real-Life Sales Negotiations', in *Discourse and Society*, Vol. 5 (4), 1994, pp. 437–62.

Dorner, Jane, *Markets and Fairs*, Wayland, London, 1973.

Goffman, Erving, 'On Cooling the Mark Out', in *Psychiatry*, 15, 1952, pp. 451–463.

——, 'On Face-Work: An Analysis of Ritual Elements in Social Interaction', in *Psychiatry*, 18, 1955, pp. 213–31.

——, *The Presentation of Self in Everyday Life*, Allen Lane, London, 1969.

——, *Behaviour in Public Places*, Free Press, New York, 1963.

Her Majesty's Stationery Office, *The Mock Auction Act*, London, 1961.

Jefferson, Gail, 'On the Organization of Laughter in Talk about Troubles', in J. M. Atkinson and John Heritage (eds), *Structures of Social Action: Studies in Conversation Analysis*, Cambridge University Press, Cambridge, 1974, pp. 346–69.

Katowich, M. A., and R. L. Diamond, 'Selling Time: Situated Transactions in a Non-Institutional Environment', in the *Sociological Quarterly*, 27, 1986, pp. 253–71.

Lemert, E. M., 'The Behavior of the Systematic Cheque Forger', in *Social Problems*, 6, 1958, pp. 141–8.

McGrath, Mary Ann, 'An Ethnography of a Gift Store: Trappings, Wrappings and Rapture', in *Journal of Retailing* (1989), 65 (4) pp. 421–49.

McIntosh, Mary, 'Thieves and Fences: Markets and Power in Professional Crime', in the *British Journal of Criminology*, 16, 3, 1976, pp. 257–66.

Maisel, Robert, 'The Flea-Market as an Action Scene', in *Urban Life and Culture*, 2, 4, Jan. 1974, pp. 488–505.

Maurer, David M., *The Big Con*, Bobbs-Merrill, Indianapolis, 1940.

—— *The American Confidence Man*, Thomas, Springfield, Ill., 1974.

Mayhew, H., *Mayhew's London Underworld*, ed. P. Quennell, Century, London, 1987. First published 1882 as 'Those Who Will Not Work', Vol. 4 of *London Labour and the London Poor*.

Miller, S. J., 'The Social Basis of Sales Behaviour', in *Social Problems*, 2, 1964, pp. 15–24.

Mulkay, Michael J., *On Humor: It's Nature and Place in Modern Society*, Basil Blackwell, New York, 1988.

Mulkay, Michael J., Colin Clark, and Trevor Pinch, 'Laughter and the Profit Motive: The Use of Humor in a Photographic Shop', 1993. In *Humor*, 6 (2) pp. 162–93

Mulkay, Michael J. and Gerard Howe, 'Laughter for Sale' in the *Sociological Review*, 42, (3), 1994, pp. 481–500.

O'Shaughnessy, Patrick, 'A Glossary of Market Traders' Argot', in *Lore and Language*, 2, 8, Jan. 1978, pp. 20–3.

Pinch, Trevor, and Colin Clark, 'The Hard Sell: "Patter-Merchanting" and the Strategic (Re)Production and Local Management of Economic Reasoning in the Sales Routines of Market Pitchers', in *Sociology*, 20, 2, 1986, pp. 169–91.

Polsky, Ned, *Hustlers, Beats and Others*, Aldine, Chicago, 1967.

Pomerantz, Anita, 'Extreme Case Formulations: A Way of Legitimizing Claims', *Human Studies*, 9:219–29, 1986.

Prus, Robert C., 'Price-Setting as Social Activity: Defining Price, Value and Profit in the Marketplace', in *Urban Life*, 14, 1, 1985, pp. 59–93.

—— , 'It's on "Sale": Vendor Perspectives on the Bargain', in the *Canadian Review of Sociology and Anthropology*, 23, 1986, pp. 72–96.

—— , *Making Sales: Influence as a Personal Accomplishment*, Sage, Newbury Park, California, 1989.

Prus, Robert C., and C. R. D. Sharper (pseud.), *Road Hustler: The Career Contingencies of Professional Card and Dice Hustlers*, Lexington Books, Lexington, 1977.

Rosnow, R. L., 'Gossip and Marketplace Psychology', in the *Journal of Communication*, 27, 1977, pp. 158–63.

Sacks, H., 'Some Technical Considerations of a Dirty Joke', in J. Schenkein (ed.), *Studies in the Organisation of Conversational Interaction*, Academic Press, New York, 1978, pp. 249–69.

Sherry, John F., Jnr, 'Market Pitching and the Ethnography of Speaking', in *Advances in Consumer Research*, Vol. 15, ed. Michael Houston, Association of Consumer Research, Provo, Utah, 1988, pp. 543–7.

—— , 'A Sociocultural Analysis of a Midwestern American Flea Market', in the *Journal of Consumer Research*, 17, June 1990, pp. 13–30.

Taylor, Laurie, *In the Underworld*, Unwin-Hyman, London 1988.

INDEX